The Sociology of Opera

The
SOCIOLOGY
of
OPERA

ROSANNE MARTORELLA

PRAEGER SPECIAL STUDIES • PRAEGER SCIENTIFIC
A J.F. BERGIN PUBLISHERS BOOK

Library of Congress Cataloging in Publication Data

Martorella, Rosanne.
   The Sociology of Opera.

   A J.F. Bergin Publishers Book.
   Bibliography.
   Includes index.
      1. Opera—United States—Social aspects. 2. Opera—
   United States—Production and direction. I. Title.
   ML1711.M38   782.1'0973   81-21049
   ISBN 0-03-059329-8   AACR2

Published in 1982 by Praeger Publishers
CBS Educational and Professional Publishing
A Division of CBS, Inc.
521 Fifth Avenue, New York, New York 10175 U.S.A.

0123456789   056   987654321

Printed in the United States of America

Photo, title page. A triumvirate of operatic decision making. Arturo Toscanini, Giulio Gatti-Casazza and Geraldine Farrar on the Metropolitan Opera stage, 1915 (*Metropolitan Opera Archives*).

*To My Father
and to the Memory of My Mother*

Contents

List of Tables

List of Charts

Preface

This analysis of opera production is concerned with the roles of performers, and their relationships to each other and to the large companies that sponsor opera. A general hypothesis of the institutionalization of the arts in contemporary society is entertained, but the study was approached from an organizational viewpoint that involved looking at artists as members of organizations, and examining opera in terms of the various aspects of production. It focuses on the consequences of financially-oriented production goals and values on the cultural product. We will see the development of musical styles as an inevitable response to the market in which they are produced; and we will examine the restrictive effects of such "determinism" on aesthetic and social norms within the musical community. Opera repertoire is determined and conditioned by the organizational complex through which the musical process evolves.

The Sociology of Opera's main focus is on the analysis of organizations that produce opera. Music history is explored to discover changes in opera production and the roles of performers in order to gain insight into the current problems of opera. This study provides clues to the changing cultural patterns in society and offers the social scientist extensive sources of data for testing the cultural and social dynamics of change, conflict, organizations, and knowledge.

Primarily, the following organizations that produce opera are studied: the Metropolitan Opera Association, the New York City Opera Company, the Seattle Opera, the Lyric Opera of Chicago, and the San Francisco Opera. These five companies represent the largest organizations that produce opera in the United States; but the analysis is relevant to other companies as well. Those which present a few performances a year may not have to contend with a payroll that includes a full-time orchestra, ballet and chorus, but they do have to perform works that are popular at the box office in order to survive. To this extent, they are similar. Perhaps the problems of the smaller companies are even heightened by part-time staffs and the need to contract star performers on a one-night basis. Short seasons and part-time staffs force these companies to depend heavily on the five major opera houses to establish musical trends, initiate new production techniques, and introduce major new talent to the United States. There are, of course, exceptions, and what occurs in the larger houses does not invariably mean innovation. However, those productions, for the most part, represent what the American public wishes to see and hear.

The following study is an outcome of several experiences I have had in connection with the performing arts. As both employee and consumer, I have seen the enormous backstage machinery, the administrative cadre, and the rehearsals necessary for a single performance, as well as the informal friendships, traditions, gossips, rivalries, and jealousies that thrive in the musical community. These activities have supplemented an enduring interest in opera. I hope that by combining sociology with a personal interest in music, I can make some contribution to the body of research on the classical performing artist.

To elicit subjective comments, opinions, interpretations of work experiences, and evaluations of the interaction among participants in an opera production, I chose the open non-directive interview as the method most suitable for this study, and taped interviews with performers, critics, managers, stage directors, and conductors. The criteria for selection were celebrity, specialty, career pattern, and vocal range, but availability became a determining factor in who was personally interviewed. Most of the elite in all phases of production have been included through the use of personal interviews and secondary interview data, that is, interviews conducted by newspaper and broadcast journalists. This study rests on the sources cited as well as on the interviews conducted.

This study would not have been possible without the time and perceptive insight provided directly or indirectly by the performers and participants who dedicate their lives to the arts. In the midst of the rigors of their schedules, managers, critics, and musicians were willing to share their feelings, and I wish to apologize for the numerous names and accounts which, for reasons of space, could not be included. I want to express gratitude to Maria Rich of Central Opera Service, to the Metropolitan Opera Archives, and to Juliette Hayes of the Lyric Opera of Chicago. Professors Lyman, Ostereicher, and Vidich gave intellectual support and have always been a source of motivation. Professor Joseph Bensman of the City University of New York expressed both an academic and personal interest in my work, and has always been available whenever I needed his guidance. My friends Rob Faulkner, Connie Munro, Jack Kamerman, Robert Perinbanayagam, and Linda Romano read the manuscript and offered suggestions. I am indebted to my mother, who knew well and empathized with the dilemmas of a working mother, and to my family, who taught me to love music and respect musicians. Finally the long hours of listening with my husband to Verdi's music, and to the visual ecstasy of Franco Zeffirelli's masterpieces, the voices of Marilyn Horne, Luciano Pavarotti, and Joan Sutherland, not only made the writing more bearable, but gave it its raison d'être.

Rosanne Martorella
New York

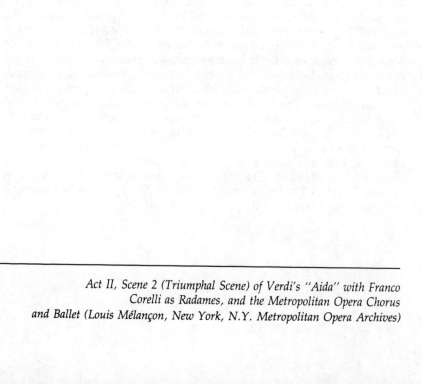

Act II, Scene 2 (Triumphal Scene) of Verdi's "Aida" with Franco Corelli as Radames, and the Metropolitan Opera Chorus and Ballet (Louis Mélançon, New York, N.Y. Metropolitan Opera Archives)

1 *Introduction*

Toward a Sociology of Opera

This book is an attempt to provide a sociological explanation for the development of operatic styles. It focuses upon the performers of opera (singers, composers, stage directors, dancers, conductors, and managers), the opera companies which produce it, and the patrons and audiences which support it. It is based on the following assumptions:

> *Music and song are social.* Musical compositions are created, and performed, by individuals. As a totality, they are part of the musical conventions of a given time. Musical expressions are inherited and shared, and are part of the language and communicative system of a culture, and social group. While one may "abstractly" deal with a musical expression as an independent aesthetic art form, its enactment, and expression, are "real" events.

> *Musicians are members of society.* All individuals are socialized into a society. Consequently, their ideas or creative acts are reflections and products of family background and the traditions and values of a social group. Musicians are also members of an artistic sub-

culture, in which they interact and exchange. Musical compositions are reacted to by other members of society. Consequently,
musicians may predicate their actions on such "anticipatory" behavior.

Music is a means of social organization. In order for music to be
expressed, it involves the interaction of the musician with other
artists, the composer, performer, as well as the audience, critics,
patrons, the publishing and recording industries. Musicians and
performers are recruited and socialized by music schools, conservatories, universities, auditions, competitions and other
professional training settings. The symphony orchestra, opera
companies, and performing arts centers, which produce music,
are involved in presenting it to the public. These organizations
are also non-profit, a fact which must be taken into account in
any discussion of a performing art today.

Sociological studies of art and artists have been dominated by
occupational sociologists — an inevitable development, given the
enormous popularity of the sub-specialty, "occupations and professions," within American sociology. However, analyzing art in the
same way as other occupations loses sight of the unique variations
of the work as highly charismatic aesthetic expressions. Consequently, studies on artists and/or performers provide a minimal contribution to a theoretical framework for the sociology of the arts. An
effort must be made to reveal the relationships between occupational
recruitment, socialization, training, and the organization of work,
with the development of artistic styles and/or aesthetic interpretations.

Studies of the interactionist tradition have done much in describing the meaning for structures among artists, and the alienation from
work which they feel. However, they fail to give credit to the macro-
cultural and institutional context within which art is expressed. These
factors provide the social structures which designate the social position of artists, the distribution of patronage, and the ideological
systems of the society, in which artists express themselves.

Similarly, organizational studies of the music industry end with
viewing musical composition in the same light as other products
which the mass culture consumes. As economics plays an increasingly
important role, analogies can be made comparing business organizations with organizations which produce art products. However,
the "production of culture" model, in emphasizing the network of
production and distribution excludes any content of the art form
itself, which has an interdependent relationship with market factors.

It concludes without saying anything of the art itself. The arts remain unique and distinct from other products, and this must be incorporated into any meaningful analysis of the sociology of the arts.

The sociology of music, especially of the European varieties such as semiotics and phenomenology, has been dominated by the aesthetic requirements of the form itself; this school of thought neglects to study the individuals doing art, and the institutional setting in which they work. Studies with this threotical commitment are more philosophical, and their interpretations are too "idealistic" to be sociological.

On the other hand, the musicologist utilizes the memoirs of musicans, early sheet music and recordings, and instruments and instrumentation of a period, to focus on musical and technological developments. His attention is somewhat different from that of the sociologist. However, his data, like that of any historian, is crucial for sociological analysis. On an interactional level, the lives of musicians, and their feelings and attitudes toward their society, art form and other artists, become data from which the sociologist departs; and, using a "vocabulary" which may include such terms as "social interaction", "conflict resolution", or "creativity," the sociologist addresses certain questions, and interprets the musician's work and life in such a way as to lend insight into the motives of artists and the causes of musical expression. Within an institutional context, the nature and extent of political authority within a society, the economic conditions of musical societies, and types of audiences and their tastes, become data from which the sociologist departs once again. In this case, institutional and market analysis, and organizational theory, provide a good beginning in the examination of the changes in operatic styles, repertoire decisions, and the social positions of opera performers. A sociology of opera, therefore, expands from musical historical data, addresses different questions, and enriches the understanding and appreciation of opera.

The interaction of the charismatic qualities of performing artists, the cultural content and values which are incorporated in their work experiences and ideologies, and the increasing specialization of their roles as artists in society, are the issues explored in this book. They provide a sociological basis for the study of opera.

How is a distinct type of performing art organization and its product, opera companies and repertoire, affected by the preferences of audiences, the controls imposed by the patrons and board members, and the amount of government and foundation subsidization? What is the relationship between the marketplace and a cultural product? Viewing "music as a process," will help evaluate the complex and interdependent relationships between the artist, the work of art, and the public. (Albrecht 1973; Barnett 1958:401–5; 1959)

Studies of painting (Hauser 1951; Antal 1948; Shapiro 1976; Kroeber 1970; Martindale 1972; Pevsner 1970; Kavolis 1968; White & White 1964), and of film (Huaco 1965; Monaco 1976) have taken a similar approach. In these cases, the authors attempt a social history, and reveal the impact of institutional factors (such as the social position of the artist, patronage, class structure, and socio-political events) on style changes.

Viewed in this way the structure of opera is revealed as a series of processes extending from artist to consumer, with an intervening and complex "multiple-channel" market that includes opera houses headed by impresarios or general managers, audiences, patrons, businessmen, corporations, governments, and foundations.

The subsystems that also affect opera are the critic, by his evaluation; the personal manager or public relations person, who acts on behalf of his client; and the publishing house or recording company, which furthers the distribution of the product.

The focus of institutional analysis in this book is on the consequences of the conditions of production for both individual and organizational functioning. The market conditions of opera — including its private patronage, mass orientation, and European traditions — have consequences for the nonprofit organization that produces opera, for the performing and nonperforming artist, and for the type of opera that is selected for presentation.

The Social Organization of Opera

The relationships among artists who are engaged in evolving productions also affect the nature of the resulting opera and the way it is produced. The accommodations among occupational roles are not easily met and often involve competing interests, which are governed by the norms of production and musical styles. Opera has historically been a battleground for the various elements of voice, instruments, dance, composers, directors, etc., with changes in the dominance of one over the others throughout time. The way these elements are integrated in the opera is significantly affected by the market conditions and the relationship between artist and consumer.

Although investigation of the relationship between the individual and the social organization antedates even the nineteenth century social philosophers, this theory has never been vigorously applied to the study of performing artists, and especially within the operatic setting. While there is an embarrassment of riches with regard to studies of factory workers, the scientific and medical professions, deviant occupations, and visual artists, there is a dearth of sociological studies of the occupational and organizational nature of the classical performing arts in America.

There is a social-psychological study of the composer (Nash 1957), dancer (Forsyth and Kolenda 1970), and instrumentalist (Kadushin 1969); an organizational analysis of symphony orchestras (Arian 1971); and popular books exploring the economics of the performing arts (Baumol and Bowen 1966; and Netzer 1978). Literature, painting, and poetry have been the subject of countless studies with various theoretical frameworks (Albrecht, Barnett, and Griff 1951). As a consequence, it was necessary to deal with musicological material, and the writings of music critics, and biographers.

The opera world is a perfect setting for the application of theories of occupations and organizations, because of the contradictory and yet interrelated interests between artists and the organizations that present and sponsor opera. Sociologists are concerned with the norms that govern the system of interrelationships within a social structure. Toward this end, an analysis is attempted of the roles of some of the performing and nonperforming personnel engaged in opera: singers, composers, general managers, conductors, stage directors, critics, and audiences. These relationships are viewed in the light of the opera's system of patronage, its nonprofit base, and the organizational complex in which the participants work, for these make up the social structure from which relationships evolve, ideas are coordinated, and musical styles are developed.

An organization, being a social group, involves the shared efforts of various individuals. To accept that as a necessary condition of social structure, however, does not involve a commitment to the consensual view of society and social organization. The writings of Simmel, Horowitz, and Blumer, for example, include a theoretical framework which takes this sociological paradox into account and presents a more realistic image of everyday activities made up of persons rather than of a "closed system." While collective behavior rests on shared perspectives, goals, definitions of situations, and vocabularies, it does not exclude the presence of conflicting demands and of "deviance" on the part of individuals who belong to a social group. (Simmel 1950; Horowitz 1962:177)

Conflict and deviance must be seen to operate within the confines of social structure — within the system of mutually established norms and values. Simmel astutely perceived both conflict and cooperation as forms of "sociation." Conflict may be a precondition for the orderly functioning of society and the degree of conflict, whether it be positive or negative (that is, whether it is an integrative or destructive influence on social structure), depends upon the social structure in which it occurs. Total disorganization may result, therefore, from some forms of conflict; on the other hand, conflict which is tolerated has some claim to legitimacy and indeed may be necessary for the functioning of the social organization.

This theory of conflict seems to account for the dynamics within an organization and explains its ability to change. In the case of opera, especially high-strung egos, schedule pressures, and artistic demands combine, and contribute to the production of an art form and to the fulfillment of personal goals as well as to the functioning of the social organization. Feuds and gossip serve to satisfy individual selves. Forsyth and Kolenda, in analyzing a ballet company, offered interesting data but fell short since they minimized competition and divergent interests of individual artists engaged within the creative unit. Although defining their problem as ". . . how collaboration is maintained in a social system that requires individual competition for rank and critical acclaim . . ." (1970:223), they subjected their data too rigidly to the "integrative pattern variables," completely losing sight of group processes and the changing nature of the social group. Contradictory perspectives were seen as always subjected to the requirements and collective goals of the social system rather than emerging as integral and dynamic aspects of it. In addition, the ballet company was seen as a closed system, with no regard for the audience, management, contract negotiations, and other forces. Paradoxically, the ballet company and the opera company are collectivities that must maintain a level of competition, given the demands of both the artists and of the art form. Conflict and deviance, therefore, become intrinsic to the functioning of the system, are institutionalized, to some extent locate the system of norms and values, and become a permanent aspect of the organization.

Defining the Problem

This book attempts to describe the opera world: its work organization, performing roles, and its marketplace including audiences and forms of patronage. In so doing, the major goal is to investigate the effects of the structure of an opera company, as well as its audience and patrons, on the cultural product. It will, to this end, investigate the nature of opera production and try to identify major, significant trends in musical styles and occupational roles, and relate these to the influence of the sources of support, including the market. It will also try to discover how the performers view each other in the larger scheme of things, their major areas of agreement or conflict, and how these are resolved in the organization of work.

The structure of modern opera is a product of centuries of social and economic shaping. To gain a clear understanding of the way in which opera works in contemporary society, the pressures and processes that influenced its growth must be examined. The very roles of the performers and the attendant staff — singers, conductors, stage-directors, chorus, dancers, instrumentalists — have evolved over time and have been shaped by various socio-economic as well as aesthetic influences, and these forces must be examined.

A modest historical analysis of how the roles of singer, composer, instrumentalist, conductor, critic, and manager have achieved their present professional status will be provided in Chapter 2. Viewed as increasingly specialized activities, their roles, particular identifications, values, and norms provide clues to the changing relationships among them as they integrate their talents within the organization. This historical review will confirm that opera has always had to contend with different and competing elements as manifested by the social position and function of the artist in society; and that this, in turn, has been affected by the prevailing system of patronage, and by audience preferences. If the social position of the artist and the changes in musical styles is seen as resulting from audience tastes and preferences, credence is given to the thesis that sociological factors are a significant force in shaping opera.

Chapter 3 analyzes the opera market in the United States. The major focus is on the patrons, the subsidies of corporations, governments, and foundations, and on the costs of production. Chapter 4 analyzes opera repertoire in the United States. It evaluates the influence of the box office and audiences on repertoire decisions and describes the effects of the market on the specific organizations that produce opera. Chapter 5 focuses on the complex organizational structures that prevail in the large companies and highlights the role of the general manager. Chapter 6 is concerned with the performers' work ethics and interrelationships in performing art organizations. Chapter 7 concludes by addressing the questions raised in the introductory chapter on the consequences of relying on the market for the shaping of a cultural product and artists' occupational roles.

In summary, then, this study shows the effects of socio-economic conditions on opera, specifically with regard to styles of performance, the organization of production, and the content of productions. It

shows that the roles of performers have been shaped by these fore-
going exigencies. Finally, it describes the manner in which the development of the various roles in the structure of opera leads to the
emergence of a social organization articulated with a minimum of
conflict and dissension.

*Backstage after a 1958 "Falstaff" with Anna Maria Canali
(Meg Page), Renata Tebaldi (Alice Ford), conductor
Tullio Serafin, Alvino Misciano (Fenton),
and Tito Gobbi (Falstaff) (Lyric Opera of Chicago)*

2 *The Rise and Development of Operatic Styles and Opera Performers*

In a somewhat panoramic view of the history of music, the role of each artist in an opera production will be investigated. The main concern here is the relationship between the social position of artists and musical styles. In this analysis, some of the following questions will be examined. Can a particular time in music history be identified in which the singer, conductor, composer, critic, director-designer or impresario emerged both as a specialist and as a professional? Next, what has been the effect of this trend toward specialization of musical styles as well as on the relationship each performer has to the others and to his function in the total production? What other factors of a socio-economic nature intervened in this process of giving priority to one artist over another, and, in turn, influenced musical styles? How has the preference for a particular artist by the patron and/or the larger audience influenced musical trends? How has the system of patronage and the nature of audiences shown a preference for a particular artist and, thereby, influenced musical trends?

Following the objective of determining the trends toward specialization, and the emergence, concomitantly, of divergent and changing styles in music both with regard to the development of attitudes toward each other and the role of each speciality in an opera production, it is necessary to look to the institutional frameworks from which such conditions have evolved. Both the position and function of musicians and singers in society will lend a clearer understanding of the nature of musical style and trends as determined by the system of patronage, and the consequences of this on the norms which govern performers' relationships to each other in organizations.

Specialization affects a performance by its ensuing divergent priorities and ideologies. Although opera has always had to contend with such diversity of specialities, what will be of interest, in succeeding chapters, is its expression today in terms of the kinds of opera produced and how they are presented — on the organization, style and content of opera. These commitments are reflections of occupations and are expressed through debates over artistic styles and standards, which have changed over time. The composer, for example, has been excluded from the production process in the leading opera houses today in contrast to his dominant position in the nineteenth century, and his changing social position in society has affected both the style and content of productions. As is evident, attention is upon performers and musical styles. In attempting to understand this process, it is necessary to use the historical studies of western music, singing, singers, and other musician-artists such as the conductor, critic, and composer.[1]

Opera as we know it today, came into being in the mid-seventeenth century. By this time, operatic form included an orchestra, a horn section, a cast of six to eight singers, and a chorus comprising the secondary roles of soldier, ladies in waiting, and the like. Opera was basically a musical event, which emphasized the role of the singer. But, before this came to be, the chronicles of opera relate a history which saw opera develop from poetry set to music.

From its beginnings as *dramma per musica*, there has been a debate as to whether opera is theater or music. This debate is crucial in the understanding of the role of the singer, and the social organization of opera. First, however, it is necessary to trace the social position of the various roles which comprise an opera.

The *Gemeinschaft* of Musical Life

Musicians, like other members of society, were affected by a social structure, which established their specific roles and statuses as well as the place occupied by their music. The magico-religious origins of music suggest that the homogeneity of the social structure was not without its effect upon the social position and function of early musicians and singers. Song was part of the ceremonies and rituals which were the center of all activity of primitive man. As a consequence, the role of the musicians was neither specialized nor secular; they performed an integral function in the ritual life of communal peoples. The first music and song, reflecting the community of experience, was less elaborate, quite undifferentiated, and more unspecialized than later forms (Rushmore 1971:7; Durkheim 1947; Nash 1964:39; Bowra 1962; Merriam 1964; Malinowski 1925:194).

Bruno Nettl, in his book, *Music in Primitive Culture*, writes:

> The typical primitive group has no specialization or professionalization; its division of labor depends almost exclusively on sex and occasionally on age; and only rarely are certain individuals proficient in any technique to a distinctive degree. All women do the same things each day, possess approximately the same skills, have the same interests; and the men's activities are equally common to all. Accordingly, the same songs are known by all the members of the group, and there is little specialization in composition, performance, or instrument-making. (1956:10)

Although music in Greek and Roman civilizations was communal, the musician enjoyed considerable prestige because he embodied the political and religious goals of the state. The musician was given a "professional" status, the ultimate in individual achievement of any citizen. Manifesting the Platonic ideal, musical expression became institutionalized in the *agones* and was reserved for free Athenians.[2]

The church became the dominant institution for hundreds of years to follow. It subjected music as well as all other forms of culture to its goals. It set standards and styles, and determined the careers of musicians and singers. Music was church music with a primary emphasis on the liturgy. A distinction between professional and clerical status was eliminated and musical achievement became the duty of churchmen, for which they were awarded status within the ecclesiastical hierarchy.[3] Sacred and secular music, as categories, were abolished; records are not available of any of the secular music of the time. The church had a virtual monopoly on musical life and inhibited innovations and specialization. All music was homophonic in style, emphasizing choir singing. Singing was in unison, and no one displayed any virtuoso technique. Frederic Dovan wrote, "The ecclesiastical period of the Middle Ages would not acknowledge interpretation in our modern sense as the individual expression of performance." (1942:45) Voice ranges, embellishments, and trills were identified with the secular life and manifested individuality and emotion. Music had to be an expression of *Gloria Dei* and the *aedificatio hominum;* Palestrina's masses and chants are the prototype of church music.

Liturgical plays date to the tenth century. In Italy, for example, by the thirteenth and fourteenth centuries, they became the Mystery Plays which were performed in piazzas and similar locations other than the church. These plays, known throughout Italy as *Sacre Rappresentazioni,* were for one or more voices, sung throughout, in *recitativo.* It is claimed that these plays, as they became more elaborate, led to the oratorio and opera by the sixteenth century.

The Secularization of Musicians and the Rise of the Performer

With the rise of the French troubadour (1150–1210), the musician gained independence. Although his was an unspecialized art requiring skills in music, voice, composition, and poetry, the troubadour's feudal and courtly life contributed to the rise of the solo performer. It was not until the Renaissance, however, that the solo performer could mature into the professional-specialist. Virtuosity, too, was left to be encouraged during this later period. The emphasis on individualism was manifested in music by secular drama, the antecedent of opera, and by the supremacy of the solo singer.

There were three types of poet-musicians at the time, reflecting a class structure with diverse tastes. The appearance of the troubadour and of the jongleur was followed by that of the minstrel, who came to fulfill the functions of both his predecessors, especially with the increasing demands for entertainment among the populace.

The troubadour, usually of noble birth, was originally a singer although later he was more exclusively involved in composition. Because of his close association with court life, particularly in politics, ". . . the ethical code of the knightly artists . . . forbade [his] being subjected to unnecessary contact with the populace." (Lang 1941:108) This furthered demands on him for composition rather than performance skills. Being gifted in the literary movements of the time and employing a more intellectual form of poetry (*trobar clus* — closed poetry) than his counterpart, the jongleur, he had greater prestige. The troubadour practiced his art for art's sake, receiving no remuneration. He was a well-trained "musician, educated in the abbeys and receiving the courses of instruction followed by young men preparing to take holy orders."[4]

The jongleur, the itinerant secular musician of the time, had a somewhat ambivalent status. Unlike the troubadour, the jongleur was not of noble birth, was feared by the church, and was envied by villagers. He traveled about the castles and towns entertaining and transmitting news in exchange for some form of remuneration. In the late middle ages, he was called the "minstrel," but the church feared his popularity. The number of minstrels grew throughout the thirteenth century, when musical life and other forms of social relationships were centered around the guilds. This form of entertainment originated in France, and had spread to Germany, Italy and Iberia with the *Minnesinger*, while in England the number of minstrels was much smaller, and the degree of their influence much less.

While specialization occurred to some extent, minstrels were skilled in music, voice, and composition. Here " . . . again emphasis was on the word and there was no idea of either vocal beauty or display for display's sake." (Rushmore, 1971:16) This secular art, writes Frederic Dovan, " . . . was a by-product of a new theory of music giving importance to poetic ideas expressed through words and language and later the voice expressed the dramatic goals leading eventually to embellishments, crescendos, etc." (1942:43) Performance could then take precedence over composition.

It took the spirit of the Renaissance to initiate appreciation of the virtuoso performer. As the medieval order declined, and along with it the domination by the church, a new structural order rose and with it its supporting ideology.

> Voluntarism, the new philosophical system which conceived will to be the dominant factor in experience and in the constitutions of the world, superseded the rationalism of the philosophers and theologians of late scholasticism. Voluntarism brought with it a strong accentuation of the individual with less reliance on the church. (Lang 1941:145)

During the Middle Ages art was considered a handicraft; during the Renaissance a work of art was thought possible only through the creative individuality and virtuosity of the artist. Thus, the Renaissance was important to the professionalization of the artist. Italy, not bound to the medieval culture of France nor dominated by the counter-reformation or Lutheranism of the northwestern countries, provided a favorable climate for the support of voluntarism. It was not until the late Gothic in the North that the anonymous composer disappears, and the individual begins to gain the recognition so deserved.

The Renaissance provided an intellectual climate conducive to the emphasis on individuality, and this affected musical styles because of the importance it afforded the solo performer. Such acceptance encouraged enormous activity among both professional and amateur musicians. Dilettantism became widespread, especially with the increased prestige given to the man of art. All aristocratic families educated their children in music, and many became competent singers, composers, and instrumentalists. Royalty, however, was not to remain the only patron of the arts.

While the emergence of musicians as specialist-performers was dependent on musical developments, it was the social conditions which nurtured a belief system which favored the growth of individuality, giving legitimacy and popularity to the performer. With the rise of the merchant cities, the mercantile classes emulated the life style of the aristocracy and so came to support artistic expressions. Given this new attitude toward the musician and his work and supported by a changing economic and political order, a public grew. Henceforth, many flocked to hear music, but they found their enjoyment in aristocratic salons, and later in the public opera houses, instead of in the churches.

The Socio-Cultural Roots of the National Traditions in Opera

From the very beginning, opera — a drama put to music — has had to contend with the balance between voice, instrumental music, drama, and dance. It has been the center for both innovation and controversy in the interpretation and integration of these elements. This study will explore the development of opera in Italy and Germany, because of their historical position in establishing major musical styles in opera and because they represent somewhat antithetical interpretations of the role given each performer in an operatic production. Each of these countries, in establishing national trends, expressed some combination or balance of the different elements that go into opera.

While musicologists can trace the origins of opera to the secular theatre of the Middle Ages and the Renaissance, the primary role of the solo singer in opera had its more immediate antecedent in the dramatic and monodic recitative created by a group of artists known as the "Florentine Camerata" toward the end of the sixteenth century

in Italy. Having their roots in the Renaissance and Baroque, literary
and artistic societies were abundant in Italy. They expanded because
of church and aristocratic patronage, and later by the support given
by the mercantile classes of the Venetian cities.

The Florentine Camerata

> met at the house of a wealthy patron, Count Bardi, and their
> members included, as well as Rinuccini, Peri and Caccini, the
> composer Vincenzo Galilei (the father of the astronomer). Be-
> tween them they evolved the idea of "recitativo" — a single vocal
> line, sung in a free, declamatory style, with simple instrumental
> support. This, solely concerned to reflect the meaning of the
> words and the inner life of the drama, did not impede the poet's
> thought as did the contrapuntal madrigal style.[5]

It is interesting to note that opera had a different emphasis in
the courts than in the Venetian opera houses. The aristocratic salons
demanded spectacular staging and costuming, while bourgeois tastes
dictated interest in the music, especially the voice.

Other European nations developed representative styles. This
present analysis of the operatic developments in Germany and Italy
is important in establishing the relationship between repertoire decisions and socio-economic factors from which these divergent styles
emerged. In investigating the nature of patronage and audiences in
both countries, it is possible to discern what influence such conditions
may have on what is selected for production. This is, of course, made
more explicit and our analysis is more complete when we begin to
analyze contemporary musical styles in the United States. We can,
however, make some national distinctions with regard to musical
developments:

> The Germans and Netherlands pursued the ideal of instrumental
> polyphony, rich in harmonic possibilities — the organ chorale
> and the fugue. . . . The Italians, on the other hand, aimed at
> perfecting the way to the sonata, the concerto, and the aria . . . its
> actual outcome was music-drama or opera, which appeared . . . in
> the last decade of the sixteenth century. (Einstein 1954:59, 80)

When Italian opera dominated the European market in the eighteenth century, it was first supported by courts of southern Germany;
but when German opera expanded to include the bourgeois patron,
Italian opera took on a different form. The rise of mercantilism, an-
tedated by the guild system, caused the growth of a middle class.
They had incomes, paid taxes, and became influential in the cultural

and intellectual life of the time. Possessing simpler tastes, they opposed the aristocratic music of the *opera seria*.[6] Love for the *Singspiel*, representing the conviviality of rural life in fairytale and mythological form, was combined with a literary tradition to create what Wagner later called *Gesamtkunstwerk* — a total art form integrating music, poetry, and drama.

In the sixteenth century, polyphony was more extensive in the northern countries and France, which initiated the spread of instrumental music and the symphony by the eighteenth century. The French contributed to the development of the lyric play and the *opera comique*. The works of Gluck and Rameau represent the masterpieces which founded the French dramatic art in music. The English, on the other hand, experimented with the ballad opera and the lyric stage.

The trend toward polyphony and contrapuntal musical lines is significant too, since it marked the beginning of a decline of the singers' monopoly on the musical market. Song was to become subjected to the requirements of instruments and musical score notation. This, in turn, facilitated the decline of the improvisatory skills of singers in early opera. It also contributed to the rise of other specialist-performers like the instrumentalist (especially the pianist and violinist) and later the conductor.

Opera as Voice versus Opera as Music

Italian music dominated all of Europe during this time; singers, composers and instrumentalists were exported to England, France, Spain, and Russia. Italy's influence was even greater in places where composers established schools, conservatories, and opera houses. Even such German masters as Gluck, Hasse, Telemann, and Mozart had to journey to the contemporary land of music. All the major Italian cities had theatres, conservatories, and church choirs — even foundling homes became training schools in musical composition and performance skills.

The Italian influence in Germany was most emphatic in Vienna (in the works of Metastasio, for example), Munich, and the Rhine cities. From the middle of the eighteenth century onward, however, Berlin became the hub of German music life. Although Germany is credited with being the home of instrumental music, when compared to the Italian bias toward the *voce*, the early eighteenth century saw a Milanese public interested in, and respectful of, symphonic music. The dramatic recitative in Germany, however, was only a step from the full realization of the orchestra as part of the dramatic action.

Rolland wrote of the national differences and possible reasons for the occurrence of such a revolutionary development in Germany.

> The Germans, on the other hand, are quite at home in the nascent symphony. Their natural taste for instrumental music, the necessity in which members of the little German Courts found themselves of confining themselves to such music, as the result of a strict application of the principles of the Reformed Church, which forbade them to maintain an opera house, the gregarious instinct which impelled the German musicians to unite in small societies, in small "colleges," in order to play together, instead of practising the individualism of the Italian *virtuosi* — all these things — everything, in short — even to the comparative inferiority of German singing, was bound to contribute to the universal development of instrumental music in Germany. Nowhere in Europe were there more schools in which it was taught, or more good orchestras. (Rolland 1915:209)

Few will disagree that musical ferment and growth at this time prevailed throughout Germany and Italy. Henry Raynor presented an interesting argument for the decline of musical composition in the pragmatic and Protestant England of the counter-reformation.

> Mercantile England had already discovered the benefits of utilitarian education for the middle classes and the poor; the upper classes did not take long to decide that it was socially demeaning to learn to play musical instruments because the playing of instruments was a profitable trade or profession. In Italy, with a less developed business life in most cities, it was natural to train musicians because both inside and outside the court life of the aristocracy, music was a common pleasure and to play in the orchestra of one of the new opera houses or to take service with a church or a nobleman did not lay the expense of apprenticeship indentures on the benevolence of those who had been responsible for a child's upkeep and training. (1972:140)

In addition to national commitments, socio-economic aspects of patronage can be seen as affecting the rise of the solo singer in Italy and other virtuoso instrumentalists in the northern countries. The French never forgot the traditions of Lully; consequently, for example, the ballet never lost its important place within the musical score. On the other hand, Gluck composed quite differently for audiences in Vienna and Italy, responding to their preferences for music or vocal technique. In 1755, he was asked to conduct performances of French *opèra comique*. In so doing, he learned to adapt his music more closely to the poetry than he had done for the Italian opera. This tendency was expressed in "Orfeo ed Euridice" (1762) — an opera written with continually melodic and important musical passages, rather than the series of segmented coloratura passages typical of his earlier works.

Patronage

Opera found patronage in private aristocratic salons, colleges, convents, and public opera houses. Everywhere there was some sort of opera and the top stars knew the value of the market. Music became so important in the eighteenth century that it represented the wealth and strength of towns, cities and nations.

The socio-political circumstances of the counter-reformation in England, as well as the growth of absolutism and mercantilism, affected the forms of patronage which supported music at this time. Different systems of patronage were reflected in the different kinds of opera of the Baroque Era, which included court opera, commercial opera, and middle class opera. (Bukofzer 1947:398) Samachson expresses clearly how patronage and audiences influenced the writings of composers, in his book, *The Fabulous World of Opera*.

> During the eighteenth century, however, the themes changed and, along with them, the nature of the comedy. Middle-class comedy replaced the traditional farcical plots handed down by the 'commedia dell' arte.' Burlesque arguments between gods and goddesses gave way to scenes of domestic misunderstanding, of master and servant at cross purposes, or of husband and wife trying to deceive each other. (1962:31)

The musician's social position was solely dependent upon the position of his patron, both private and public. Yorke-Lang in depicting musical life in the courts of Vienna, Dresden, Berlin, and Stuttgart, addressed the personalities of Frederick the Great and Maria Antonia because their relations with musicians in their employment characterize the bondage that musicians were accustomed to at this time. Since opera symbolized the supreme in musical baroque, it was used as a means of "conspicuous consumption," driving courts to bankruptcy and decline. They competed with each other in trying to lure artists away from each other's court by offering higher pensions and political status. Unfortunately, musicians were subjected to court whims; commissions glorified birthdays, weddings, and other ceremonial festivities. Memoirs and biographies are full of accounts of exploitation by these despotic patrons. (Yorke-Lang 1954:355; Pleasants 1966:48; Westrup 1955:98).[7]

Another musicologist has described the ideology that supported the showy productions commissioned by court patronage:

There were productions with a startling sumptuosity and a dizzy refusal to consider expense. . . . Where a composer of force and genius did not control the production, someone else, usually the artist-designer responsible for the machinery and setting and concerned with the creation of spectacular effects, took charge; in this latter case, the music became secondary to whatever visual excitements could be threaded into the story. . . . Even if a highly cultured aristocrat flattered his guests when he assumed their familiarity with mythological subject-matter set to severe music, a natural refusal to be out of the intellectual sway made highbrow style into a court convention . . . [and] was intended to manifest the grandeur of the authority who sponsored it; therefore, it had to be grand. The cost was not counted because the symbolic value of opera was reckoned to be worth whatever exorbitant sums were spent on it. (Raynor 1972:165)

Public patronage was represented by the free cities which controlled the musical life of the burghers and the churches. The guilds established standards, regulations for tests, and a system of municipal hierarchy for public commissions. In comparison to the private patron:

> musicians were well aware of the security afforded by public employment . . . because of their security and their more 'orderly' organization . . . . Self-supporting composers who made their living from the proceeds of their music did not exist . . . . The dependence on an aristocratic patron put the musician in the servant class. . . . Under the collective patronage of the churches and cities the musician enjoyed the same independence as did the craftsmen of the middle class. Civic employment in a prosperous city carried almost as much social prestige as court employment. (Bukofzer 1947:401–5)

The amateurism which spread in fifteenth-century, German-speaking Europe did much to produce generations of music lovers. Religious brotherhoods and fraternities took music quite seriously as an intellectual art. They imposed competitions for entrance to apprenticeship programs and required vigorous training in composition and singing. They offered no competition to the professional in that their activity was seen as an enjoyable, moral, and serious art. The *Meistersinger* was given authority and status; he represented an educated, leisured middle class who adopted and emulated aristocratic life styles and ideas. These collectively became the basis for a public audience.

where/what

→The academy, an association in which musicians got together to share ideas and perform for each other, eventually led to the modern concert hall. Students and amateurs realized the importance of these academies as a market for their music, and traveling *virtuosi* had to contact these groups in order to perform their works.

During the Baroque Era, however, opera was performed in the North solely in aristocratic salons, and this practice inhibited the growth of a public audience. Manfred Bukofzer (1947) claims that private performance insured a sounder and closer relationship between the composer and the audience, or between production and consumption. The aristocracy commissioned and understood the works performed, while the later development of the concert hall demanded the role of a critic to act as an intermediary between the composer and a less sophisticated audience.

Although the Italian influence throughout Europe in the eighteenth century was extensive, other song and opera did not succumb to the Metastasian style. The German *singspiel*, for example, featured simple melodies and folklike solo songs. Gluck in Paris, and Mozart in Vienna took off in their own directions, and certainly paved the way for the later work of Wagner and Weber in Germany.

The Virtuoso Singer

In Italy, musical preferences in style, and, consequently preferences for specific performers, developed with particular systems of patronage, which regional differences and national distinctions created. By the late seventeenth century, the Venetian mercantile class, unlike the aristocratic and religious patrons of Rome and Florence at the time, had established opera houses that produced public spectacles. By taking opera out of aristocratic salons, they established a commercial public; and it was a public that showed a preference for superstars, vocal *virtuosi*, and dramatic spectacles. Such a public created the demand for opera. Orphanages, previously papal choir schools, supplied the market by training singers and musicians and later became the schools for the musical training of *castrati*.

For almost two centuries, singers ruled the stage, and made both composers and librettists subservient to their wishes. During the seventeenth century, not only was music written for a particular singer and his/her vocal technique, but singers often changed the scores at their whim.

There were four well-known prima donnas born in the year 1700: Faustina Bordoni, Francesca Cuzzoni, Regina Minotti, and Vittoria

Tresa. They primarily centered at the court of Mantua, at the public opera house of Venice, and at the court of Dresden, then the center of German opera (Pahlen 1973:11). Later prima donnas included Vittoria Archilei, Adriana Basile, Leonora Baroni, and Catarina Martinelli. They led long and healthy lives, and were adored and entertained at the finest and most luxurious courts of Europe throughout the seventeenth and eighteenth centuries. They experimented with and provided the foundation for *bel canto* (beautiful and fine singing). Their supremacy in musical circles was only interrupted by the age of the *castrati*.

Venetian opera became known as "solo opera," the aria carrying the emotion and the climactic themes. Like other art of the Baroque Era, display and ornamentation was an end in itself. The *opera seria* provided the musical counterpart of baroque art. Arias were the high point of the opera — and practically the entire opera was a series of arias linked by *recitativo secco*, accompanied by a cello or harpsichord. The improvisatory nature of trills, *appogiaturas*, crescendos, and the like, afforded the solo singer the esteemed virtuoso position in baroque music. The solo singer dominated the market of the seventeenth and early eighteenth centuries. This artistic freedom was quite a departure from the religious and medieval polyphonic style in which voice ranges adhered strictly to the general design and the expression of individual talent was prohibited.

The Venetian opera houses were the first public opera houses in which tickets were sold to finance productions. Raynor astutely analyzes the role of the box office, and the social values which came to support the production of opera in the Venetian cities:

> Venice in 1637, like Hamburg half a century later, was as conscious of its own grandeur and of its status as a city attracting vast numbers of tourists as any court might be. Though commercial opera run for a profit could not afford to indulge in costly machinery and great choruses, it won its popularity partly as a manifestation of civic, rather than individual power; opera meant no less as a symbol to merchant princes than it did to Mantua, Florence, Ferrara and in a short time Vienna, where it was a recognized declaration of political authority and wealth. (Raynor 1972:169)

In Venice, at this time, there was an unusual bias toward the display of vocal technique. Little attention was given to the composer's aim and the requirements of the musical score. Unlike the later Wagnerian audience, the eighteenth century listener would have been uneasy with the orchestra's dominance. The mania for spectacle and virtuosity was epitomized by the adoration given a particular solo singer of "mistaken" identity as outcries of "bravo" and "viva il coltello" echoed through the opera houses. Audiences listened to an unusually high and beautiful coloratura vocal range contained in the body of a tall, broad-shouldered, hairless male — the *castrato*. Institutions grew all over Italy for their training and provided a black market for castrated boys. By the late seventeenth century, the *castrati* had monopolized the singing market. Gluck and Mozart wrote early operas with specific *castrati* in mind. For a few (Farinelli, Caffarelli, and Carestini), after initial vigorous training and a monastic life style, the rewards were bountiful. Musical and political positions were granted in the courts of Germany, Spain, Portugal, Scandinavia, Austria, Russia, and Italy.[8] The *castrati* gradually disappeared by the early nineteenth century. Napoleon, before his fall, had issued a decree outlawing castration, and as religious beliefs began to tolerate women on the stage, females reappeared.

The *castrati* period lent prestige to the coloratura voice range, thereby establishing a musical tradition that was important in the history of singing and musical interpretation. It also led to the adulation of the coloratura voice of the *prima donna* — the "first lady" of the opera company.

The era of Guiditta Pasta, the first "Norma," Giulia Grisi, Angelica Catalani, Henriette Sontag and Maria Malibran was from 1820 to 1835. *Primi Uomini* included Boschi, Montagnana, Fischer, Garcia and Rubini. It was a time when singers reigned supreme, and although there were musical conventions to conform to, vocalists had the freedom to compose or improvise at certain sections throughout an opera. Henry Pleasants, in his well-known book, *The Great Singers*, 1966, provides examples of such individual improvisation by displaying the musical scores of Catalani. Of these scores (see pp. 24–25), he writes,

> There was no telling whose music might turn up in any opera in which Catalani sang. Here are the famous —some thought them infamous — variations she sang to Paisiello's 'Nel cor più non mi sento' and which she introduced into 'Il fanatico per la musica.' They are a good example of the overembellishment of a simple tune that characterized the decadence of the age of 'bel canto.' (1966:114–5)

Many of the singers of this time also had the distinction of having Rossini, Bellini, and Donizetti write operatic roles with them in mind. A distinction bestowed; however, this led to type-casting, and specialization of vocal range, which were unheard of prior to this time.

Another "Golden Age of Singing" occurred between 1880 and the First World War. During this time, singing underwent great changes. As the baroque faded, mythological heroes and stories gave way to real people and events. *Opera buffa* experimented with different themes and plots, and gave importance to the male roles, which were once secondary. Concomitant musical development in orchestration encouraged the singer to add a dramatic dimension to his/her technique — a dimension which has steadily gained in importance to the present day. Callas' predecessors of this time were the German, Wilhelmine Schroder-Devrient, and the "singing actress," Pauline *(1850-70)* Viardot-Garcia. They did much to establish the norms of today, which dictate a harmony between vocal technique and dramatic characterization.

By the nineteenth century — through the works of Verdi, Rossini, Donizetti and Bellini — the Italians had assured the solo singer a place in the mainstream of the plot, because of the emphasis upon melody and the importance of arias and recitative passages. The female voice took on added importance with the decline of the *castrati*. The male counterpart (*primo uomo*) was given importance in the works of Rossini, Verdi, and later Wagner, but the bass had to wait for later developments in the comic *opera buffa*. The growth of large concert halls and auditoriums accelerated the demand for stronger and larger voices, both male and female.

The *opera seria* and the voices of the *castrati* created what is known today as the first age of *bel canto*. This extremely important development irretrievably established virtuosity as an interpretative and creative art in opera performances. While there was virtuosity in the *agones* of ancient Greece and later in the solo parts of the liturgy, this unique interpretation firmly established virtuosity, later to be transferred to other musical specialists.

> We know how the first instrumental virtuosos were inspired by vocal polyphony, transcribing sacred and secular songs and adapting them according to the resources of their instrument and their own ingenuity. (Pincherele 1963:32)

Instrumentalists — like Liszt, Rubinstein, Paganini, and Wieniawski, to name a few — were praised for their virtuoso talents. Along with these *virtuosi*, the singer came to be viewed as a "creator," as his performance also required the skill of interpreting the works of other artists.

> *Bel canto* was, in other words, a performer's art, with the composer serving the singer as the song writer or arranger serves

> the popular singer or instrumental jazz soloist today, and with the singer granted a liberty to depart from the written notes conceivable today only in popular music or in the part of the older generation of Jewish cantors . . . . He was expected, even required, to depart from the letter of the score, and he was judged by the imagination, taste, daring and refinement of his invention. (Pleasants 1966:24)

Improvisation contributed to the rise of virtuosity, but had unfortunate effects upon the composer[9]. His musical aims were considered secondary to the showy and skilled displays of singers. Even today, the definition of virtuosity, as physical technique, subjugates musical requirements to the performer's interpretative skill. Marc Pincherele alludes to the mass appeal of *virtuosi* and accepts their role because of their ability to captivate audiences and generate further interest in music. He writes, "The virtuoso soloist is more accessible because he is less abstract, by an outward charm, he is more effective. . . ." (1963:39) Ironically, with the rise of virtuosity came a shift in definition which included "performance" as an art in itself, as a response to audience preferences, especially Italian audiences, in the eighteenth century. This has further contributed to the marginal position of the composer[10].

The Audience and the Critic

The improvisatory and *bel canto* nature of the Italian opera did not take hold in the northern countries. They experimented instead with different and even antithetical musical styles. Protestant church music, a long German literary tradition, and the rise of mercantilism created an urban bourgeois class with a taste for rural and communal themes which came to be expressed as part of the total theatrical setting. The northern countries esteemed the composer of opera, and later the composer-performer and instrumentalist. Although the German *Lied*, the counterpart to *bel canto* singing, was respected, the emphasis was on the requirements of theatrical staging and musicianship rather than on the solo prima donna. The *Lied*, for example, was reserved for recitals and individual display. With the German tendency toward the adoration of the instrumentalist, virtuoso commitments were established which contributed to the rise of the orchestra and the virtuoso-conductor of the following century.

The values of the middle class and the communal nature of northern German music also manifested themselves in the church music of the early Baroque Era. Unlike its Catholic counterpart, German religious music demanded the participation of congregations and became so popular that choral societies, *Kantoreien,* other informal amateur organizations proliferated. Such amateur participation led, by the late seventeenth century, to instrumental dilettantism. (Brockway 1941:374)

Amateur groups were supported by the church, became quite universal, and created an unprecedented demand for performers. Dilettantes became performing musicians at public concerts organized by choral societies. Musical historians claim that the public concert hall, rarely found in the Baroque Era, dates from about the middle of the eighteenth century when the town concert societies were founded. They continued to proliferate into the nineteenth century. The numerous concerts held by musical societies were important since they took music out of the parish church, thereby secularizing instrumental music.

Musical societies are said to have created a widespread love of music that had the potential for creating a listening audience, rather than a performing public. The various strata of the upper bourgeoisie provided such an audience with leisure and financial backing. Subscription audiences were not uncommon. Handel's budgetary burdens as a composer-performer-impresario with The Royal Academy of Music in England were not unlike those of today's impresarios. Subscribers in those days, however, sought to make a profit by treating their subscriptions like investment shares in the companies.

The concerts soon became the settings for composer-performers like Mozart and Beethoven to perform their works for subscription audiences. Public concerts did much to introduce instrumental music, highlight the role of the composer-performer, and provide a showplace for the display of the virtuoso. Raynor summarizes the relation of public concerts to opera:

> In spite of Beethoven's glorification of the public concert, in those cities where opera was linked to a court, and to displays of social grandeur, orchestral music continued to take second place to dramatic music. There is no reason whatever to regard opera as an "aristocratic" form and the symphony as in some way essentially "middle class;" but it was in the towns where opera was not a special entertainment fervently supported by royalty and the socially great that the concert achieved parity of esteem with the socially grander form. Wagner's failure to establish regular professional concerts in Dresden in the 1840s shows that the official devotion to opera persisted long after Beethoven's death. (Raynor 1972:329)

The rise of these public concerts is interesting in the light of the thesis that socio-economic forces shape the organization of opera. The concerts met the demands of a middle class audience. This public audience paid homage to the instrumentalist (composer-performer) and contributed to the emergence of the role of the critic. As the market for public concerts was expanded and even became international in scope, ". . . the cult of *Wunderkinder*, so popular in the nineteenth century, got under way." (Lang 1941: 723).

As musical concerts became widespread, an audience grew composed of listeners with varying degrees of sophistication. The critic, for a time, supplied such a public with musical tastes by his critical evaluations of performances and increasingly functioned as an intermediary between the musical and lay communities. The first music critics appeared in the eighteenth century and were the elite of musical society, being either composers or theoreticians. Max Graf describes their role and their commitments to the Age of Reason:

> The glorification of human reason which is the chief characteristic of the eighteenth century assumes an admiration for science and for scientific culture. Hence, the enlightened musician was the cultured musician, not a mere artisan without knowledge of the spiritual achievements of his age. Men like Mattheson and Telemann were, as their books prove, laden with erudition; and when they walked gravely through the streets of Hamburg, with their black cloaks swelled out by the sea breeze, the passers-by respected them as they respected the earnest senators and the fanatic preachers of the city. (Graf 1946:47)

The critics' commitments to the enlightenment and the Age of Reason inevitably paved the way for their confrontation with baroque opera. Musicologists claim that the art of criticism developed in the eighteenth century as a response to the Italian style of singing. In the Classical Age, the spread of musical magazines encouraged musical criticism, and the critics' influence was heightened once their work began to appear in the "daily newspapers." Max Graf claims that it was not until Haydn and Mozart had died and Beethoven had established his fame that criticism began to appear in the dailies. In the musical magazines, critical style had taken a heavy, intellectual and scientific approach. Graf writes that, by 1810, there had been significant changes.

> [Music criticism for the general public] . . . too, left the theoreticians and entered the house of music lovers and amateurs; . . . this change in style was similar to the change that

brought about the rise of classical English prose — plain, clear, and efficient — of the eighteenth century. The change was early apparent in the magazines edited by Hiller. Their language began to approach the daily life of the common reader. (Graf 1946: 115)

And this more popular style and language of musical criticism did much to incorporate as well as respond to the demands of the middle class audience. As public concerts broke from amateur associations, and became increasingly widespread, musical criticism began to appear in the daily newspapers.

As Romanticism approached, bringing with it an adoration of the composer, composer-critics like Weber, Berlioz, Robert Schumann, and Liszt took to the pen to defend their music. This was quite different from the approach of the noble man of letters, the theoretician, who had cultivated an intimacy with musicians. By the middle of the nineteenth century, criticism had become professionalized and part of the dailies. Graf wrote of the new critic's inevitable allegiance to his public:

> The music critics of the new industrial age sided with the readers of the papers — who looked for entertainers in theatres and concert halls of an evening . . . . Such was the condition of things, when Richard Wagner turned his colorful imagination upon myths and legends, gods and heroes, and put them on the stage of the opera house. (Graf 1946: 225)

The non-composing critic, who was perhaps better trained in the skills of journalism than the artist-critic, was the thinker, writer, and aesthetician whose criticisms were based on well-formulated principles. The artist-critic, in contrast, viewed his skill in musical composition as his raison d'être. The modern critic faces particular problems due to both to his affiliation with the mass media and the extent of his occupational specialization. Since the eighteenth century, he has become more concerned with writing evaluations than with actually engaging in composition or performance.

Unlike his predecessor in Europe, who was considered a literary critic or personality, the modern critic is looked on as a specialized reporter, identified with and given status contingent on the publication for which he writes.[11] Others free-lance or are associated with educational institutions. Albrecht points to the kinds of media that evaluate the output of artists, but he does not view their role as essential in the marketing process. He writes that publications in which reviews or critical evaluations appear range from:

> the local newspaper to that of the New York Times, or the London Times, both of which produce "magazine" sections or

supplements devoted to literature and the arts, as well as other types of publications . . . *Harper's,* the *Atlantic,* the *Saturday Review* and the *New York Review of Books.* . . [and] are usually free from politics or biases that may characterize any particular periodical. (1973:7)

The emergence of the critic was, however, connected with the emergence of music, and in particular opera, as a form of public entertainment. If the public was going to pay for entertainment, it had to receive some kind of assurance from some "authority" that it was either likely to get its money's worth or that it had indeed obtained value the previous night. The critic in a sense became the middleman between consumers on the one hand and artists and producers on the other.

Today, given the reliance of the mass audience on the media, the feature writer serves the function of expressing the needed appreciation for musical events, thus stimulating the lay public to go to performances of serious music. In fact, major newspapers appear to allot as much space to biographies, interviews, and other interest stories as they do to the actual reporting and/or criticism of musical events. The critic's specialized functions in relation to the demands of both the media and public have created a controversy over his role. Is it reporting of music events as "facts" or is it musical criticism involving aesthetic appraisal and interpretation? To the musical community, the latter is known as the musician's critic, while the former is reserved for the public.

The Composer-Performer

Socio-cultural values and particular forms of patronage led to differences in musical orientation and the rise of specialists. Private and middle-class patronage, manifested at first by the subscription audience, brought about a demand for the virtuoso performer. Dilettante instrumentalists and choral groups in Northern Europe extended the taste of these audiences for the composer-performer, while aristocratic and Venetian families favored the singer's interpretation and the *bel canto* style. For some time, the soloist overshadowed the composer, until Northern bourgeois tastes and Protestant interests facilitated the emphasis on instrumentalists and the composer-performer came to compete with the singer. Both social class and ethnic group were seen as affecting musical styles; for example, the middle class in Germany preferred instrumental music and the *Meistersinger* while the German courts paralleled the Italian cities' love of opera.

The Italians pioneered in the markings of articulation, while the Germans made innovations in musical orchestration. Composers, at this time, also were the performers of their own works, and some composer-*virtuosi* of the eighteenth century included Tartini, Vivaldi, Mozart, Beethoven, and Corelli. Capable of combining both composition and performance skills, the composer-performer of the late eighteenth and early nineteenth centuries came to dominate the virtuoso market. Those composers capable of virtuosity in performance achieved in the nineteenth century the kind of eminence the singer had enjoyed in the eighteenth century. As musical criticism and historiography came to be dominated by German critics and historians, the composer was increasingly viewed as embodying the ultimate in musicianship. Music historians have, to some extent, neglected performers and singers in their analyses, and this bias may be explained by the traditions established during this time.

The composer-performer was an early stage in the process of professionalization and specialization of the performer, conductor and composer. With the publication of music, the composer became more involved in performing of other works, and the publisher took over from the impresario as intermediary between the composer and his audience.[12] The composer no longer composed in response to a patron's whim. Instead, by the end of the nineteenth century

> to all intents and purposes, he had become a court conductor whose primary task was to see that the growing repertory — its standardization was a very slow process—was adequately rehearsed and performed. . . . [T]he breakdown of the old system took the composer effectively out of practical music-making, unless he were also a virtuoso instrumentalist or conductor. It robbed him, not only of his opportunity to work in close collaboration with other musicians, but also of his chance to forge a close, potentially creative association with his audience. That is to say, it took away his direct social function. (Raynor 1972: 352–3)

The prestige of the composer is indicated by the fact that Beethoven was welcomed as an honored guest in upper class circles; ". . . his aristocratic patrons were well-educated amateurs and realized that the composer in Beethoven should receive encouragement over the virtuoso" (Lang 1941:757). In contrast, Haydn wore a lackey's garment and was treated like a servant in the German courts.

The middle class, however, admired the *performance* skills of Beethoven, Schubert, Mendelssohn, Schumann, Chopin and later Liszt and Paganini, creating an enormous market for these traveling *virtuosi*. The increasingly widespread organization of public concerts did much to highlight the virtuoso until this dimension of the artist finally took precedence over his skills in composition.

The specialist-performer represented the artist with perhaps a less sophisticated, and a less abstract knowledge of music. "Recitals in the modern sense began only in the eighteen thirties, with the generation of Liszt, Thalberg, and Clara Wieck Schumann. Before their time a solo recital on the piano or a public performance of a piano sonata was a rarity" (Lang 1941: 967). The number of amateur instrumentalists who became popular composer-performers grew.

Hindemith stresses the revolutionary impact music publishing had in contributing to the specialization of the composer-performer into independent professions of composer and performer.

> By the time Arnulf wrote his treatise in the early nineteenth century, the situation had changed, notation had become sufficiently reliable to free the performers from the fetters of dull imitation, and with the development of more particular music, they were obliged to lift their musical accomplishments to a higher level of general intelligence with the knowledge of notation and harmony, the composer's craft also developed more and more into a highly specialized art instead of a rather esoteric branch of science. This more efficient and more elaborate method of composing led to an ever increasing strain exerted on the musical material, which forced the performers to adapt themselves to demands heretofore unknown. Once used to these new conditions, they started inventing new technical devices and virtuoso tricks of their own which, in turn, again influenced the composers' technique. The immediate effect of all this was a revolution of the performer and his work. From now on, the composer was dependent on the performer. (Hindemith 1969:130–1)

By the end of the nineteenth century, artists had specialized ". . . into 'Beethoven players,' 'Chopin players,' 'Wagnerian tenors,' 'conductors of Russian music,' etc." (Lang 1941:967) The composer-performer, however, personified the spirit of Romanticism, the ultimate in virtuosity combining both creation and interpretation. This had undoubted consequences on later attitudes toward performers. And the Romanticism of the nineteenth century served to legitimize the eventual supremacy of performers over composers:

> With the classicists romanticized, an era of growing individualism and interpretive subjectivism set in. Not the classic counterbalance of content and form, but the performer's individuality, gradually appears as the driving force of a personalized interpretation . . . . The interpreter no longer 'performs.' He 'repro-

duces' the art work . . . . As the nineteenth century progresses, the romantic performer becomes more and more an appeal to the listener's imagination, to the subconscious, which is more exciting than the plea of a baroque interpreter for conscious intellectual understanding. (Dovan 1942:155)

The dangers of emphasizing a performer's skill over the creative act of composition is indicated in the following remarks by Dennison Nash in his study of the American composer:

> An increase in the specialization or division of labor may very well be the basic condition from which all of the aforementioned conditions of music in modern society are derived. The composer has become more and more a specialist-performer. He has tended to jettison other skills (e.g. instrumentation) for the sake of his creative art. At the same time, increasing numbers of specialists stand between him and the audience. (Nash 1952:45)

This statement is especially important in the context of the present argument on the effect of patronage on musical style reflected by the social position of the artist. Musicologists and sociologists both agree that a change in patronage from private to public contributed to the "alienation" of the composer; he became farther and farther removed from his audience. The composer of the eighteenth and nineteenth centuries composed for people he knew, and was in close contact with his composition from the moment it was commissioned to its execution. Today, execution involves a complex organization with highly specialized activities and a management doing the job that had been once considered the function of the composer who created the work. His former authority and status have indeed been taken away.

The relationship between art and society as manifested in the social position of the artist in specific market situations, or in systems of patronage, is explicitly stated in the following quotation:

> The major change in the market relations of the Renaissance artist was primarily from religious to secular patronage. While the artist had lower social status, the relationship of the artist to his consumer was a close one. The artist participated in and knew the life of his patrons . . . . The rise of a large middle class in the eighteenth and nineteenth centuries resulted in a mass market for art . . . . With mass audiences whose obligation was the purchase of a ticket, or a book, rather than employment of the artist, art reached monumental proportions. The full symphony orchestra became the characteristic expression of music and it per-

formed for large audiences in architecturally appropriate halls.
(Bensman and Gerver 1958)

The transition to the performer as a specialist, irrespective of his
ability to compose, is revealed in the biographies and memoirs of
famous pianists, violinists, singers, and conductors of the late nineteenth century. The lives of Bruno Walter, Fritz Kreisler, Niccolo
Paganini, and others, symbolize and confirm the final phases of specialization in the arts. The role of the music publishing industry, an
expanding audience which preferred *virtuosi*, and the concept of
"performance" as a creative act, all contributed to the influential role
performers have today in dictating musical styles and trends. In addition, the audience, as a paying and listening entity, was in immediate contact with the performer and was satisfied when the artist
performed well. Indeed, the "star system" was an embodiment of an
audience-dictated preference for performers with heroic stature. This
made it possible for individuals to attract audiences and to keep them
over a period of years.

The Conductor

The conductor as we know him today has his immediate roots in the
nineteenth century. Conducting, however, goes as far back as the
late seventeenth century operas and possibly before, if one considers
the "leadership" requirements of the choir and vocal ensemble of
earlier periods. Paul Hindemith wrote of the earliest description of
the conductor in the "Tractatus de Musica" of Elias Solomon, a clerical
music writer of the late thirteenth century:

> He is one of the singers, and according to Elias 'has to know
> everything about the music to be sung. He beats time with his
> hand on the book and gives the cues and rests to the
> singers' . . . . Elias' conductor has essentially the same obliga-
> tions our conductors have, the difference being that nowadays
> the practising, correcting and prompting is done at the re-
> hearsal . . . . Unfamiliar to us is the complete lack of emphasis
> on the leader's work, the tendency to keep him the *primus inter
> pares*. (Hindemith 1969:136–7)

The conductors' relative dictatorship over the musical hierarchy
at present has been facilitated by the development of orchestration
and by twentieth-century innovations and norms in production, staging, and instrumentation. The late seventeenth and eighteenth cen-

turies saw the composer-conductor as conducting from the bow, clavier, or piano and sharing his responsibility with other instrumentalists. Eighteenth century leadership especially was delegated to two individuals: the chief violinist, known as the "leader," and the keyboard player, known as the "conductor." In opera, composer-conductors were the general rule. With the publication of music came the added obligation of musicians to add other composers' works to their repertories. Harold Schonberg claims that until the rise of the modern conductor as "performer-interpreter," his fame was measured more by his skill at composition than by conducting (1967:90). As a result, musical norms have changed and along with this the notion of what is musically aesthetic and tasteful. In comparing the norms of the eighteenth century, Schonberg writes of the expected role of the conductor at that time:

> His concepts as a performance musician, and hence as conductor, were governed by the eighteenth century concept of 'taste.' Taste in those days meant something quite different from what it does today. When we say that a present day musician has taste, we take it to mean that he follows the notes, keeps his own personality to a minimum, tries to reproduce the ideas of the composer as diligently and honestly as possible. But, taste in the eighteenth century involved precisely the opposite: the ability of the performing musician to embellish or even improve the ideas of the composer. The notes were the ground plan, and they only served to stimulate the ideas of the performer. If the performer made of those notes something grand, logical, imaginative, he had good taste. If he indulged in rapid display work, or in other ways displayed a conventional and commonplace mind, his taste was suspect. (1967:51)

This freedom continued into the late nineteenth and early twentieth centuries primarily due to the giants, Berlioz and Wagner. Although they indicated quite precisely the musical and staging demands of their own compositions, this did not inhibit them from re-interpreting works of earlier composers. Their genius, vanity, and following acted to legitimate their alterations. Ironically, they were establishing a trend which acted to inhibit such freedoms for generations to follow.

> They were not worried much about the letter of the score; they were always more interested in its spirit. . . . This, he did "only with the object of making the existing version produce the effect I desired." Not what Gluck desired: what I desired. But, that was part of the rules of romanticism, and Wagner was one

of the arch-romantics. In romanticism, the ego was all-important, the performer on the level of the creator, and one's aspirations were much more important than any such vague thing as scholarship or fidelity to the printed note. (Schonberg 1967:133)

The *Weltanschauung* of the latter part of the nineteenth century found its counterpart in music in the rise of symphonic and operatic interpretations of Wagner. *Gesamtkunstwerk*[13] did much to establish the supremacy of the conductor.

With more sophisticated orchestration and composition, and the increasing size of the orchestra, the late nineteenth and early twentieth centuries resulted in a redefinition of the conductor's role. Conducting came to be viewed as an art in itself — as an art of "performance" — its prime function being "interpretation." This was reinforced by the romantic notions of freedom and individuality; and until today, a performance was measured by a conductor's ability to "interpret" another's composition.[14]

In the twentieth century because of the importance attached to scientific knowledge and university affiliation, those thought to be truly great conductors are those who capture and retain the phrasing, tempo, and historicity of original composers. Today any performer, instrumentalist, singer, or conductor who has this ability, and returns to original manuscripts, or uses old instruments and techniques in order to retain the stylistic motives of the composer, is admired. The singer who merely embellishes without a fuller sense of the music (verbalized as "musicianship") is criticized. With this new orientation, the conductor is known more for his skill in conducting than composition and is a far cry from the multi-functional composer-performer, or *Kappelmeister*, of the eighteenth and nineteenth centuries. Toscanini is a case in point: his style set revolutionary trends for future conductors. Hans von Bulow's success was also based primarily upon his conducting. On the other hand, Gustav Mahler and Richard Strauss were well-known as composers as well as conductors and achieved fame on both grounds.

It was possible to invest conductors with "star quality" since they played individuated and central roles in a symphony or opera. Once again mass audiences could be made to focus on a star; this time the conductor had elicited their interest, loyalty, and financial support. This trend has had its effect upon the role of the singer. Orchestration and the ensuing rise and even dominance of other performers has led Henry Pleasants to correctly claim that styles have been established with the composer and public as the focus and the singer has come to be seen as an accompaniment. (1966)

With the public's acceptance of the composer rather than singer as the dominant figure in the lyric theatre, and of the conductor as the composer's plenipotentiary, the singer's formerly more or less exclusive intimacy with the public came to be regarded as improper and even indecent . . . . Such exceptional artists as Grisi, Patti, and Melba could perpetuate the older relationship of singer and public, in which the composer served the singer's courtship of the listener; but the repertoire that favored this relationship could not withstand the popularity of the new operas. (Pleasants 1970:340)

There was a counterpart to this trend of thinking for the virtuoso instrumentalist. Individual technique and display would be secondary to the general aim of the composition. Performance would be, in Virgil Thomson's term, "collectivistic." The function of integrating the different elements, however, was given to the conductor. With the declining influence of the composer, the changes in musical styles, and the proliferation of works by nineteenth-century composers, it is the conductor who has been given the role of reinterpreting and recreating these works. This development will be made clearer in the analysis of the organization and content of opera among the leading opera houses in the United States today.

Conclusion

It has been established that the emergence of the various artistic roles that comprise the modern operatic-symphonic structure are connected to the socio-economic changes that have occurred in western society. Increasingly, these roles have become professionalized; there has been a growing interdependence between artists' specialties, their status, aesthetic norms, and the structure of the market. As social institutions have become specialized and market relations have changed, the social position of artists, the nature of their roles, and the cultural product have also changed. Opera grew as a reconciliation of word and music. At present, the debate continues as to whether opera should be dominated by voice, music or theater. The debate has always existed, and has always dictated different positions for the performers. Both the audiences and the system of patronage showed varying degrees of preference for the composer, singer, director, or conductor. These preferences, in turn, affected the artists' relative positions of prestige and status in the musical community and, consequently, their authority in the determination of musical styles.

From early Greek times, until well into the eighteenth century, musicians had to contend with some system of private patronage, which was historically shared by the nobility, the clergy, and the courts. Before the advent of a secular and finally bureaucratic milieu, the artist was an integral part of the social activities of the group and was subservient to his patron. The growth of municipalities contributed to the eventual "professional" status of the musician, but the modern function of the performer has more immediate roots in the composer-performer who emerged by the mid-nineteenth century.

At that time, public concerts, reflecting the demands of a bourgeois audience, encouraged the decline of the role of singer, since audiences came to admire the virtuosity of the composer-performer and finally the instrumentalist. Supported by the public patronage of the middle class, which bought tickets, and the spirit of romanticism, which valued individuality and freedom, the virtuoso performer evolved as a significant force in setting musical styles. The consumption of music gradually shifted from the nobility and clergy to the middle class, but retained an "elite" position among the arts and as a symbol of status. The baroque style and splendor of court opera were transported to the commercial opera house and along with them went preferences for super-star singers performing compositions which were originally commissioned by aristocratic patrons.

The growth of opera was not merely a function of talent and technology, but also of the values and norms of behavior reflected in the system of patronage and audiences' tastes. These forces acted interdependently, stimulating the emergence of artists as specialized performers. They, in turn, affected certain musical styles. The development of specialization, with ensuing divergent perspectives, is manifested in present day conflicts over artistic styles, standards, the role of performing artists in a single production, and their status in the opera community.

The next step is to examine this art form in the United States today. How is musical style — as represented by the repertoire favored by the major opera organizations — influenced by audiences, private patrons, foundations, and corporations? The demands of audiences are surely considered and reflected in repertoire decisions. The analysis will further examine the consequences of these developments on the relationships among artists. The conflicts, accommodations, and adjustments, as well as the indicators of star-status, are rooted in the changes occurring in the audience-artist relationship. It will be profitable to see how the organization responds to the exigencies of the market.

Notes

[1]Music history relies upon innovations in printing, which occurred around 1500, the development of the phonograph, which occurred around the end of the nineteenth century, and upon autobiographies, memoirs, archeological evidence, paintings, reliefs, poetry, and literature. For a discussion of the role of performers in music history and especially addressing the rise of the professional, see: Romain Rolland 1922; Henry Raynor 1972; and Jack Westrup 1955.

[2]The *agones* were contests in athletics, chariot and horse-racing, music, drama, literature, poetry reading, etc. *Eros* is the bridge between ideas and phenomenon: *nomos* implies "harmony," which is a musical expression of the norms of moral conduct; analogy exists between the movements of the soul and the musical progression (Lang 1941:13–14). Cf. Homeric epics, Plato's Timaeius, Laws, Georgias, Philebus, and the Republic. See Rolland 1915:19–20 and Loft 1950.

[3]The famous *Schola Lectorum* (of early Jewish and Christian tradition) were clerical schools in which men and boys learned to sing the psalms at religious services to assist the clergy, and training centers for the famous *castrati* of the seventeenth century. (Lang 1969:24, 33, 52; Rolland 1915:14; Einstein 1954:30; Henderson 1921:17; Rushmore 1971:12).

[4]Rutebeuf (1230–80) a veritable Francois Villon of the late thirteenth century, was the first real subjective, individual and independent lyric poet of the middle ages (Henderson 1921:49; cf. Lang 1969:111).

[5]Orrey 1972:16; Grout 1965:34; Raynor 1972:155; Honigsheim 1973:216. Rolland reminds us of the simplicity of taking a particular creation and isolating it quite independent of the arts and intellectual development. He traces the growth of opera, therefore, to the *sacre rappresentazioni* and the *maggi of Tuscany* which represented the application of music to words and recited passages.

[6]Eric Bloom (1971:478) defines *opera seria* as ". . . serious opera in Italian. A type of eighteenth century opera especially cultivated by the librettist Zeno Metastasio treating mythological heroic historical subjects. The musical treatment is mainly by recitatives and arias, more rarely duets and other concerto numbers of choruses."

[7]The aristocratic salons inhibited innovations in music since they could house only small ensembles. This explains the proliferation of chamber pieces during the time.

[8]Physical changes accompanied castration, which was usually performed when a boy was nine to twelve years of age. The intention was to prolong the growth of the vocal chords thus affording a soprano voice range. For an excellent discussion of the *castrati* and biographies of the famous ones, see Pleasants 1966; and Rushmore 1971:17–21. Herriot

[9]In the older sense, *virtuosity* described an excellent musician displaying knowledge and skill of other than his specific art, be it the voice, composition, or instrument. Critics for generations have been critical of the virtuoso when

a display of skill and technique seems to overshadow requirements of the score. See, for example, Kuhnau's satirical account of a German masquerading as an Italian virtuoso, in *Der Musicalische Ouack-Salber*, Rolland 1915:17–18. In the current usage, the term has meant ". . . a physical pleasure in skill, in agility, insatiable muscular activity, a pleasure in conquering, in dazzling, in subjugating by his person the thousand-headed public . . ." Pincherele 1963:17.

[10]See Hindemith 1969:132–33; Thomson 1939; Henderson 1938:152; Pleasants 1966:25–6; and Dovan 1942.

[11]For example, Richard Aldrich (1863–1937) of the *The New York Times* and *Tribune*, Hermann Finck (1854–1926) of the *Post*, Virgil Thomson of the *The New York Times*.

[12]Verdi's long and close relationship with his publisher, Ricordi, attests to the importance of the publisher as intermediary between composer and audience. This role had formerly been played by the impresario, who produced the composer's works. See Martin 1973.

[13]*Gesamtkunstwerk* can be defined as a music-dramatic unity. See Lang 1941:883; Dovan 1942:276–84.

[14]For a discussion of performance as "interpretation," see Lang 1947:963; Dovan 1942:311; Donal Henahan, "Mozart, Bach and the Great Divide," *The New York Times*, 1972; 9, regarding the use of original manuscripts and instruments in the 1972 Summer Mozart Festival at the New York Philharmonic; and Pincherele 1963:52–66.

The Metropolitan Opera House, Lincoln Center,
New York (Metropolitan Opera Archives)

3 *The Economics of Opera*

From Private to Public Support:

Although musical values in the United States have incorporated European artistic traditions, musical life was assured here only when it proved profitable and awarded social prestige to its consumers. Lacking national traditions of its own, opera in the United States tried to incorporate as much as possible from Europe; large companies followed the European model in their repertoire and casting. Henry Pleasants, an astute observer of the American musical scene, explains:

> This time factor [World War I] is essential to the critical comprehension of what happened to serious music. Technical exhaustion coincided with sociological obsolescence and an aesthetic decay. All coincided with the ultimate agony of the nineteenth century on the battlefield of Europe in the First World War . . . . One of the singularities of world civilization no longer European is the habit of its intellectuals to think of culture in European terms. As though culture were somehow exclusively synonymous with European accomplishments and tastes in music, painting, sculpture, architecture and literature. (Pleasants 1970:6)

Since the 1930s, although reorganized as a nonprofit association
with control independent of those who owned it, American opera
has expressed the conceptions of boards of directors and their wives.
It has also had to reconcile its patrician roots and controls with the
demands of an urban middle class. Opera's problems have been aggravated by the enormous rise in production costs and the changing
nature of philanthropy in the United States. Selling tickets has made
opera more responsive to the demands of the "box office;" consequently, the costs and popularity of productions influence decision-
making more than concern for the future of either the art form or the
artist. These developments have coincided with and were contingent
upon the rise of a commercially-oriented industry, encompassing
large-scale organizations of management, public relations men,
unions, journals, and "incorporated" music centers. Opera in America can only be understood in the light of this institutionalization,
which has brought an increasing professionalization and bureaucratization to the arts.

Perhaps an analogy can be made to the social functions of opera
in Europe during the early nineteenth century. There, as in the United
States, opera proved successful when it met the musical tastes of its
audience, and, when it was appropriate to the social conditions of
the city. In his history of the Metropolitan Opera, which disturbed
the descendants of the aristocratic patrons of the turn of the century,
Kolodin satirically described how the architecture of the house revealed the social status of its patrons and paralleled the social life of
New York. He wrote:

> It is not inappropriate commentary that certain of the box
> holders whose families built the house, lived in it as long as it
> suited their purposes, and abandoned it when it no longer did,
> still receive, on the average, $1,200 in interest annually. Assum-
> ing that they are sufficiently interested to subscribe for the
> ancestral box of the preferred Monday, they continue to attend
> the opera without charge, and actually without an assessment.
> The current cost of a once-a-week box subscription would be
> $1,080. . . .
> If you "owned", you were "in"; if you merely "rented," you
> were more than out — you were socially nonexistent. Needless
> to say, those who "rented" swallowed their unhappiness with
> this caste system, but extended it a bit farther by looking down
> on those who neither owned nor rented, but merely bought tick-
> ets. Some place in the house there was a dividing line between
> those who looked down on each other and those who looked at

the stage, but I have not, in fifteen years of research, been able to determine just where it began. (1966:48–50)

A short anecdote describing the emergence of opera in America as a capitalist enterprise is illuminating in its allusion to the "Protestant Ethic," which frowned upon all forms of entertainment. In the 1850s, America's greatest showman, P.T. Barnum, devised and established the first promotional concert tour for Jenny Lind, the "Swedish Nightingale." To ensure success, he had to create an audience and a desire for future tours. Stressing Lind's Protestant-orphan background, her purity, and her charitableness, he organized a fantastically successful tour, even though the critics commented on the circus-like atmosphere of his promotional practices. The Lind tour marked the beginning of opera in America, and a strong enthusiasm for an art form that was previously considered "immoral" and too "Catholic" (Hitchcock 1969).

With the rise of urban centers and an influx of immigrant populations, secular music became increasingly middle class, but retained strong European allegiances which have, to date, fostered a distrust of experimentation in modern repertoire. Opera is a European import, which has formed the tradition of serious music in America, especially since the middle of the nineteenth century, and is distinct from the vernacular of religious and ragtime music.

Nineteenth-century music gradually broke away from the aristocratic soirees and came to be performed at cathedral services. Public concerts, under the control of artists' managers, increased in response to the demands of a middle class audience, which had an affinity for more simplistic styles of music and resisted both complexity and innovation. The growing sheet music industry encouraged the growth of amateurism and a life style of musical consumption. Because audiences glorified the performing artist, the composer had to look for a patron elsewhere. "One result of the adulation of virtuosos was an emphasis on the performance of music, rather than on the composer, or even the music itself . . . on the means rather than the end" (Hitchcock 1969:51).

Such popularity made the performer somewhat more secure. Although subjected to fluctuating tastes and traditions from 1860 to 1920, the performer gradually became professionalized by musical conservatories, university affiliation, professional societies, and journals of music. Public support for the opera was expressed through the university, but the university also functioned in training and experimentation not destined for the mass market. The university

The Met then & now

has provided jobs for musicians and opportunities for performance of compositions which would not otherwise be presented.

The history of the Metropolitan Opera more specifically reflects the institutional changes, having been transformed from a lucrative and prestigious enterprise in about 1880 to a nonprofit public association by 1932. In the beginning, it was manipulated by the rich, who owned stock, received large dividends, and more importantly, owned their much-sought-after box seats for the entire season. Prior to its establishment as a nonprofit association, the roles of the board and management overlapped, making it difficult to distinguish between those who managed and those who owned. But since then, there has been at least a "theoretical" separation between the board and the management.

The Metropolitan struggled to overcome the effects of the Depression of 1929 and the many deficit years that followed to present the greatest voices in each generation only to have its image distorted and its loyalties divided, especially during the war as a result of its international commitments; and, finally, to create a dynasty at Lincoln Center, with its grandiose production and maintenance facilities, its fifty-two week season, union demands, and insignificant attempts to offset its internationalism. Repertoire and casting decisions have not been without their detractors, especially during the twenty-two year regime of Rudolph Bing. The social and economic factors discussed above can well account for the decisions made by a company like the Metropolitan.

The shift which began during the Depression from a status-granting and profitable institution to one beset by economic problems is made clear by Irving Kolodin's remarks:

> For reasons clearly discernible, an economic domination replaced the social one. Kahn's place in this . . . was that of a monarch, but a limited one. He had every power but that of leader. . . . So long as he obeyed the rules, the ownership fraction was quite content that he amuse them, even on occasions, uplift them. If what was tendered was just plain dull, it disappeared soon enough anyway. Around a nuclear core of Wagner, Verdi and Puccini — the Father, Son and Holy Ghost of the Metropolitan orthodoxy — Gatti spun a pattern intricate, diverting, ear-filling, and profitable. When the economic system on which it was based gave way, it followed suit, magnetically, inevitably. . . . With the depression came the realization, in slackened support and lessened attendance, that opera could not endure on the patronage of those who supported it by habit rather than volition. Soon enough the most firmly grounded habit — pay-

ment on the assessment for boxes — would be uprooted. The roots, it was already evident, would have to be transplanted into a deeper, more fertile soil to those who valued the Metropolitan as a home of opera rather of social display (1966:453).

Kolodin suggests that the Metropolitan Opera Company, led by Conried and Maurice Grau prior to Giulio Gatti-Casazza's administration, combined both social prestige and profit. When he took over in 1908, Gatti was able to convince his backers that he wouldn't lose money. His success is attributed to the international glamour and fame of a truly golden age in singing characterized by artists like Caruso, Muzio, Ferrar, Galli-Curci, and many others. Edward Johnson, who reigned between 1935 and 1950, sought to maintain a balanced budget, but with the inclusion of American singers. To achieve this end, he produced only the most popular operas and concentrated on raising the level of staging and production technology. The final "collectivisation" came and was firmly established during the Bing regime, from 1950 to 1972. The backstage machinery grew as Bing revamped staging and continued to employ European singers, backed by an American company of "covers," chorus, orchestra and ballet. Superstars in the fields of directing, singing and conducting were cast in productions from the classical period. Significant changes occurred in staging and directing especially with the innovations made in stage technology during this time. In the most popular productions, where he could afford to be extravagant, Bing commissioned designers, and directors from outside of opera. The era prior to the 1960s was one of increased audiences, and enlarged repertoire; the era of the 1970s and 1980s are marked by economic conditions which threatened the survival of opera in America.

The Growth of Opera Activity Across the United States

The growth of the Metropolitan Opera, and the New York City Opera, both located in New York City, was characteristic of the enormous expansion of activity across the nation. In the 1960s, many new independent organizations and large art centers were organized, and by 1980, there were over 200 art centers, including eighty-six professional opera companies. All have experienced increases in attendance, facilities, number of performances, paid personnel, and maintenance costs in the past decade.

The extent of this growth, in addition, varied with the size of the operating budget. In the period 1965–69, there was more expansion of smaller companies (with annual budgets ranging from $5,000 to $49,999 and $50,000 to $249,999), than of companies with budgets of $250,000 and over. In contrast, companies on a larger scale declined; only fifteen were established from 1960 to 1964, and twelve, 1965 to 1969. Two factors may account for this; the high cost of starting large-scale organizations, and the foundation and government support to smaller companies during this period (NCA 1973:158–60). In 1970, Central Opera Service reported in a survey the existence of forty opera companies with budgets over $100,000. By 1980, the number of opera companies with budgets over $100,000 had jumped to 109. Inflation within the ten-year period can account for this unfortunate statistic.

Most of the opera in the United States is produced by a handful of large and well-known opera companies, each of which has an established season, a staff, an orchestra, and a repertory company. Of these companies, only three offer annual contracts to their chorus, ballet, and orchestra members. Very often, musicians are contractually committed not only to opera, but also to ballet, dance, or theater. Other performances are produced by companies offering only a few performances each year, touring companies, summer theaters, and other workshop groups. Approximately 40 percent of productions are produced by university workshops. American works are more often produced by university workshops and regional companies like Houston, Minnesota, and Lake George. (See Appendix B)

40% of prod. in Univ.

An analysis of professional opera companies in the United States reveals that they fall into three major divisions. The Metropolitan is at the forefront, a "star" both inside and outside the United States. Its budget alone is larger than those of the next four largest opera houses combined. It offers an annual contract to its chorus, orchestra and ballet, and is known as an "international" company, featuring predominantly foreign operas, and engaging "superstars" on a per-performance basis. The second category is the next four largest companies: the New York City Opera, the San Francisco Opera, the Lyric Opera of Chicago, and the Seattle Opera Company. The Lyric and San Francisco companies, although somewhat smaller than the Metropolitan, are similar in their tendency to engage international stars. The New York City Opera has always been and continues to be considered an "American" company, which features American singers, contemporary repertory, and ensemble singing.

The five have achieved international recognition. Their seasons vary in length. The Metropolitan no longer refers to "seasons" since their contracts for chorus, ballet and orchestra personnel run for fifty-two weeks. Their main programming is scheduled from mid-September to April, in addition to a national tour, and "Opera in the Parks" of New York City. The New York City Opera offers a fall and spring season of about two months each, and also goes on tour.

The third group of opera companies are called "civic opera," and may present two to a dozen productions in a season. They are the pride of our smaller cities, sometimes engaging international stars, but generally hiring a company made up of American singers who have had extensive training and experience in the provincial opera houses of Europe. These regional companies conduct extensive tours providing experience to young American singers, and exposing opera to audiences, often for the first time.

A comparison of the extent and nature of activity among non-profit professional companies with those of college workshops and university-affiliated groups will show that there has been considerable growth of opera organizations both on college campuses and in towns and cities across the nation, but colleges have shown more activity. The significant questions are: What is being produced? And for whom? Opera companies perform for far larger audiences than colleges, and college auditoriums are small compared to the stadiums and art centers. Of the five large opera houses, the seating capacity is as follows: The Metropolitan Opera, 3,600; Lyric Opera of Chicago, 3,500; San Francisco Opera, 3,000; Seattle Opera House, 2,875; and New York City Opera, 2,500.

Table 1 compares opera activity among professional companies and colleges and reveals that companies produced more opera performances, with a total of 6,782, during the 1979–80 season than colleges, with a total of 2,609. During this season, a total of 986 organizations presented opera. Of these, 109 were considered "major" professional opera companies with membership in the American Guild of Musicians and Artists, and budgets over $100,000. A further sixty-eight companies had budgets between $25,000 and $99,000. In addition, there are 390 festivals, clubs and theater groups which presented opera. The remainder, almost 50 percent of opera companies in the United States, are relatively small subsidized college and university workshops, which numbered 419 in 1980.

During the 1979–80 season, there was a record number of 9,391 performances. Maria Rich, Director of Central Opera Service, remarking on the survey statistics presented in table 1, has written:

> We are looking back at the biggest U.S. opera season yet. Performances in 1979–80 increased by about 10 percent over the previous year, continuing the steady growth and doubling the number of performances during the past decade. Thanks to larger halls and bigger attendance, audience figures rose about 125 per-

TABLE 1

TYPE OF ORGANIZATION, REPERTOIRE PERFORMED,
BUDGET SIZE, AND NUMBER OF PERFORMANCES

		79–80	78–79	77–78	76–77	74–75	69–70	64–65	54–55
PERFORMING GROUPS									
Companies: over $100,000 budget		109	95	78	68	54	35	27	na
Companies: other		458	456	458	424	335	266	296	280
College/University workshops		419	415	420	422	418	347	409	167
	Total	986	966	956	914	807	648	732	447
Number of Performances									
Standard repertoire		5,482	5,181	5,191	4,574	4,097	3,011	2,643	1,844
Contemporary foreign repertoire		548	609	523	622	2,331	1,768	1,533	1,373
Contemporary American repertoire		3,361	2,764	2,092	2,193				
	Total	9,391	8,554	7,806	7,389	6,428	4,779	4,176	3,217
Musicals (not included in total)		1,397	1,430	906	217				
		(10,788)	(9,984)	(8,712)	(7,606)				
Number of Operas Performed									
Standard		237	242	237	226	209	178	167	103
Contemporary (foreign)		47	54	55	44	71	163	164	107
Contemporary (American)		213	202	156	157	107			
	Total	497	498	448	427	387	341	331	210
Musicals (not included in total)		104	72	43	34				
World Premieres		79	64	42	33	16	17		
American Premieres		22	18	21	14	11	18		
Audiences (in millions)		10.7	9.94	9.76	9.20	8.00	4.60		
Expenses (in millions)									
Companies: over $100,000 budget		$133.6	$111.5	$96.3	$79.7		$36.5		
Companies: $25,000–$99,999 budgets		3.7	3.8	4.4	3.5				
All others		38.5	31.1	29.8	27.2				
	Total	$175.8	$146.4	$130.5	$110.4				

DETAIL OF PERFORMING GROUPS

		Number of Companies		Number of Performances	
		1979–80	1978–79	1979–80	1978–79
Companies: budget over $1 million		16	15		
Companies: budget over $500,000		22	15		
Companies: budget over $200,000		31	29		
Companies: budget over $100,000		40	36		
	sub-total	109	95	2,779	2,442
Companies: budget over $50,000		42	37		
Companies: budget over $25,000		26	36		
	sub-total	68	73	784	869
Orchestras/Festivals/Choruses		124	125		
Avocational/Clubs, etc.		183	187		
Theatres (non-profit)		83	71		
	sub-total	390	383	3,219	2,777
Total Companies		567	551		
College/University Workshops		419	415	2,609	2,466
Total Opera Producing Organizations		986	966	9,391	8,554

SOURCE: Rich, Maria, "Central Opera Service Annual Survey Statistics," *Central Opera Service Bulletin*, V.22, #3, New York: Central Opera Service, Fall, 1980, p. 32.

cent over the same period to 10.7 million, with another 2.5 million enjoying educational programs. Even companies that added extra performances reported larger audiences per night, and there was a general increase in subscription sales. (Rich 1980:32)

The semi-professional and college groups have given more opportunities to young American singers, but they have primarily seen their function as pedagogical. Abram Chasins claims that "the college campus today is the largest consumer and dispenser of musical art . . . buying 75 percent of professional activities in the United States." (1973:74) Their losses, resulting from the productions of contemporary and experimental works, have led them to rely heavily on aid from university departments, foundations, and government, particularly through the National Endowment for the Arts and the National Council of the Arts.

Table 1 also shows the number of performances according to the type of production, standard or contemporary.[1] Table 1 does show increased activity due to the emergence of new opera companies and college workshops, and the increased number of productions and performances in each of the years where data was available. Within the twenty-five-year period, 1955–80, organizations presenting opera doubled, the number of performances tripled, and both the standard and contemporary repertoires were expanded. Standard repertoire outnumbered contemporary, with a total of 5,482 performances that were presented from 237 productions in the 1979–1980 season, while contemporary repertoire added 3,361 performances of 213 productions. This is important to the analysis since it reveals that while college/university workshops presented over 3,000 performances, they were to much smaller audiences, and their productions concentrated on the contemporary repertoire. The larger companies would not be able to sustain the losses that would be incurred by producing these less popular works.

While the United States trains artists, and many feel they are the best educated and most skilled, there is no market to absorb them. Europe has been saturated with American singers eager to establish careers, but Europeans have become increasingly unwilling to accept American singers, probably because of national commitments and labor pressures. The small towns and municipalities of Austria, Germany, Italy, and Britain have government-supported opera companies which provide jobs for those who are not employed by the large houses of the major cities. This has resulted in a market that is wider and more flexible in comparison to America. There is no counterpart to this system in the United States. Our universities have become esoteric training centers, often alienating themselves further from the mass market by producing works for musicians rather than for the general public. On the other hand, all but one of our commercial houses, the New York City Opera, are international and offer the largest monetary rewards for star performers.

The difficult domestic situation has been aggravated by unpredictable career developments, intense competition, sporadic work opportunities, the costs of touring and private lessons, low salaries, and the long years when there was neither a music journal nor a research organization. As a result of this precarious situation, music complexes like Lincoln Center lack group cohesiveness, and competition among the various arts houses is not uncommon. Sometimes, they do not even know of each others' forthcoming schedules; perhaps their indifference reveals their competition. Programs may overlap, as they did when the New York City Opera and the Metropolitan Opera both performed "La Traviata" in the same season.

Budgetary problems have been complicated by the overall market situation and the expansion of performing arts centers. The 1960s saw a large growth of building in the arts — which contributed to the erroneous notion that there was a culture boom in America. With federal, state, and local aid available, cities across the nation sought to develop arts centers, rather than build individual structures to house the performing arts. Lincoln Center in New York City, the Kennedy Center in Washington, D.C., Milwaukee's Performing Arts Center, The Dorothy Chandler Pavilion in Los Angeles, the National Arts and Recreation Center in Ithaca, New York, and hundreds of others around the United States confirm the national influence of arts centers. Their indiscriminate growth has left companies with enormous and strangling maintenance costs. Expenses increase while productivity and income remain stable, so huge deficits are the norm. Such an insecure economic base and the uncertain employment opportunities seem to refute the much publicized "culture boom of the 1960s."

Dick Netzer clearly explains the cause of the economic dilemma in the arts.

> Private markets work efficiently, in economic terms, only if the costs of production meet certain criteria. One such criterion is the absence of economies of scale in production, that is, reductions in cost per unit of output as total output increases. (In the arts, the unit of output may be a consumer visit to a museum or an individual's attendance at a performance.) The economically efficient price to charge is the cost of providing an additional unit

of output, but in situations of declining unit costs, a price set at that level will be below the average cost of all units of output and will result in a deficit. (1978:25)

Rather than face destruction, companies use the box office receipts to determine what is to be produced. "Successful" productions reappear season after season, while those with less audience appeal are dropped from the repertoire unless a foundation can be induced to support them. Productions that do not sell are not thought to be the responsibility of commercial houses. Some companies have survived, and rely upon foundation monies, such as that given by the Ford Foundation since 1975. Maria Rich addresses the importance of the Ford Foundation report, and writes:

> Financial stress, however, is showing for the arts for the first time in some years. At the time of this writing (1980), shortly after the close of the season . . . twenty of the 109 major companies indicated they have not yet covered expenses, either de facto or through pledges. This does not necessarily mean the demise of these companies, but it points the way toward high-interest loans and deferred deficits. This used to be a generally accepted practice but was almost totally eliminated during the second half of the seventies, following the successful four-year Ford Foundation grant program addressing the specific problems of cash reserve and accumulated operating deficits. In return for assistance, the companies had to prove to be self-sustaining once the deferred debts were wiped out. Since then, we have witnessed much greater financial stability among large opera companies. (1980:32)

While this has been a superficial overview of the market, it serves to emphasize the desperate plight of the performing opera. An analysis of production costs is necessary to understand the causes of the "desperation gap" — the disparity between income and expenses. The structure of the organizations is contingent upon the nature of the performing arts, in which productivity and income cannot rise with the costs of production. This, in turn, affects the styles of production, or the repertoire and provides the framework in which meanings and ideologies of work evolve.

Expenditures

Between 1970 and 1980, the economy's double digit inflation has not been without its effect on the arts. For example, between those years the number of companies listed as "major" organizations with budgets over $100,000 rose from forty to seventy-eight. In addition, total operating expenditures for all opera companies in the United States in 1970 was $38,743,000, and by 1980, the budget of the Metropolitan alone approached this figure. The Ford Foundation study, *The Finances of the Performing Arts* (1974), found that four companies (excluding the Metropolitan) had budgets of over $1 million in 1970; by 1980, this number had risen to sixteen. Table 2 reveals a one-year change, and an increase in expenditures among all opera companies given the inflationary trend.

Table 3 outlines a 1978 survey, conducted by Opera America, a service organization for professional opera companies in North, Central and South America, which indicates that opera companies spend approximately 52 to 74 percent of their budget on personnel. Smaller companies spend more on administrative/production expenses since they have to rent the house, scenery, costumes, etc. from other sources. Opera America also reported an attendance of over 4½ million in 1978, with television and radio listeners totalling over 87 million. (1980:13)

Expenditures are the costs of operating an opera company, and these costs may be divided into two major categories. The first category includes salaries and fees for: regular performing artists and guest artists; regular and guest directors and conductors; stage managers, instructors, creative designers, and technical staff; production or (nonperforming) personnel such as stagehands, crew and shop; policymaking administrative personnel; supervisory personnel; and clerical, box office, and front of house personnel. The second category encompasses nonsalary costs: scenery, costume, light and sound; royalties, scores, scripts, transportation and per diem; facilities rental; financing and maintenance of own facilities; facilities depreciation; nonfacility depreciation; nonsalary subscription and promotion costs;

TABLE 2
NUMBER OF OPERA COMPANIES
BY BUDGET SIZE

	Total	
Budget Size	1978–79	1979–80
Over $1 million	15	16
Over $500,000	15	22
Over $200,000	29	31
Over $100,000	36	40

SOURCE: Rich, Maria, "U.S. Opera Survey 1979–80," *Opera News*, November 22, 1980, p. 32.

TABLE 3
OPERA EXPENSES
BY BUDGET SIZE

	Personnel	Non-Personnel
Under $150,000	52.9	47.1
$150,000 to $500,000	64.2	35.8
$500,000 to $1 million	66.9	33.1
Over $1 million	70.3	29.7
Metropolitan Opera	74.4	25.6
Canadian Companies	65.1	34.9

SOURCE: Opera America Profile, 1978, p. 13

fundraising costs and fees; and interest on nonmortgage loans. Table 3 contains comparisons of expenditures between different size organizations.

Opera budgets are determined by: artistic quality, as reflected in artistic fees; the kind of repertoire, as reflected in costs of mounting new productions, or revamping expensive old ones; the number of productions, as reflected in larger rehearsals and maintenance costs of scenery; and the length of the season, as reflected in maintenance costs. The single most expensive allocation, in opera companies of all sizes, is for performing/artistic salaries which account for about forty-five percent of the Metropolitan Opera's budget, and around the same percentage for the smaller opera companies. Analysis of the percentage distribution of expenditures reveals that the Metropolitan spends disproportionately more for non-artistic salaries than do smaller companies, who spend more on renting their scenery, auditoriums and the like (nonsalary production cost category).

Negotiations between management and the American Guild of Musical Artists, representing members of the chorus and ballet, reveal that these segments of opera consume the smallest part of the artistic budget of salary fees.[2] This group has traditionally been the last to fight for higher wages and better working conditions. This fact is a consequence of the art form itself — opera has always been a vehicle for the voice, and solo singers have demanded the highest fees being at the pinnacle of the operatic status system.

Members of the chorus, ballet, and orchestra, as well as other artists paid by the week make up the unionized performing personnel in music organizations. Principals and solo singers establish individual contracts with management. They usually exceed the minimal fees established by AGMA. The Metropolitan Opera is the largest permanent organization in the live performing arts — that is, employing its staff for fifty-two weeks — and it is in large companies that management resists increases because it is in large companies that high labor cost ratios exist.

Opera has to negotiate with more unions than any of the other performing arts. Music organizations differ from profit-making organizations in private industry and labor relations reflect their structure and the nature of the work activity. Its unique features are its personnel expenses, its non-profit base, its extreme complexity, and the overlapping of functions given the relatively small number of artists (Moskow 1960).

The enormous complexity of operations, and the specialization and coordination of activities (see Chapter V) is revealed in the number of diverse union groups represented in the large music organizations. One can count twenty-three different unions that are involved and some unions include performers: the American Federation of Musicians (AFM-musicians, conductors, librarians, arrangers, copyists, orchestra), American Guild of Musical Artists (AGMA-singers, choristers, choreographers, dancers, stage directors, stage managers), Directors Guild of America (DGA-composers, and lyricists), Society of Stage Directors and Choreographers (SSD&C); and, for the supportive personnel, International Alliance of Theatrical Stage Employees (ATSE), the International Brotherhood of Electrical Workers, the International Union of Operating Engineers (OE), and the Service Employee International Union (SEIU-ushers, guards, etc.)[3]

The Metropolitan bargains with seventeen different unions, four of which are locals of the International Alliance of Theatrical Stage Employees (IATSE); Chicago negotiates with seven unions, New York City Opera with seven, and each has a separate history and a unique set of problems. Inevitably, negotiations by one union affect the others, and this aggravates the situation further.

Secondly, the nature of the organizations, including both their nonprofit base and musical goal, gives artists a high degree of bargaining power because they can't be easily replaced. However, the lack of outside job opportunities and the fact that musicians probably do not want to do anything else reduce the likelihood of their striking. A recent article in *The New York Times* reported that, except for the small percentage of superstars, the aspiring American singer averages $5,000 annual pay. (Daley 1980:26) "The non-profit employer operates at a considerable deficit so that the market mechanism found in private industry does not regulate the allocation of resources in the same way." (Moskow 1960:26)

A brief review of the circumstances involved in the recent orchestra strike at the Metropolitan highlights the economic dilemma within opera, and its current problems with regard to labor relations. In 1980, the leader of AFM, which employs 1,962 people, asked for a 12½ percent raise during the next two years, and two additional weeks off to supplement the then current five weeks vacation. The Met's offer was a 9½ percent raise the first year, 9 percent the second, and an additional week of vacation and increased benefits.

Opera musicians, harboring long felt feelings of neglect, and non-recognition ("we're 'pit' musicians") held strong to their demands. The four-performance a week issue became the most difficult to resolve with the management. Three months of negotiations, political fighting, the cancellation of eighty performances, and the resurgence of ill feelings resulted. Finally the orchestra musicians won most of their demands, but the ramifications are still to be felt nationally (Serrin 1980:B4; Henahan 1980:49).

Income

The income of established commercial companies comes mainly from ticket sales, recording and broadcasting rights, program advertisements, house rentals, and restaurant-theater concessions, though these are sometimes supplemented by contributions and grants. In any event, income has not kept pace with sky-rocketing salaries, maintenance fees, and staging costs. Deficits have become the norm, and increased productivity cannot fill the gap. The Opera America survey estimates that the receipts of the average opera companies from audience and ticket sales is approximately 56.4 percent of their income, while individual donors contributed on the average 12.8 percent, foundations, 6.7 percent, guilds, 10.2 percent, local and state government, 5.4 percent, corporations, 4.7 percent, and the federal government, 3.8 percent (1978:13). The Ford Foundation Report (1974) addresses the factors which contribute to the capacity of a company's income to offset expenses.

> The extent to which expenses can be met by earned income depends upon a large number of factors. They include the size and income level of the population served, the appeal of the art form and its repertoire, the cost of mounting new productions, the number of performances of each production which can be presented, the cost of each performance (which involves the wage

rates of the performers as well as their number, the cost of other
personnel required to be present, and various nonpersonnel
costs), administrative costs, the ticket price level, the size of the
theater or auditorium, and the length of season.

Table 4 outlines the percentage distribution of earned income for
the 1970–71 season, by budget size, with the Metropolitan Opera
listed separately because of the enormity of its budget. Income from
tickets sales represents 63 percent of total income for the Metropolitan
Opera, and a high of 91 percent for opera companies with budgets
of $500,000 to $1,000,000. As a result of this data, it can be concluded
that the Metropolitan Opera is successful in its ability to offset costs
from private contributions. Government support seems to have
helped the smallest companies, as well as those four opera companies
(Seattle Opera, Lyric Opera of Chicago, San Francisco Opera, and
New York City Opera) just below the size of the Metropolitan Opera.

Expenditures are a result of the nature of the art form; and, opera
is by far the most expensive performing art to produce. Its "labor
intensiveness" is inimical to the problem, and one that cannot be
resolved at the expense of reducing, or curtailing salary scales. The
salaries of performers, similar to the allied-health professionals, did
not keep up with other labor demands prior to 1970. Nor can costs
be lowered at the expense of artistic quality. Income, however, unlike
expenditures, is somewhat flexible responding to higher ticket prices,
house rentals, contributions, and the like — all contributing to "unearned" income to offset rising costs. While attempts have been made
in this direction, and accounts for the survival of these opera companies throughout the last inflationary decade, a review of the budgets for these companies testifies to the severity of the economic
situation.

The expenditures and incomes of the opera companies is summarized in table 5, for the ten-year period 1971 to 1980. The income
presented excludes "unearned" income, which predominantly comes
from contributions as discussed above. As expected, deficits appear
in all the seasons, and represent the following approximate percentages of the total budgets: Metropolitan Opera (30 percent), Lyric
Opera of Chicago (60 percent), San Francisco Opera (46 percent),
Seattle Opera (53 percent). The deficit for the Metropolitan Opera
went from $4 million in 1971 to $13.2 million by 1980; and it doubled
for both the Lyric Opera of Chicago, and the San Francisco Opera
within the past five years. Seattle Opera has maintained a similar
budget since 1977, with income representing $1.1 million, and ex-
penses totalling $2.3 million. The Metropolitan's budget has climbed

TABLE 4
PERCENTAGE DISTRIBUTION OF EARNED INCOME 1970-71

| | Budget Size | | | | Metropolitan Opera |
	Under $250,000 (13)	$250,000 to $500,000 (9)	$500,000 to $1,000,000 (4)	Over $1,000,000 (4)	
Subscription ticket income	38	38	45	59	42
Single/block ticket income	34	22	43	25	20
Student/block ticket income	5	3	3	1	1
Total main season ticket income	77	63	91	85	63
Other performance ticket income	1	8	0	5	4
Total ticket income	78	71	91	90	67
Services income from government sources	6	1	0	4	1
Services income from other sources	11	13	1	3	16
Total services income	17	14	1	7	17
Recordings/films/radio/TV	0	0	0	0	3
Total nonticket performance income	17	14	1	7	20
Total performance income	95	85	92	97	87
Income from performances of other groups	0	7	0	0	0
School/class/training income	0	0	0	0	0
Other nonperformance earned income	5	8	8	3	13
Total nonperformance income	5	15	8	3	13

SOURCE: *The Finances of the Performing Arts*, Volume I, (A Survey of 166 Professional Nonprofit Resident Theaters, Operas, Symphonies, Ballets, and Modern Dance Companies). New York: Ford Foundation, 1974:63.

TABLE 5

COMPARISON OF EXPENDITURES AND INCOME

	1971-72	1972-73	1973-74	1974-75	1975-76	1976-77	1977-78	1978-79	1979-80
Metropolitan Opera	$19.8/ 15.6	$22.4/ 16.4	$24.3/ 16.5	$25.7/ 16.7	$27.9/ 18.5	$28.6/ 17.4	$31.5/ 19.1	$34.6/ 22.7	$39.6/ 26.4
New York City Opera					$6.7/*	$6.3/	$8.2/	$9.8/	$10.4/
Lyric Opera of Chicago	$3.2/ 2				$5.6/ 2.3	$6.4/ 2.7	$7.1/ 3.0	$8.8/ 3.1	$10.0/ 4.1
San Francisco Opera	$3.2/ 2				$5.0/ 3.2	$6.3/ 3.4	$6.6/ 4.0	$7.4/ 4.8	$9.4/ 5.8
Seattle Opera							$2.3/ 1.4	$2.6/ 1.3	$2.3/ 1.1

*NOTE: Income excludes contributions. Figures represent millions of dollars.

*Since New York City Opera is part of City Center of Music and Drama, Inc., income levels could not be observed.

to almost $40 million by 1980, and is equal to the combined budgets of the other major four companies herein analyzed.

Table 6 outlines the expenditures in greater detail, summarizing the costs for performing and non-performing artistic salaries, administrative and production expenses. The organization's "labor intensiveness" is exemplified by the fact that performing artistic salaries assumes the greatest share of the budget, and (depending on each of the companies' own classification) represents from 41 percent to 71 percent of total expenses. Although the budgets vary in size (from $3 million to $40 million in 1980), the percent distributions are closely related, except for the salaries paid to artists by the New York City Opera, which accounted for 71 percent of the total budget. The average allocation for artistic salaries is approximately 55 percent, while administrative costs assumed 45 percent, and non-salary production costs assumed 27 percent of the expenditures for the companies listed.

The Metropolitan Opera

The Metropolitan Opera remains one of the greatest international opera houses. Its weekly Saturday broadcasts have brought opera potentially to every household in America. It is not only a giant in opera, but a model to other opera houses. It is also the place where singers dream of appearing one day.

The total income of the Met — including ticket sales and "other" income from recordings, broadcast rights, program advertisements, house rentals, and gift shop sales — comes nowhere near meeting the cost of production. Without the tremendous increase in contributions, during the years examined in Tables 4, 5 and 6, and considering the present growth in production costs, the deficit would have proven disastrous. The Metropolitan's greatest attempt, in its history, to offset deficits has been to establish a $100 million endowment fund (Centennial Endowment Fund), which hopes to yield $8 to $10 million annually in interest, which will go toward its deficit, and insure the stability of this international house.

Chart 1 shows the finances of the Metropolitan over a ten-year period from 1970 to 1979. Throughout most of the seasons represented in the chart, expenditures grew at a faster rate than income. In the sixties, the deficit was not great, but then there was a sharp reversal at the beginning of the seventies due to a growth in the season, increased performances and productions, a fifty-two week contract for practically the whole artistic and technical staff, a move in 1965 to the new opera house at Lincoln Center, and a strike in the 1969–70

TABLE 6
PERCENTAGE DISTRIBUTION OF EXPENDITURES 1979–80

	Metropolitan Opera	New York City Opera	Lyric Opera of Chicago	San Francisco Opera	Seattle Opera
Performing artistic salaries	37.1%	71%	15%	38%	16.6%
Total artistic	61.6%	1%**	41%	59%***	41.6%
Administrative	12.1%		21%	19%	25.5%
Nonsalary production costs	18.5%	25%	38%	19%	31.5%
Miscellaneous	7.8%	3%		2.7%	
Total opera expenditures ($million)	$39.6	$10.8	$9.3	$9.4	$3.2

*The following figures are approximate since the opera companies did not have similar
  category listing expenditures.
**Royalties
***Stage transfer, storage and technical, and affiliate artists included in this category.
SOURCE: 1979–1980 Annual Reports.

season. The strike reduced the number of performances by a third,
and ticket income by 40 percent. In 1965, (not shown in the Chart)
the expenditures jumped over $4 million due to the move to the new
house which enlarged audience capacity, the backstage area, and
added three underground levels for rehearsals, storage and office
space.

The early seventies saw a decline in attendance, both by the
subscribers, and at the box office; gone were the days of a ten-year
wait to be a privileged Met subscriber. During the sixties, attendance
averaged 95 percent, but it dropped by 20 percent by 1970. The
strike (1969–70), general inflation, the middle class flight into the
suburbs, and higher ticket prices, contributed to the decline in attendance.

Since 1970, as Chart 1 reveals, the Metropolitan has operated at
increased deficits; however, contributions during the 1970–79 period
managed to offset these deficits. During this period, the production
costs had risen from a little over $16 million in 1970 to more than
$39 million in 1979. In 1970, income was $10 million; by 1979, it was
two and one half times that at $26.4 million. Therefore, as expen-
ditures of ticket prices, musicians' salaries, and the consumer
price index doubled, contributions almost quadrupled during
1970–80. If this did not occur, the Metropolitan Opera would be
closed today.

CHART 1. Metropolitan Opera Financial Summary, 1960-1979*

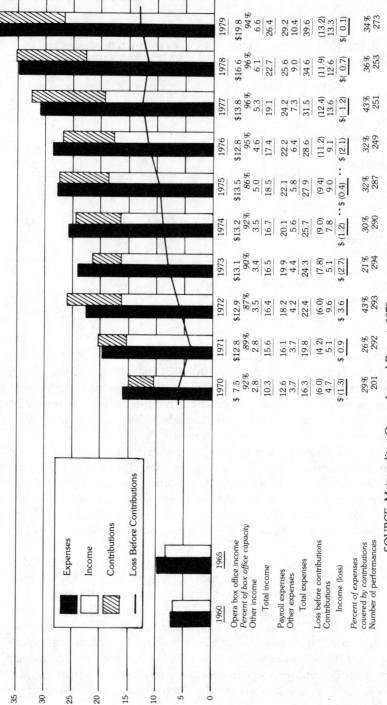

	1970	1971	1972	1973	1974	1975	1976	1977	1978	1979
Opera box office income	$ 7.5	$12.8	$12.9	$13.1	$13.2	$13.5	$12.8	$13.8	$16.6	$19.8
Percent of box office capacity	92%	89%	87%	90%	92%	86%	95%	96%	96%	94%
Other income	2.8	2.8	3.5	3.4	3.5	5.0	4.6	5.3	6.1	6.6
Total income	10.3	15.6	16.4	16.5	16.7	18.5	17.4	19.1	22.7	26.4
Payroll expenses	12.6	16.1	18.2	19.9	20.1	22.1	22.2	24.2	25.6	29.2
Other expenses	3.7	3.7	4.2	4.4	5.6	5.8	6.4	7.3	9.0	10.4
Total expenses	16.3	19.8	22.4	24.3	25.7	27.9	28.6	31.5	34.6	39.6
Loss before contributions	(6.0)	(4.2)	(6.0)	(7.8)	(9.0)	(9.4)	(11.2)	(12.4)	(11.9)	(13.2)
Contributions	4.7	5.1	9.6	5.1	7.8	9.0	9.1	13.6	12.6	13.3
Income (loss)	$(1.3)	$ 0.9	$ 3.6	$(2.7)	$(1.2)	** $(0.4)	$(2.1)	$(1.2)	$(0.7)	$(0.1)
Percent of expenses covered by contributions	29%	26%	43%	21%	30%	32%	32%	43%	36%	34%
Number of performances	201	292	293	294	290	287	249	251	253	273

Legend:
- Expenses
- Income
- Contributions
- Loss Before Contributions

SOURCE: Metropolitan Opera Annual Report, 1979.

* In millions.

The San Francisco Opera

The San Francisco Opera, although fifty-eight years old, has acquired international acclaim within the last twenty years under the leadership of Kurt Herbert Adler. Demand for subscription tickets has increased its schedule of performances to a three month fall season, with an audience of over 200,000 throughout the San Francisco area. By 1980, the company engaged its own orchestra, and included, in addition to the San Francisco Opera, the Western Opera Theater, the Summer Training Program and Performances, Concerts, and the American Opera Theater. It also tours Los Angeles. It, like other opera companies, has charted a year -round operation for both artistic and financial reasons.

Table 6, in outlining the distribution of expenditures for the five major opera companies, has revealed that the San Francisco company spent approximately 5.5 million dollars on artistic salaries in 1980. A review of the specific allocations for expenditures reveals a disproportionate increase in this category since 1975, in comparison to other costs. For example, from 1975 to 1976 the amount allocated to artistic fees rose $1 million; from 1976 to 1978, it rose approximately $500,000 each year, and jumped 1.5 million dollars for the 1979–80 season.

Since the San Francisco Opera must pay for the opera house rental, and does not have a permanent stage production shop, their production costs are proportionately higher than the other companies — accounting for almost $2 million in 1979–80 season. The gap between expenditures and income is outlined in table 5, and reveals a loss (before contributions) of approximately 2 to 4 million dollars from 1975 to 1980. Earned income represented 55.6 percent of total income for the 1978–79 season (chart 2). Like the Metropolitan, San Francisco has been saved by individual contributions, which accounted for 75 percent of total contributions. The annual report (1979) summarizes its budget problems, and attempts to stabilize its deficit.

> Why do we incur a deficit? The problem is very simple, the remedy not so simple. Our costs, through the ravages of inflation which seem to have no end, keep increasing at a rate faster than our income. Revenue from ticket sales ranges in the area of 60 percent of our costs . . . a high percentage. . . . Every effort is made to keep costs to a minimum consistent with maintenance of quality, and we will not compromise on quality . . . . Our long-term goal is to build our Endowment Funds to at least $5,000,000. The income from these funds will not serve to balance the operating expenses of the Association, but will contribute

CHART 2. San Francisco Opera Financial Summary, 1978-1979

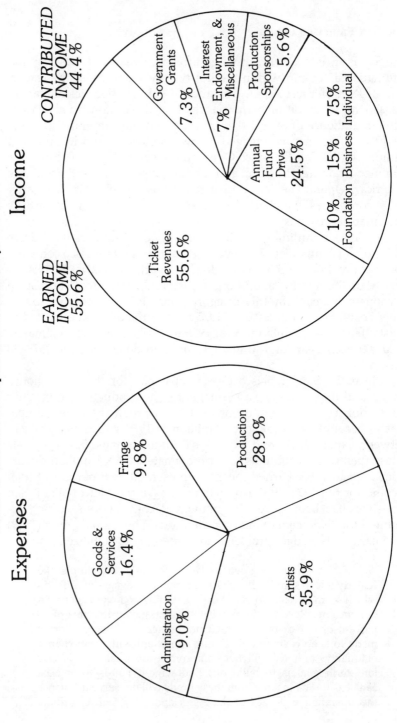

Expenses

Income

toward meeting the increasing annual deficit and help to secure the Association's future.

The New York City Opera

Tables 5 and 6 include the income and expenditures for the New York City Opera. While exact figures could not be discerned from the published budgets, it is evident that earned income in no way meets the costs of production. A review of the contributions received (private, corporate and government), indicates that the New York City Opera receives approximaely 30 percent of its total income from contributions, which include in rank order: private individuals, foundations, New York State Council of the Arts, the National Endowment of the Arts, and the City of New York.

As in other opera houses, the largest segment of the budget is spent on salaries. Although the figure representing salaries has increased yearly, from 68 percent in 1975 to 74 percent in 1980, salaries have not increased proportionately to total budget increases. In 1975, the budget was 6.7 million dollars, and in 1980, it was 10.4 million dollars. Production costs (including scenery, costumes, and staging) account for approximately 7 percent of the total budget for the years 1976–80. In 1975, production costs represented an unusual high of 15 percent given the fact that the bicentennial year was celebrated by several new operas.

The Lyric Opera of Chicago

Within six months in 1954, a three-week opera season was announced in Chicago. This was made possible by the unbounded energy and wit of Carol Fox, Nicola Rescigno, a conductor, and Lawrence V. Kelly, a real estate businessman who loved opera. From the beginning, under the management of Carol Fox, Lyric Opera filled the seasons with the top superstars of the time, and was credited with numerous debuts, premieres and new productions. It was an unprecedented season in 1954 since it represented the American debut of the "unattainable" Maria Callas, starring in Bellini's "Norma." High expectations were soon fulfilled as it became applauded as one of the great opera companies on the international scene. Presently, it has a four-and-one-half-month season. In 1980 it gave thirty-nine performances, of five productions. It recently established, with National Endowment for the Arts funds, a system of "annual apprenticeships" for singers which serves as a pool for the chorus. These singers occasionally sing in secondary roles and possibly fill "cover" positions.

From 1954 to 1980, Lyric Opera's budget went from $287, 676 (including eight productions, sixteen performances), to $10 million (including five productions, sixty-seven performances). Income fell short of around $50,000 in 1954, and by 1980, it had to raise almost $6 million to cover expenses.

The Seattle Opera

In fifteen years, the Seattle Opera Company has grown to rank alongside institutions with histories of European and urban support. It was established in 1964 when a group of Seattle financiers and music impresarios hired Glynn Ross, who merged the Western Opera Company, and the Seattle Opera, then the opera committee of the Seattle Symphony (Salem 1976:59). Presently, it boasts a six month season scattered throughout the year, and in 1980, it presented thirty-one performances, of five productions to an audience of over 100,000. Within the past three years, its budget has averaged a little over two million dollars.

Unearned Income

It is evident from the data presented above that earned income cannot meet the costs of opera production. In such a "labor intensive" market, costs cannot be reduced, except at the expense of artistic quality. Administrators have had to look for other sources of income to balance their budgets. Private philanthropy, including contributions from private donors, foundations, corporations, and special campaigns, helps make up the deficits. Community art councils and other forms of government support represent the public source of funds. Foundations and corporations have been the most recent sources of financial aid to the arts, but still comprise the smallest portion, compared with individual donations. However, foundations and corporations are responsible for the change in philanthropy in the United States, and for the increases in unearned income. Contributions of unearned income are usually in response to efforts to fill the gap between expenditures and box office receipts, but there are aspects not controlled by opera companies, as the Ford Foundation study reports:

> The pattern of unearned income is determined by factors
> outside the control of most performing arts organizations. . . . The

Unearned income (handwritten annotation)

greater importance of United Art Funds among smaller than among larger operas is due either to the fact that United Art Funds are more prevalent in cities that have smaller operas or that larger operas more frequently elect to conduct their own fundraising campaigns rather than accept contributions from United Art Funds. (A frequent condition of contributions from United Art Funds is that the recipient not conduct a campaign for additional local contributions.) The changes that occur are the result of changes in policy of agencies that are usually outside the immediate local scene. (Ford Foundation 1975:75–79).

It is estimated that unearned income represents approximately 40 percent of the total income of opera companies. Table 7 specifically outlines the percentage distribution of unearned income for opera companies, by budget size. Most unearned income comes from the private individual (from 25 percent to 55 percent), businesses (from 3 percent to 11 percent), and foundations (from 7 percent to 14 percent), and accounts for 86 percent of the Metropolitan's contributions, and from 69 percent to 82 percent for the other opera companies. The larger companies do not accept United Art Fund Contributions because of the fact that they would have to reject other private campaign efforts, which, in any case, yield more than the United Art Funds. Government support represents the smallest percentage distribution when compared to private patronage.

Federal and local grants appear to come to the aid of the smaller companies, while state government grants have come to the aid of the larger companies. This government subsidization was due to the large effort made nationwide by the New York State Council on the Arts. Federal and state government grants have appeared on the scene only recently since 1965, with the establishment of the National Endowment for the Arts and the State Arts Councils.

The Private Patron

The term "private patron," as used here, includes individuals who contribute under their personal names as "patrons," as well as fundraising committees and councils affiliated with opera companies, and contributions from subscribers. Their contributions include monies given for specific purposes (for the commission of a new work, or for rehearsals), and for general purposes (for donations placed in general funds or applied against the annual deficit).[4] In the past, only 2 percent of all private philanthropy has come to the arts; health and education have been given priority allocations by foundations. However, the Rockefellers have been the latest benefactors of Lincoln

TABLE 7
PERCENT DISTRIBUTION OF UNEARNED INCOME 1970–71

	Budget Size of Opera				
	Under $250,000 (13)	$250,000 to $500,000 (9)	$500,000 to $1,000,000 (4)	Over $1,000,000 (4)	Metropolitan Opera
Individual contributions	24	19	57	47	55
Business contributions	3	11	6	14	11
Combined/United Art Fund contributions	22	20	0	5	0
Local foundation contributions	7	16	10	11	14
Other local contributions	13	13	5	5	6
Total local nongovernment contributions	*69*	*79*	*78*	*82*	*86*
Federal government grants	10	11	8	0	0
State government grants	3	0	2	5	8
Local government grants	6	4	6	6	5
Total government grants	*19*	*15*	*16*	*11*	*13*
National foundation grants	12	6	6	6	0
Total government/national foundation grants	**31**	**21**	**22**	**17**	**13**
Total contributed/grant income	**100**	**100**	**100**	**99**	**99**
Total local contributions/grants	75	83	84	87	91
Corpus earnings used for operations	0	0	0	1	1

SOURCE: *The Finances of the Performing Arts*, V. I., A Survey of 166 Professional Nonprofit Resident Theaters, Operas, Symphonies, Ballets, and Modern Dance Companies. Ford Foundation, 1975: 77.

Center with gifts totaling more than $30 million. Over $75 million was privately raised for Lincoln Center, with the private donor making the largest contribution. A total of $145,770,000 in individual donations was contributed to the arts in New York State alone in 1971. In 1980, donations were over $13 million to the Metropolitan Opera alone!

The Corporation

The Baumol and Bowen book, *The Performing Arts — The Economic Dilemma*, (1966) focused needed attention on the arts and was used to secure increased support from corporations and business councils.[5] Contributions were made in the form of direct cash gifts, matching grants, and securities. Corporations not only provided for the purchase of tickets, but also for the needed media advertising, and for the commissioning of works. Personnel, space, and equipment were loaned for the improvement of community art centers. Management and tax advisers contributed their services. Of the ten most generous donations, two were given to the Metropolitan Opera by Eastern Airlines and the American Export Lines, Inc.

Dr. Frank Stanton was Chairman of the Business Committee for the Arts, Inc. (BCA), when it was formed in 1967 to stimulate business contributions to the arts. At the Central Opera Service Convention in 1973, he reported on the increasing activities of corporations in the arts. He said that corporations donated over $22 million in 1965 and over $56 million in 1970. Perhaps another $50 million could realistically be included, he thought, if one considers the expense accounts large businesses allow their executives. He estimated a total of $70 million in actual contributions in 1972, and an equal amount in business expense accounts to total $140 million directly and indirectly contributed to the arts in 1972. By 1979, this figure rose to an incredible $436 million. Fifteen corporations gave over $1 million each.

Of the eighty new Metropolitan productions done between 1950 and 1972, approximately sixty-five were sponsored by private individuals or by corporations. But in 1963, these sources comprised less than 1 percent of all private contributions for new productions. Texaco, Inc. has been the exclusive corporate sponsor of the Metropolitan's Saturday afternoon broadcasts. Other corporations, including Eastern Airlines and Glen Alden Corporation, have contributed to new productions of "Aida," Wagner's Ring Cycle, "Cavalleria," and "Pagliacci." During the 1971–72 drive, 381 corporations contributed a total of $1,214,241. All the top ten New York-based corporations in the *Fortune* "500" list of major United States Corporations have contributed to the Lincoln Center Consolidated Corporate Fund Drive.

BCA reports that in 1979, sixty-nine corporations gave specifically to opera companies. While a number of the regional and civic companies across the United States have shared their generous support, the Metropolitan and Lyric Opera of Chicago have seemed to benefit the most from corporate support. Their status, long history, urban location, and media exposure account for this trend. Corporate philanthropy to the arts appears to be the fastest growing source of contributions, and may well become the largest aspect of all corporate philanthropy in the future.

The Foundation

Institutional support — including foundations, universities, unions, and corporations — accounted for only about 5 percent of private philanthropy in 1964; but foundations have increased their donations to the arts, and these contributions have become more accessible due to the changes in tax laws. In New York State, private foundations contributed 28 percent or $12.7 million of total 1970–71 private funding. This came from approximately 200 different foundations and represented a total of 326 different grants (NCA 1973:27). Foundation grants are often short-term on a per-project basis. Traditionally foundations have contributed to education and the sciences. Health and welfare have seen increases in allocations; in comparison, the arts have received the least amount of help. Millsap's recent study on private foundations (1980) reports over 22,000 foundations registered with the Internal Revenue Service, with assets totalling more than $32 billion — of these foundations, 1,300 show an interest in the arts. However, there are over 250,000 organizations actively seeking their aid in the arts, humanities and education.

The Ford Foundation, the richest philanthropic organization in the world, expanded to include the arts in 1957. Like the Ford Foundation, other smaller foundations are geared toward limiting grants to specific programs, such as helping in the education and training of individual artists or helping companies rehearse new productions. The Martha Baird Rockefeller Fund for Music, for example, is limited to small grants of $300,000 to organizations with annual budgets of less than $800,000 per year, and $15,000 to individual artists. Over the past fifteen years, its largest grant has been $15,000. Waldemar Nielsen, while summarizing the Avalon Foundation's allocations, wrote of its conservative bent which is not uncommon in foundation activities in all of the arts.[6] On the Ford Foundation he writes:

> In twenty-nine years of operations (since 1969) . . . it granted a
> total of $15 million for fine arts and conservations. . . . Its per-

THE ECONOMICS OF OPERA   71

formance reflects the interest of a cultivated and civic-minded woman of fundamentally conservative trend. . . . In cultural areas, its major grants were to the Metropolitan, the New York Philharmonic, and the Bronx Zoo. . . . But fundamentally, the foundation operated on the principle that it could best serve social needs by helping to sustain and improve the work of reputable existing institutions, not by breaking new ground (Nielsen 1973:222-3).

The Ford Foundation has been comparatively active in the arts and 1966 proved an unusually good year for grants to symphony orchestras with the initiation of a ten-year $80 million commitment. After 1966 with McGeorge Bundy as President, there was a shift in emphasis. The humanities and education lost allocations; funds for national affairs were greatly increased; and the arts showed a decline from 25.2 percent in 1966, to 9.8 percent in 1969, and to 4 percent in 1980. The allocations made in the area of national affairs rose from 8.3 percent to 20.6 percent by 1969 (Taubman 1971). Over the fifteen-year period from 1957 to 1971, the Ford Foundation committed $232 million to the arts (see chart 3) prompting Howard Taubman of *The New York Times* to write that their role was: ". . . probably unsurpassed in world history, even by the Medicis or the most ambitious and daring of Popes" (1971).

The Ford Foundation's activity in opera has predominantly included grants to performing arts organizations. The contributions during the 1960s were for new productions, expanded seasons, student performances, and the commissioning of new works. It is especially proud of its grants to the Seattle Opera and the Center Opera Company of Minneapolis for the commissioning of experimental operas (Ford Foundation Report 1980:9). Other grants went to training young singers, and indirectly to opera from publishing, recording, or school performances. During the 1970s, Ford's help to opera reflected the economic dilemma in the arts. The subsidies contributed less to expansion and commissioning of contemporary opera, and more to offset operating budgets, provide long-term planning assistance and insure greater managerial effectiveness within opera companies.

From 1970–75, the Ford Foundation continued a generous trend to opera programs with gifts amounting to $9,483,049. A great portion of this money was donated for "Cash Reserve Programs" to the better known companies and regional associations. The Cash Reserve Program was explained as follows.

Each grant is made on a one-time, non-renewable basis, and has two key features: first, if a group has an accumulated oper-

**CHART 3. Ford Foundation's Activity in the Arts:
Grants and Projects, 1957-1971***

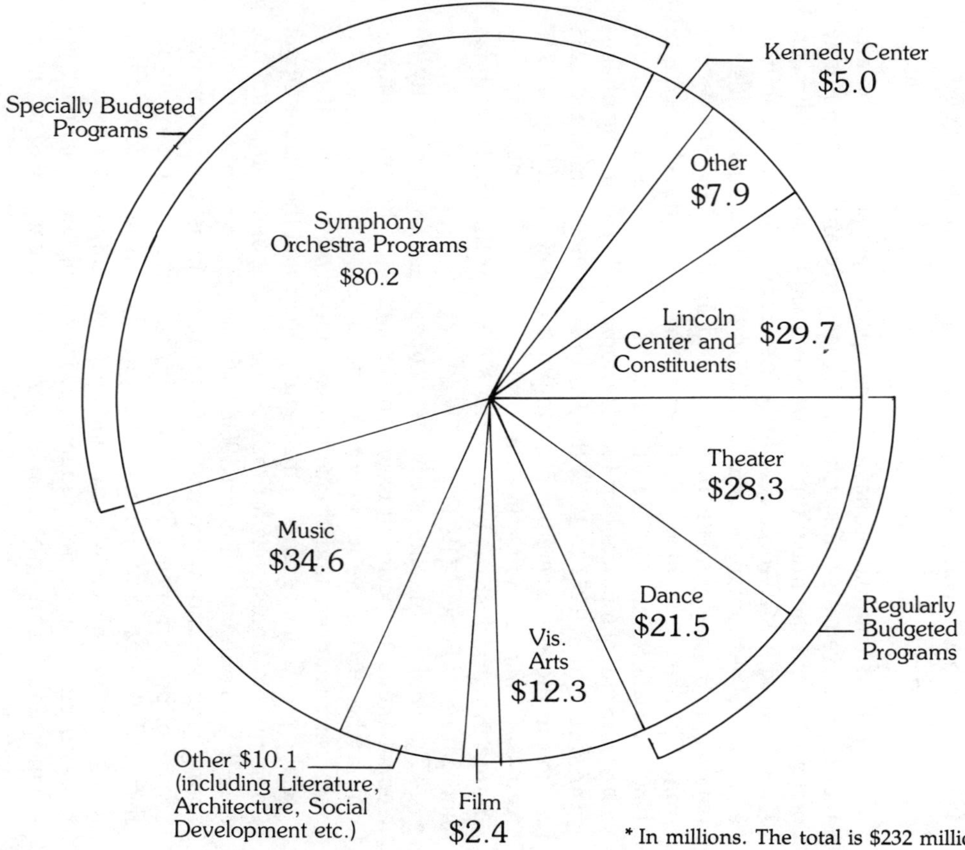

Kennedy Center
$5.0

Other
$7.9

Lincoln
Center and
Constituents $29.7

Theater
$28.3

Regularly
Budgeted
Programs

Dance
$21.5

Vis.
Arts
$12.3

Film
$2.4

Other $10.1
(including Literature,
Architecture, Social
Development etc.)

Music
$34.6

Symphony
Orchestra Programs
$80.2

Specially Budgeted
Programs

* In millions. The total is $232 million.

ating loss. . . . second, the grants will provide each company with a revolving cash reserve fund, separate from the company's operating account, over a four-year span. . . . The program thus gives the group and its board of directors powerful incentives both to broaden the base of contributors and to avoid the creation of new operating losses (Ford Foundation, Arts Program Report 1971:6).

During the last five years, while Ford has still been paying their grant commitments, new grants totalled only $350,000 — a substantial decrease in allocations. A recent press release by the Ford Foundation outlined six major themes that the foundation will concentrate on over the next six years. Although the arts program can be included under the themes mentioned, it does not have its own independence (Ford Foundation 1981).

The Government

Government support for musical arts has been small and indirect. Through tax exemptions, land grants, urban renewal programs, park and recreation subsidies, and Title II which provided funds through state education programs, the arts have benefited. Tax exemptions for philanthropy and contributions by private donors, an indirect government subsidy, accounts for a large proportion of private donations in opera. Direct government grants totaled 5 percent of the total income to the arts in New York State, or $8.8 million, and was distributed among 336 organizations in 1970–71. That amount was almost equivalent to the Metropolitan's total private contributions for 1972–1973.

Government involvement in the arts dates back to the New Deal of the 1930s. Several theater, writing, and music projects were initiated at that time. However, the WPA projects were phased out with the impact of WW II. From 1955 to 1961, cultural projects which traveled abroad were supported. A federal advisory commission, which took its mission seriously, was established during the Kennedy administration, and August Heckscher became the first presidential consultant in cultural affairs. Shortly after Kennedy's death, the Senate approved a bill establishing a National Arts Foundation; soon after, the National Council on the Arts Bill was passed, but this bill had no grants to award. In 1965, Johnson introduced a bill which provided for actual grants to support nonprofit arts organizations, establishing the National Foundation on the Arts and Humanities (Netzer 1978:58–9). However, Partnership for the Arts, an organization for the arts, has been set up as a lobby and works through arts councils, business and civic leaders, and politicians to initiate greater monetary allocations to the arts. Although some community arts councils existed in the 1940s, they really didn't begin to proliferate until the 1960s.

The major funding agency of the government, The National Endowment of the Arts (NEA-Public Law 89–209), provides matching grants to assist professional opera companies in extending touring activities and expanding opera audiences. Its emphasis is on getting opera to smaller communities and to schools; improving performance quality, providing intern opportunities for young artists, strengthening organization and improving fund-raising techniques, and in cooperation for other opera companies, eliminating duplication of expenses for sets and costumes. Grants may be provided to sponsoring organizations to increase regional distribution of opera. Those eligible include opera-producing companies of regional or national impact, sponsoring organizations whose services benefit a group of opera companies on a regional basis, and a limited number of professional and educational institutions. NEA allocated $600,000 in 1968, $410,000 in 1969, $951,000 in 1970, and $125 million by 1980.

NEA's grants to music programs totalled over $5 million from 1966 to 1970, and over $41 million in the four-year period, from 1971 to 1974 (Netzer 1978:64–5). In 1980, it specifically gave $4.2 million to opera-musical theater companies to aid young artists, unfamiliar works, commissioning of new works, touring groups, and to cover production costs.

While the Metropolitan Opera received almost $2 million from local, state and federal subsidies, it received the largest grant of all NEA funding in the Opera-Musical Theater Program, totalling $750,000. This was directed to defray the costs of producing Berg's "Lulu." New York City Opera received $265,000, Seattle $200,000, Lyric Opera of Chicago, $210,000, and San Francisco Opera $385,000. Most of this money was allocated to cover the costs of new productions, or the production of unpopular operas, which would have otherwise never been selected for presentation (NEA 1980). These grants account for a fraction of the company's budget (for example, 2 percent of the Metropolitan's; 2½ percent of New York City Opera's; 4 percent of San Francisco's.

Europeans, on the other hand, ". . . tend to feel that cultural activities make an essential and irreplaceable contribution to human life and the general welfare, and therefore qualify for public support" (Metropolitan Opera Association 1972:27). Consequently, government subsidies to the Vienna State Opera, Hamburg Opera, Munich Opera, and the Royal Opera of Sweden amount to two-thirds of their expenses. Britain's contribution to Covent Garden is 42 percent of its total income.

The issue always raised is whether government support will affect program selection. The repertoires of the European houses and of regional companies and universities of the United States seem to indicate that government subsidy has provided for greater freedom. In fact, 61 percent of performing arts groups and 60 percent of the visual arts groups represented in a recent study feel that they were limited "a lot" in their activities by shortage of funds (NCA 1973:175). However, when asked if government support would have some influence on their programming, music organizations indicated:

> There is little doubt in their minds that greater government support would have some influence on the programming of individual organizations. . . . The smaller organizations feel most of all that their programming would be influenced by greater government funding (NCA 1973:175).

This statement is somewhat ambiguous. Does it mean that large organizations which are established and well-known do not need to legitimate themselves for support so that their present repertoire reflects audience approval? Would smaller organizations, in applying for government aid, have to change their current selections to serve more communal and educational interests? Or does this mean that smaller companies cannot sustain themselves without government support, and that larger companies would utilize government funds for special projects, or for giving Americans more musical opportunities?

It has been shown that the need for government subsidy is mandatory if our nation wishes to be represented in the arts. Given the stature of its opera houses, symphony orchestras and ballet companies, in many cases the United States is at the avant-garde. There is no doubt that government subsidy has benefited the regional companies across the nation, and represents increased support to the larger opera companies. In addition to receiving direct monies, recipients of NEA gain prestigious and credibility. Other private sources, especially corporations, are eager to contribute to prestigious NEA winners. Thus, government support generates other subsidies.

A Political Consciousness for the Arts

The economic impasse, caused by a constantly widening gap between income and expenses, has stimulated board members, executive directors, and chairmen in the arts to vigorously seek financial support from the obvious as yet untapped patron of the future: the government.

The planners thought that, in asking the biggest business in America for help, a particular definition and role of the arts had to be "legitimated" with a style and vocabulary politicans, lawyers, and bankers could understand. In turn, state arts councils, regional companies, board members, and corporations, sought to "organize" by forming coalitions on a national level within the ideological frame of "art for the community."

To organize the fragmented and diverse interests of each of the performing arts, a common cause was necessary. Individual attempts at fund-raising and frequent competition among organizations had to take secondary positions. Each organization had come to realize that in numbers there was strength. Because of the unbearable economic burdens, a viable coalition was in the making by the early seventies. Board members applied legal and organizational skills to the arts. Numerous committees, forums, and conventions were formed. The obvious place to begin was in coordinating the various fund-raising committees and councils of individual companies. Next came the integration of arts centers, regions, and councils under the Partnership for the Arts. This council, aided in opera by the Central Opera Service, established a complex communications network on a national level.

Prior to the formation of the Partnership for the Arts, and Opera America, founded in 1970, Central Opera Service had, for over ten years, provided the public with information on opera companies and their repertoire. It distributed available data, and did a lot of information gathering of its own, thus providing for an exchange of ideas and issues among companies. Its political orientation was not evident until the rise of NEA in 1965, when the financial need was made visible by the publication of *The Performing Arts—The Economic Dilemma* and *The Rockefeller Report On the Future of Theatre, Dance and Music in America*. Management began to say — "This is it! We've done our job and the arts just can't survive unless the government steps in to help." This was no half-hearted approach. The campaign was direct, concisely verbalized, and loud. Amyas Ames, Chairman of Lincoln Center, has been the most outspoken arts representative to lobby for government support. Through his testimony before the Select Subcommittee on Education of the House of Representatives, he has done much to spur activity in this area.

There are now thirty-three non-performing arts organizations, foundations, councils, and guilds (see appendix) that are, in one way or another, actively engaged in lobbying. The various state councils and their regional constituents have been incorporated under the Associated Councils of the Arts (ACA). This has insured a liaison with politicians in state legislatures and with the federal government. Other committees, like the BCA and the Lincoln Center Consolidated Corporate Fund Drive, act to spur corporate interest and consciousness of the arts. Individual guilds and committees as well as individual devotees have lobbied for appropriation bills in both the Senate and House.

Businessmen sitting on boards provide their legal and organizational expertise, as well as the influential personal contacts required for an effective coalition. Schonberg has commented on art as "big business" saying,

> that the arts in America are authentically Big Business, as fully worthy of Federal help as Lockheed or Grumman (the arts employ more, spend more, take in more) . . . . [T]he leaders of symphony orchestras, opera houses, museums, and drama companies throughout the country are solid businessmen, not radicals or egg-heads, anxious to throw away money in a great cultural boondoggle. (1973:19).

In another article, he wrote:

> The National Endowment advised by the various arts councils and Partnership for the Arts, is not going to scatter money around promiscuously. Partnership for the Arts, for one, has worked up a very severe set of criteria for organizations seeking aid, and has also suggested that the total of state and Federal help for any organization should not exceed the amount of private support that organizations can raise. The people running American cultural organizations are not radicals; they are bankers, brokers, philanthropists, and businessmen who are as much exponents of private enterprise as anybody in the inner circles of the present Government. (1973)

The arts are run by businessmen from the American corporate world and their strategies reflect their business orientation. Consider the consequences, for example, of the "criteria" established by the Partnership for the Arts under which companies are deemed "eligible" to apply. The criteria include the following factors: 1) the quality of the art company, 2) its public service activities, 3) the contributions received from the private sector, 4) and—most important—the needs of the institution for providing its overall services for the community. As one can see, the smaller, avant-garde groups, or those who need a start will probably have less of a chance of receiving government aid. Ironically, the "big" corporations or art dynasties are likely to benefit most, since they already have the necessary technical expertise and institutional stability to accumulate large funds from the private sector.

In an attempt to provide public information on the arts to the community and to politicians and, thereby, to generate an interest and awareness of the needs of the arts, art councils have undertaken studies. They have commissioned consultant firms, formed volunteer committees, or engaged the services of Central Opera Service and the National Research Center on the Arts. What is significant is the part these data have played in providing for a justificatory and ideological definition: the arts reflect the needs and interests of the community. They have pointed to the enormous concert attendance, the "ethnic" programs supported by arts centers, and the effect of inflation on the arts. The appropriations, it is argued, represent a meager 10 percent of the $2 billion spent yearly by the American people on the non-profit arts. All of these statistics pointed to the ubiquity of the arts and the nationwide need for the arts. This then became the rationale and legitimation for public support. According to NCA:

> Non-profit cultural organizations employ 33,000 people — as many persons as the (New York) State steel industry. The operating expenditures of non-profit cultural institutions, $350 million, are more than half the operating expenditures of the State's agricultural business . . . . Arts and cultural institutions in New York State have a total estimated value of more than $6-million in assets, properties, and holdings, equivalent to the national holdings of General Motors Corporation. . . . The arts swell the tourist industry, which is a $3.5 billion activity in the State. The salaries of those working in the arts are taxed and all those buildings and activities are customers of the local trades (1973).

Thus the statistics continue to be accumulated and poured forth to legitimate art, but not on a philosophical level or for its own sake. We have shown that a "big business" approach to opera did much to illuminate the desperate need for government support and to provide ideological legitimations for the role of the arts in American society. It is however, a sad comment on American society that politicians and bankers had to be convinced of the need for art by the use of big business tactics and ideologies.

The final step of such lobbying was to rid art of its "elitist" image and align it with cross-cultural, cross-class and cross-geographic aims.

The study *Arts and the People* (1973) did much to stress the importance which individuals from all classes, interest groups, and neighborhoods attach to the arts. It views the arts as reflective of ethnic diversity, and finally points to the relation of the arts to social problems. Thus the report says that

> this is true in the city and country and regardless of social background or age. In New York City schools where absenteeism in public high schools rises about 28 percent in some cases, it drops to 5 percent for arts activities (NCA 1973b).

In 1966, at the Central Opera Service Convention in Washington, Charles Young, then the Chairman of the Executive Committee of the National Council of the Arts, defined the role of the arts in a democratic setting;

> I think the reason the public subsidy is necessary is because we are moving as a democracy to the place where the arts are no longer the province of the elite; where we must increasingly take care of both quality and quantity . . . and stress the importance of always keeping the artist — the performer, as well as the creative artist — as the focal point, whether the discussion revolved around artistic administration or budgets. (1966).

Opera, perhaps more than other performing arts, has had to work toward severing itself from its patrician roots and its image as an "elite" institution. A more realistic approach might be to acknowledge opera's elite position, and insure its aesthetic standards. Government support should absolve opera companies from the necessity of pandering to the market, and encourage the production of works other than those which are "public, democratic, and mass-supported". Patrons of the past favored particular operas and had preferences for superstars, and a larger middle-class public emulated their tastes. Now businessmen tell government that according to business criteria, this kind of opera is what the public wants. This in turn, will not liberate artistic decision-making from a total dependence on the market.

Summary

The preceding has been an attempt to analyze the economic base of the opera, by outlining the income, expenses, deficits, and contributions to the leading opera companies, and by demonstrating an increasing need for government support. This analysis has, in one way, laid the foundation for the following chapter, which will focus on the roles of audiences and the box office, and their effect upon repertoire.

The data on the opera companies have revealed an enormous gap between income and expenses which has been aggravated by an alarming rise in production costs, primarily due to artistic salaries, and staging and technical fees. But one cannot blame inflation, unions, and featherbedding, as Baumol and Bowen suggested. The artistic organization, by its very nature, cannot be compared to a business firm, in which increased output can generate increased profit in order to affect increased costs. Opera production necessarily operates with consistent deficits, an unusual practice in a nation that prides itself on successful private enterprise. Because of continuous economic pressure, opera has been forced to consolidate into a few major commercial companies, which perform for longer seasons and which, in doing so, must guarantee fifty-two week contracts to their artists. The operating expenses of these arts centers have forced administrators to undertake rational planning in an attempt to control costs and tap additional sources of income.

These realities exist and are not helped by either the behavior of fund raisers or the attitudes of Congress. Foundations, government, and corporations, attempting to control "risk capital" involved in philanthropy (which itself is an irrational and contradictory position), support only established and stable organizations as revealed by their lack of support of individual artists, works of an experimental nature, or companies who wish to establish themselves. While there are fund-raisers and foundations solely devoted to the latter, they are rare and have limited funds. In addition, the national guidelines, stipulating that federal support should not exceed the amount an organization can raise on its own, contribute greatly to restricting recipients to companies that produce standard repertoire. Companies and productions that are exploratory and "risk taking" do not seem to have the bargaining power or political support needed for fund raising.

It is difficult to discern the consequences of the economic pressure on opera because of the secrecy of decision-making in its boardrooms and the general unwillingness of managers and directors to discuss the crass monetary aspects of opera production. Long and endless arguments about possible government influence on repertoire have deflected attention from the possible effects the present dependencies may have on contemporary musical trends. Repertoire is always presented as an artistic matter, but interviews, gossip, and informal reporting reveal the interdependence of artistic and financial matters.

Long-term union contracts still have the performer facing economic insecurity. Although the Metropolitan Opera orchestra and a few others like the New York Philharmonic and the Boston Symphony have fifty-two week contracts, their financial position still remains precarious. At best, security is assured for the very few superstars, and even they are subject to the vagaries of an international market for performers. Such conditions work both for and against the success of even the star virtuoso. Yet managers know that box office returns increase with the making of stars such as Maria Callas, Beverly Sills, Joan Sutherland, Leonard Bernstein, Margot Fonteyn, or Franco Zeffirelli. Columbia Artists Management, Inc. knows well the box office effect of its superstars, as did the late Sol Hurok. The consequences of institutionalization for both performers and for the creation of new art are many and debatable. As professionals, artists have gained independence from the traditions and dominance of popes, countesses, and kings; now they are subjected to the requirements of the "production" goals of "non-profit" organizations. Their sense of alienation is compensated for by the satisfaction of being "professional," i.e., economically secure. Artists are bound by a system of rights and values which they think are for their own benefit, yet the same system ensures that as performers they are subject to pressures from the organizations that employ them.

Opera, like other art forms, has gone through periods in which it has had to struggle to survive. Finally, by its affiliation with arts centers, it has established itself as an ongoing institution. In the process, it has been manipulated and used as a status-granting institution; there has been a peculiar shift in what opera stands for in the light of its aristocratic traditions. Presently, it is redefining itself in a typically American way as "practical, democratic, egalitarian, expedient, and middle-class" in order to acquire governmental patronage.

Creative and performing artists, with differing professional interests and musical interpretations, work daily within this milieu. The remaining chapters will focus on how this non-profit structure affects the cultural product (repertoire), the occupational roles of artists, and the meaning of their work. Performers' experiences vis-a-vis each other and the values they internalize in coming to terms with these circumstances will be examined; for this setting provides the social structure in which defenses are created and ideologically interpreted, personal feelings are suppressed, and conflicts are tolerated.

Notes

[1]It is extremely difficult to delineate the historical periods which represent the end of "standard" repertoire and the beginning of "contemporary." Both popular and stylistic trends affect the usage of these terms and complicate their definitions. However, for the purposes of this study, the term "standard" will be used to include all opera composed prior to and including the life of Puccini, and "contemporary" for the period following Puccini to the present.

[2]Annual orchestra musicians' salaries range from $37,000 to $40,000 in 1980.

[3]Concert-goers will recall that in 1973 in New York City, there were four major strikes, by the Museum of Modern Art, the New York City Ballet, the Philharmonic Orchestra, and the New York City Opera. Each of these strikes reflected the cost squeeze in the arts. They have contributed to the redefinition of the roles of the artists in terms of unions, contracts, and employee relationships. They have also affected relationships among significant others including managers, union delegates, lawyers who negotiate with art administrators on behalf of artists, and the periphery of artistic friends and professional colleagues.

[4]For more readings on the private patron, see *Philanthropic Digest*; Tom Buckley, "The Cost of Putting Footprints in Sands of Time," *The New York Times*, October 17, 1973, p. 49; Donal Henahan, "Philharmonic Hall Gets Eight Million Gift," *The New York Times*, September 21, 1973, p.1; and Milton Gussow, "Mrs. Newhouse Gives Papp $1 Million," *The New York Times*, May 31, 1973, p. 50.

[5]The Baumol and Bowen book (Twentieth Century Fund, 1966) also encouraged the publications of the following books and reports revealing the extent of support by these groups: Richard Eells, *The Corporation and the Arts.* (New York: Macmillan & Company, 1967); *The Conference Board Record* (New York: National Industrial Conference Board, 1968) A. Gingrich, *Business and the Arts* (New York: Paul S. Erikson, Inc., 1969) and *A Guide to Corporate Giving in the Arts* (American Council for the Arts, 1980.)

[6]See Howard Klein, "Do We Dare Help the Artist Who Dares?", *The New York Times*, June 10, 1973, pp. 17 and 37 for a discussion of foundations who play it safe by supporting only established and legitimate organizations rather than "risking" with individual artists or more experimental companies and works.

[7]For a discussion of the difficulties of passing bills for government subsidization in the arts, see Donal Henahan, "Will Congress Pass the Comedy and Drama to the People," *The New York Times*, June 17, 1973, p. 17; Harold C. Schonberg, "Was the Cheering Premature," *The New York Times*, June 1973; Milton Gussow, "National Endowment Puts Government Into Role of Major Patron of the Arts," *The New York Times*, August 12, 1973, p. 1; Terri Cornwell Eakin, "Democracy and the Arts," in Kamerman and Martorella, eds., *Performers and Performances: The Social Organization of Artistic Work* (forthcoming).

By popular demand, the Lyric Opera of Chicago scheduled additional performances of "La Bohème" in 1973. (Lyric Opera of Chicago)

4 *Musical Tastes: The Interplay Between Box Office and Repertoire*

The opera audience includes those who buy tickets, through box office and subscription series, the private patron, and other contributors — including the foundations, the corporations, and the government. Selection of repertoire is made in response to these groups; it is by purchasing tickets that audiences express their preferences.

The economic analysis in preceding chapters focused on the costs of production and became the basis for the assertion that the selection of repertoire is dictated by those who support opera, since the dependence of opera on such market conditions has set limitations on what can be produced. Repertoire reflects a compromise between public tastes, private patronage, and the preference of musical directors and superstars. The repertoire of the leading houses over the past years since their initiation is reviewed in this chapter to discover whether any dominant styles prevail. The chapter will thus conclude the analysis of the opera market which, in the preceding chapter, demonstrated the "non-profit" base in the arts.

Balancing Artistic Values and Production Costs

In producing any art form, the ideal relationship between costs and what is selected for presentation would be one of mutual independence. Producing an opera puts into motion a large organizational complex, requiring the talents and expertise of performing and non-performing personnel, which caters to audiences who buy tickets; this situation is far from ideal. Production costs often take precedence over artistic and musical considerations. This economic problem has, unfortunately, led to the resolution of artistic problems in terms of financial considerations. Sensitive to the dangers of such a situation, Baumol and Bowen in their economic study of the arts wrote:

> Artistic judgements defying business calculations enter at every step. In the profit-seeking business world these are clearcut measures of effectiveness, the income account and the balance sheet. For the nonprofit organization . . . although a diminishing deficit might seem to indicate effective business management, this is not necessarily the case. It might simply reflect an increasing failure to meet artistic obligations. (1966:1961)

A preoccupation with production costs is reflected in an increasingly "rational" approach in planning future seasons, in making repertoire decisions, and in exploring the public appeal of the "product." Costs are scrutinized and attempts are made to control them. More and more, the board member whose function once was to raise income, now aids management in "controlling" the costs of the product. This he does both by his legal and financial expertise as a lawyer or banker, and by his influential contacts with financiers and corporations who provide additional sources of income. Musical directors, conductors, and performers, dissatisfied with proposed budget cuts, find themselves at odds with board members and managers who influence artistic decisions by reducing rehearsal time, limiting the size of the chorus and the number of supernumeraries, and restricting the budget for scenery, etc. An internationally known opera administrator, Rolf Liebermann, makes no secret of his "rational" approach given the "realities" which exist, and says:

> But to begin with, you must be effective. Then you can start to be philosophical . . . . One shouldn't talk about one's artistic mission. If you have to produce an automobile, or what-ever, you have to produce it for a price. It's exactly the same in opera. It's an organization that sells opera performances. (Heyworth 1971)

Pierre Boulez, director of the New York Philharmonic, remarks in a radio broadcast that low costs affect his daily work and decision-making:

It's very important. For instance, if you want to do a work which is unknown or a new work, a twentieth century work for the first time, you have to carefully plan the program because we have four rehearsals and if we want to have extra rehearsals for a new program, we have to pay for it, and the costs are really soaring to a point that we can't afford any more. If we have a big work and large orchestra and soloists you can do that only once or twice a year and you can't rehearse anew very often. The programs of the season are a result of dialogue with guests then looking at the economy . . . if the program will fit the budget. (1973)

One singer who was more resigned to the economic constraints in opera, spoke of how the economics of opera determines what is produced:

One of the reasons — for Meyerbeer, I'm sure, is slightly out of vogue — is that an opera like "Les Hugenots" is just too expensive to mount today. Five or six different acts, enormous ballet, a battle scene, on-stage massacre scene. It would take so much money to present an opera like this that the management feels, and rightfully so, it's just not worth it, so this is why we have organizations like Concert Opera Society, the Carnegie Hall thing who do obscure pieces that you wouldn't likely see on stage.

Another singer, Jess Thomas, regretfully remarked that opera according to American standards ". . . is seen in terms of how much it makes." Manager Herman Krawitz, describes quite matter of factly how he estimates costs:

I would base it on estimates and have to say, you want to do this, it'll cost you so much. It'll take X amount of dollars. I could tell you by whom we hired. When you engage Zeffirelli, you have an expensive production . . . figure this two years in advance including shoptime. Bing always wanted quality and I did too . . . . What you get, you spend . . . . We knew where we were in finances. Give or take a certain amount. In total, I came pretty close to predicting costs. It's not as hard as it sounds (1973).

Schuyler Chapin, General Manager of the Metropolitan Opera in 1973, talked about the importance of controlling costs as he ruefully remarked:

Part of the solution is keeping tight control of expenses and we are carrying out a concentrated program to reduce costs. But there are limits to the economies which can be made without impairing artistic excellence (1973).

In a long letter written to Lowell Wadmond in 1952, Rudolph Bing reveals the confrontation between musical values and economic constraints within the artistic organization:

> The question of whether an operation like ours is run extravagantly or economically is answered by the facts of whether people are overpaid, whether there are too many people in various departments, whether time or materials are wasted, etc., etc. . . . It is unrealistic to say "here is $150,000 and go ahead and make three new productions." The only realistic way is to ask what three new productions will cost and then provide the funds accordingly. . . . I could offer you innumerable cases where and how we have cut expenses and saved money but — and this brings me to the first part of my letter — we, of course, operate on an expensive level and this is the basic question . . . . These obligations as I see them, and I admit this frankly, are in the first place artistic. The Metropolitan Opera will be judged by future critics on its artistic merits and not on deficits or profits (1972:228–31).

But the excessive costs in producing opera are poignantly revealed by the losses incurred night after night. These losses serve to justify the overzealous preoccupation with costs by art administrators. Even capacity houses do not necessarily reduce the deficit. Operas which are "box office" successes are measured according to the costs per performance in order to see which operas are the most expensive to produce. Table 8 is based on data taken from a Metropolitan study. Operas are ranked according to their dollar loss per performance. The total amount of ticket sales is reflected in box office percentage (percent of house capacity sold). "Aida," with the highest box office capacity, incurs the largest loss per performance, $29,000, while "La Boheme" and "Carmen" with smaller capacities, are cheaper to produce and lose $14,500 and $18,000 respectively. The average loss per performance stands at about $20,000.

In describing the Metropolitan Opera Association study, the financial director remarked:

> We've done some interesting analysis. Things that fill the house aren't most economical! The board went crazy when this was presented. They do not like surprises . . . . For example, "Aida" is most expensive, no matter how full the house is. You can't make much from it. I analyzed all the operas in terms of how much we lose (1973).

TABLE 8
NET LOSS PER PERFORMANCE
METROPOLITAN OPERA 1972

	Box Office		Variable*	Loss per
	%	$	Costs	Performance
Aida	98	$49,000	$28,500	$29,000
Cav/Pag	90	45,000	23,500	28,500
Salome	75	37,500	15,000	27,500
Walküre	96	48,000	23,000	25,500
Siegfried	97	48,500	23,000	24,500
Sonnambula	77	38,500	13,000	24,500
Orfeo	70	35,000	9,000	24,000
Ballo	80	40,000	13,000	23,000
Macbeth	84	42,000	14,500	22,500
Lucia	85	42,500	14,000	21,500
Tosca	90	45,000	16,000	21,000
Grimes	75	37,500	8,000	20,500
Pique Dame	80	40,000	9,500	19,500
Trovatore	99	49,500	19,000	19,500
Don Giovanni	88	44,000	13,000	19,000
Faust	89	44,500	13,000	18,500
Rosenkavalier	97	48,500	16,500	18,000
Carmen	98	49,500	17,000	18,000
Traviata	93	46,500	14,000	17,500
Romeo	80	40,000	7,500	17,500
Otello	95	47,500	14,000	16,500
Rigoletto	90	45,000	11,000	16,000
Norma	99	49,500	14,500	15,000
Flute	92	46,500	11,000	15,000
Boheme	93	46,500	11,000	14,500
Fille	98	49,000	13,000	14,000
Butterfly	94	47,000	10,000	13,000
Barber	99	49,500	17,500	13,000

SOURCE: Metropolitan Opera Association, 1972.
*Variable Costs are losses incurred beyond $60,000 average cost per performance.

Although the table covers a span of only five months in one season, it illuminates a trend in repertoire at the Metropolitan: audiences have a preference for the larger and more spectacular productions, such as "Aida" and "Die Walkure," and for star vehicles like "La Fille du Regiment." Since the beginnings of the Metropolitan, its aristocratic patrons have tended to prefer Italian opera, with the Wagnerians gaining control over repertoire from time to time. Star selection is an important additional factor in filling the house. There is no doubt, for example, that the popularity of "La Fille du Regiment"

was due to the performances of Joan Sutherland and Luciano Pavarotti; "Lucia," another favorite, dropped to 84 percent house capacity
when the lead was sung by other than a "superstar."

Table 8 further clarifies the losses per performance by isolating
the sums representing fees for the artists and "extras." These fees
are represented in the table as "variable" costs since they are contingent upon individual, per-performance agreements rather than annual contracts. They vary from night to night. "Variable" costs
include solo artists' fees, salaries for extra stagehands and supernumeraries, as well as the expense of additional lighting, costuming
and scenery above the average cost allocated for each performance.
Ticket sales are given in both dollars and percentages of house capacity. The average fixed cost stands at $60,000 per performance.

The operas incurring the greatest losses are the "grand" productions of Verdi and Wagner and those for which four or more
superstars are engaged. "Aida," "Siegfried," and "Die Walküre" fall
into the first category, with losses of $29,000, $24,500 and $27,500.
Those employing four or more superstars include "Cavalleria Rusticana" and "Pagliacci," "Die Walküre," and "Siegfried." These productions have total losses at $28,500, $25,500 and $24,500.

Of those operas with high variable costs, "Trovatore," "Siegfried," "Die Walküre," and "Lucia Di Lammermoor" may be able to
offset these costs by ticket sales. This was the case with "Trovatore,"
which with a 98 percent house brought in $49,500, and reduced var-
iable costs to $19,500. On the other hand, "Salome" had a relatively
lower variable cost, $15,000, than the other operas, but could not
sustain this loss. At 75 per cent house capacity, its box office receipts
brought in only $37,500, resulting in a loss of $27,500.

In conclusion, the net loss per performance varies with the popularity of both the opera itself and the cast. The costs of the large
dramatic operas that require expensive staging, a superstar, and extras fees may be partially offset by box office receipts. Total losses
are cut back by reducing the number of performances of the expensive
productions.

As part of the overall planning, the managers have made a self-
conscious and deliberate attempt to develop advanced public relations
techniques. To offset its drop in attendance, the Metropolitan, for
example, has instituted promotional activities such as student and
senior citizen discounts, the use of credit cards, student rushes (tickets
sold one hour before a performance), extended mailings, and guild
and benefit performances on premiere nights. This year as director
of the New York City Opera, Beverly Sills has even lowered the costs
of tickets hoping to increase total attendance rates. Artistic produc-

tions are increasingly referred to as "products." The terminology reflects a concern for their market potential. One manager says that the urge to produce compositions that sell varies with the seriousness of the deficit.

> When things are a little tight, we have to pull in our reins. There are times when we plan something which is a little less secure than something else, that will influence the decision. The weight may fall on the side of something which is more secure from the standpoint of audience popularity. Certainly that cannot be the sole bargaining factor or else you're sacrificing artistic standards. You have to compromise and objectively you can't do everything we want to and so all of these factors have to be plugged in and hopefully we come to a decision that will be viable from all standpoints.

Advertising, too, has to be included. This technique is new to the arts and especially to the Metropolitan which has often boasted about its long waiting lists for subscription. A manager outlined a recent campaign and expressed an ambivalent attitude toward it:

> Since the new house, we've had new problems. There's more "packaging" than selling which needs much more time. It's nice to say that we're 98% sold out. . . . Now there's always campaigning. . . . This is an ad that could sell some tickets:
>
> ". . . CARMEN MAKES LOVE ON WEEKDAYS AS ON WEEKENDS. . . ."
>
> I don't really care as long as we have a response for these series. They are the hardest to sell . . . hard to sell because New York City has changed. It's a weekend city . . . advertisements had to be jazzy because they wanted to stress that we don't keep our stars for the weekends. . . .
> It's too bad we have to learn how to package the same old product, as you, an opera buff, know . . . it's like your life style going to the opera and we have to think of bringing the audience in. We have to package the same old product which is "grand old opera" and basically our repertoire is the standard repertoire, about 90%.

A recent report on the arts in New York State revealed an increase in funds allocated for public relations and advertising. These will become even greater in the future, especially for the large music organizations. Dance and theatre organizations, on the other hand, foresee greater expenditures for administrative staff and for desperately needed building facilities.

Concern with production costs has become part of the daily decision making in opera. A preoccupation with cost has led to close supervision and control and a tendency to view opera as a "product" that has to be made "marketable."

The Audience

The box office is the most obvious "measure" of public preferences, and represents approximately 60 percent of the operating incomes for the Metropolitan, Chicago, and San Francisco Operas. Each percentage point of box office returns is equivalent to $100,000 in income; a decline in attendance can produce disastrous deficits. The Metropolitan's 1971–72 season was marked by a reduction from 89 percent to 87 percent of capacity; fortunately, the figure rose in 1972–73 to 90 percent. This situation is aggravated when ticket prices reach their peak. Analysis of production costs reveals that even "box office" productions do not guarantee balanced budgets, but submission to box office demands insures greater financial security and has come to be justified because it means survival. Although accurate prediction of the box office returns is not always possible, prudent management is well aware of the "winners" and what audiences want. A rare or unfamiliar work by Verdi, Wagner, or Puccini is a sure hit, even more so when superstars are engaged for these new productions. One is reminded of a statement by Edward Johnson who, as manager of the Metropolitan from 1935 to 1950, remarked, "Opera depends for its prosperity on Verdi, Wagner, and Puccini." Increases in costs also force music organizations to rely more heavily on subscription performances. Subscriptions fill the house in more than half of the total opera performances.

The opera audience is highly diverse and heterogeneous. Among those who go to the opera two or three times a week are patrons, claques and fans; the subscriber and occasional opera goer attend less frequently. Subscribers and occasional opera goers, however, remain the largest and most conservative group of consumers. A survey of opera audiences conducted by the National Council of the Arts indicates that opera, like all art forms, has been affected by the mass media. Audiences are exposed to opera through television and radio more frequently than through actual live performance. Opera and ballet, have the lowest attendance rate among the performing arts.

Opera still remains a symbol of social status to the patrons[1]; many attend two or three times a week. The serious advocates include the sycophants who belong to a diva, including claques, as well as the fans who love opera no matter who is singing. These frequent attenders are the most knowledgeable, are adamant in their preferences in repertoire and casting, and are eager to share their knowledge regarding the folklore, gossip, and history of opera. Income and education are important variables in determining attendance, and studies report that operagoers are predominantly white upper-middle-class college graduates who are professionals or teachers (NCA 1974: 12–15; DiMaggio and Useem 1978).

who attends opera Characterist.

The Box Office

Although managers are preoccupied with public tastes and feel they know what they are, they have never conducted studies of their audiences. To management, audiences have been defined somewhat categorically, as those who purchase tickets at a particular price; the product's profit ceiling is determined by the highest ticket price that the box office can bear.

In John Mueller's analysis of symphony orchestras in the United States, he views repertoire as a reflection of the demands of different groups and includes:

> the standard and familiar items, of "box office" numbers, of modern and unhackneyed compositions, experimental novelties to satisfy the intelligent patron and members of a cult, some pieces for light relief, and a certain minimum number of regional representatives. It is not easy to reconcile these conflicting demands with one another, or with the rules of prudent management (Mueller 1951:47).

Box office predominantly responds to the "standard" repertoire — works that have survived a competitive selection over time. One could estimate that about 75 percent of a season's repertoire includes the "mainliners," while 10–25 percent are new productions, the remainder being contemporary or experimental works. The public's ubiquitous influence is verified in the following quote in which William Schuman, a celebrated composer, measures the worth of his own works by their popularity. Regretting the nonperformance of his large symphonies or dissonant pieces, he continued:

> It bothers me . . . . I am never bothered by works that are not performed much because they haven't had an audience success. But, for example, my violin concerto had great acclaim and has always had audience success and is rarely played by violinists.

I don't understand it. I would understand with works that don't go with an audience. I have no feelings about those. I think the time is much more critical for American composers now with symphony orchestras because they are becoming less adventuresome. (Schuman 1973)

Few would disagree, although clear documentation is lacking in this study, that superstars insure box office success. One publicist remarked, "Yes, that's what makes box office. Superstars are stars known by the public, that is box office!" (Williamson 1972) Another was asked if he thought the star system was declining, and to that he emphatically replied:

No! This is wishful thinking on the part of conductors and directors. Everywhere there is a star system. It has to be. It's the only way one will sell tickets. No opera house first goes for ensemble. They try ultimately but first they must see that a Corelli or Nilsson is available (Gravina 1973).

Inevitably, the manager admits his dependence for box office returns on the stars and on the audiences who support them. One manager's ambivalence was expressed defensively, ". . . but there is a difference in developing one's own stars. Certainly, this company has never brought in international stars who have made their reputations elsewhere. . . ."

While blaming the star for interfering with the plans of the house and demanding high wages, managers also complain of audiences and the forced concession to their tastes. Journalists, like others of the musical community, express a somewhat condescending attitude towards the rank and file; one says of audiences:

I don't know what the audience wants. They want big stars. First of all, they want opera they know . . . like baseball, they want big names. . . . Again any serious intellectual artist . . . any serious opera goer would prefer ensemble. Wouldn't you? I am not talking about the average opera goer, Mr. and Mrs. Schwartz, who go to two or three or four performances a year and want something they won't have to suffer through. They even suffer through Aida which seems long and even Carmen.

And a serious opera fan remarks:

The trouble today at the Met, is that artists know they're not, for the most part, going to be booed. . . . Today too many artists are products of publicity. And the American public goes to opera like it was TV. . . . Here I am, they say, entertain me. They don't understand that they have to put something into it themselves.

Ironically, private, corporate, and now government funding comes to support "popular" compositions. The same is true in the financing of new productions. One manager justifies his concessions to public tastes by their ability to insure future donations:

> If you are given a donation, you spend it. If you examine the records, we did very well. The public was excited, they sent checks. . . . Our assets are good. We have money around — in art, real estate, we own the old building and grounds. We left it in a very very healthy condition (Met). A wonderful staff. Everything was paid for. All the equipment in first-class condition. When I came, everything was in shambles from typewriters to everything.

And so the cycle is complete. For the majority of performances and companies, the most popular operas are produced because people are willing to purchase tickets and patrons are willing to contribute funds to supplement the costs of popular pieces. Philanthropy responds to what is currently popular; opera, therefore, is publicly acclaimed and becomes a status symbol for the donor.

With the growth of audiences and the mass media, the roles of publicists, public relations people, personal managers, and critics have grown. They play important roles as intermediaries between the artist and the public. They contribute to the creation of images that the public responds to and often accepts.[2] Musicians and critics alike contend that the role of the critic has been overemphasized, especially in regard to the power he possesses in influencing careers, commissions, and repertoire plans. In the classical field, however, the need for the critic is probably underestimated. His evaluations represent one of the few public estimates of the worth of a performance in a market which desperately relies on audiences. His influence has been due primarily to the fact that musical knowledge and training are limited to a small fraction of the "listening" audience and to the fact that audiences in America were reared by the mass media and have come to rely on the critic. American audiences are less likely than others to trust their own feelings and appraisals of what they see and hear.

The critic, however, is ambivalent about whom he writes for and what his function is. There are musician's critics, public's critics, journalist-interviewers, and feature writers — all stimulating an interest in the field. There is a hierarchy based on the critic's interest, specific experience, and training. Schonberg, music critic of *The New York Times*, told me in an interview that he requires his staff to have had training in music. Donal Henahan, writing on Shaw's genius, revealed that it was Shaw's special gift in writing — a style metaphorically connoting the feelings, images, and tempo of the content — that supported his vast knowledge of music technique. (1973:13). Because of the lack of newspapers in New York today, Harold Schonberg's criticisms in *The New York Times* have much more power than most and are seriously read by musicians and audiences alike. The critic is accused by musicians of making or breaking their careers — or by managers of not giving particular productions a fair chance and causing box office sales to decline. The critic is sometimes disdainfully accused of being more preoccupied with showing off his journalistic skills than with simply dealing in musical aesthetics.

Publicists, public relations people, and others who work for the performer-as-client try to get as much publicity and coverage of upcoming events as possible through advertisement, feature stories, etc. Their function is to generate an interest and demand where perhaps none would otherwise have existed. A star performer's virtuosity and technical display are easily understood by mass audiences without the knowledge required for appreciation of "ensemble," German opera, and other more avant-garde operas. Members of the media are not without blame in fostering star personalities and the adulation of the virtuoso rather than an interest in the art form. The majority continue to attend performances to hear "so and so." One publicist, admired for her unreserved and blunt manner quite uncommon in the public relations industry, blames members of her profession for their inability to stimulate people to attend concerts:

> I'm pretty tired of hearing this whining about the public's declining interest in classical concerts. I think it's the participants and the promoters who are really declining. The same old tired people, doing the same old tired things in the same old tired way. Is that any way to attract today's masses?

Inevitably any discussion of audiences raises the familiar and somewhat anachronistic issue of music for the masses. While it is not the intent here to focus exclusively on one issue, it has been emphasized that reliance on box office sales has created an overdependence on public tastes; and this has often had a detrimental effect on artistic and musical standards. There is an increasing tendency toward selecting the most popular repertoire rather than what may be more artistic and musical. Harris Green of *The New York Times* (1973) raised the "music for the masses" issue and is highly critical of altering musical standards. He is especially critical of the use of visual effects and other "gimmicks" to sell classical repertoire to less sophisticated audiences. This tendency not only affects what is produced but how it is produced. For example, productions which have been done to emphasize the showy are expensive and often miscast because a particular superstar wanted a debut in a new production. These effects constitute a lowering of artistic quality and a concern with other than musical values. An excess of costuming, staging, lighting, and other "dramatic" effects (e.g. pantomine, excessive gesturing and the changing tempo of the music to conform to bodily movements), are specific manifestations of the unfortunate need to make it "appealing" to audiences. Sycophants, too, are guilty of this in supporting the virtuoso display of the stars they adulate.

On the other hand, complete freedom in repertoire selection, which could be had with additional funds from the government, may not alter the standardization of the past fifty years. In addition, a situation of total independence from the market may result in companies producing works which are totally removed from present day audiences. Paradoxically, the market is essential for an art form to survive and it forces the art to communicate with the individuals it addresses.

There is no doubt that box office favoritism is a significant factor in deciding what gets produced. Francis Robinson, well-known in the opera world, and long affiliated with the Metropolitan, was asked who determined artistic standards. He responded:

> The public. We put it as ABC, Aida, Boheme and Carmen and Sir Rudolph used to say, "they know the masterpieces;" and it's not just because they heard about it. They know and feel the difference immediately. They demand and want the best (1971).

An assistant manager, wanting to remain anonymous, referred to the Metropolitan Opera as a "petrified and fossilized house" because of the need to sell tickets; he included other American institutions in his criticisms. Chicago, La Scala, and Covent Garden, he found, were not so rigid in repertoire, because of supplements provided by the government. He further went on to blame the subscription system. "Sure income is needed," he said, "but it has led to a conservative, even reactionary, repertoire."

Another assistant manager of the Metropolitan expressed dissatisfaction with the situation in which repertoire selections are made on the basis of what sells, which included operas that are known as "star" vehicles. "Look at next year's repertoire. It's conservative. I

don't know why they are doing 'Don Giovanni;' 'Hoffman' is for Sutherland; 'Troyens' is more adventurous; 'The Italian in Algers' is for Horne. . . ."
And yet, defensive of criticism of "unventuresome repertoire," he continued:

> We took more chances than we get credit for. Conventional works come out sometimes safe. We gambled. You know the press says we didn't take chances. When we did they condemned us with a lack of understanding . . . . They killed the work "Rake's Progress". The sense of experimentation. I am not saying they should like the things they don't like. They always get into that unventuresome repertoire but they forget the times we did. . . . He didn't want all those Bohemes and Toscas but they are a hit. They go well with the audience. The critics encouraged it whether they were aware of it or not. When we gambled they reacted. Artists want a full audience. Unless they are given the feeling that they are doing some good, artists don't like to do unpopular works.

Rolf Liebermann, who achieved great success and acclaim as general manager of the Hamburg Opera and who now leads the Paris Opera, summarized the Metropolitan's problem in a *New York Times* interview:

> The problem with the Metropolitan is that one is always dependent on the goodwill of people who may or may not be willing to help, so that one can never plan on a really secure budget. That's one dangerous thing. The other is that if the budget is based on a 96% box office, then that excludes everything risky and anything modern (1971).

And a newly appointed Music Director of the Metropolitan in 1972 summed up the irreversible set of circumstances:

> I don't think the repertoire of the Met is so terrible. In a big house one cannot afford to risk too much. I wonder whether it is just to say that the City Opera does avant-garde things and so-and-so and the Met doesn't. Look, I don't want to fight them, but their budget and their possibilities on a much smaller scale almost call for that "little better." They have the chance to try more because it doesn't cost so much money. The Met is the largest opera house in the world and cannot afford to be too audacious, but, of course, it should improve on its repertory.[3]

Carol Fox, general manager of the Lyric Opera of Chicago, has gone even further in asserting that it may not be her job to produce repertoire which is risky and, thereby, accepts the ideology of survival:

> Our audience might take a lot of hearing to comprehend and enjoy them. And I don't know that it's our purpose to do all these things. The most important purpose is to content the public, to get them to come, and bit by bit to indoctrinate them to the new. (Jenkins 1972)

A "White Paper" published by the Metropolitan Opera admits to this inevitable and unfortunate consequence for organizations dependent on box office and compares opera houses abroad that have government support:

> It has also been said that subsidy means greater freedom and opportunity to experiment than dependence exclusively on box office allows. Where the government makes up the difference between box office income and expenses (about 70% in Germany and as high as 90% in Sweden), it is much easier to plan a more adventurous repertory and not worry about selling tickets to works which are artistically worthwhile but have not yet had sufficient exposure to the public to be popular (1971).

An attempt has been made to indicate some of the subtle and difficult economic and social conditions leading to the development of and total concession, to mass tastes. Two concomitant circumstances have evolved: the growth of the mass audience, and an impending financial crisis. Although opera has always had economic constraints, the costs of producing opera today have made it more perilous, thus inhibiting its development. These expenses have resulted in a takeover by "production costs," manifested by a concern for box office returns so overzealous that future planning becomes predicated on what "sells."

The Distribution of Standard and Contemporary Repertoire

If one looks carefully at what is produced, it is possible to analyze the nature of the organization of opera. Repertoire becomes a significant factor since it reflects audience demands and the response to it by administrators. If, as in the case of the large companies that

One of the most popular operas in the United States is Puccini's "La Bohème." The Cafe Momus's second act of "La Bohème," designed for the Lyric Opera of Chicago in 1972 by Pier-Luigi Pizzi (Lyric Opera of Chicago)

are caught in the financial squeeze, every opportunity to increase the
box office receipts is taken, popular operas will be selected and superstars will be cast in major roles. It may then be concluded that
there is a direct relationship between the selection of opera repertoire
and the structure of the market.

Table 1 (see p. 48–49) outlined the number of professional companies, and opera university workshops in the United States. It also
compared standard and contemporary repertoire trends from 1954 to
1980. The standard repertoire accounted for 1,844 performances in
1954–55, 2,643 performances in 1964–65, 4,097 performances in
1974–75, and 5,482 performances by 1980. Contemporary foreign repertoire dropped from 1,844 in 1954–55 to 548 by 1980. Contemporary
American repertoire showed an increase from 2,193 reported in
1976–77 to 3,361 in 1980.

The contemporary operas appear primarily in the college market.
The repertories of the five major companies in the United States were
predominantly made of standard operas. At first glance, the figures
in the tables that follow seem to indicate that there is a "fair" representation of contemporary works and that commissions and new
productions are not uncommon. But, for the most part, this is true
only among university-based organizations and is not characteristic
of the commercial market. In addition, the audiences on college campuses represent only a small fraction of the total opera-going public.
The audience for the standard repertoire is much larger than the
figures would seem to indicate.

We will begin by outlining the most popular operas in the United
States. Table 9 shows the top ten productions for the period
1966–1972. Puccini's "La Boheme" heads the list with 1,023 productions. "Il Barbiere di Siviglia" was performed 870 times, "Le Nozze
di Figaro", 800, "Traviata" 759, "Madame Butterfly" 707, "Die Fle-
dermaus" 673, "Carmen" 661, "Cosi Fan Tutte" 558, "Hansel and
Gretel" 534, and "Tosca" 504. This list is dominated by Italian opera
composed during the nineteenth century. They are all melodic, and
are structured to compliment aria singing.

In the five year period, 1966–72, Puccini was the most popular
composer. Table 10 gives the total number of performances by composer. Puccini was followed by Mozart, Verdi, Rossini and Donizetti,
in that order.

The data revealed by Tables 9 and 10 come as no surprise especially following the economic analysis. The productions, as well as
the composers that are most popular, include works from the "standard" repertoire and are the staple of opera houses across the nation.

TABLE 9
MOST POPULAR OPERAS IN THE
UNITED STATES, 1966–72

	Number of Performances
La Bohème	1,023
Il Barbiere di Siviglia	870
Le Nozze di Figaro	800
Traviata	759
Madame Butterfly	707
Die Fledermaus	673
Carmen	661
Cosi Fan Tutte	558
Hansel and Gretel	534
Tosca	404

SOURCE: Central Opera Service, New York City, *Opera Repertory 1966–1972*, (New York: Central Opera Service Bulletin, 1972).

TABLE 10
MOST POPULAR STANDARD COMPOSERS
IN THE UNITED STATES, 1966–72

	Number of Performances
Puccini	3,228
Mozart	2,564
Verdi	2,254
Rossini	1,187
Donizetti	1,029
Gounod	442
Offenbach	411
Pergolesi	358
Mascagni	359
Leoncavallo	299
Wagner	261

SOURCE: Central Opera Service, New York City, *Opera Repertory 1966–1972*, (New York: Central Opera Service Bulletin, 1972).

Table 11 shows the number of performances of the seven most popular productions within the contemporary repertoire for the same six-year period, 1966–72. Other well-known contemporary composers performed included Barber, Moore, Foss, Floyd, Stravinsky, Ginastera, and Copland. Most of these works were not produced by the major companies, but appeared in opera workshop productions, summer theaters, touring companies, and regional opera houses. The exception is the New York City Opera which has maintained a policy of producing contemporary and unfamiliar repertoire.

The Metropolitan Opera Repertoire

The Metropolitan Opera is the oldest and most famous opera company considered in this book. Since its initiation in 1883, it has led in prestige and grandour around the world. Consequently, its deccisions with regard to repertoire selection establish standards, and serve as a model for many other companies throughout the United States. Since the top stars appear on its stage, recordings have reflected its premieres and new productions. Table 12 lists the total number of performances by composer. Verdi is the most produced composer, having appeared in eighty-four seasons of its eighty-six year history. Of the thirty operas that Verdi composed, the Metropolitan has produced fifteen, with a total of 2,710 performances. Ten productions of Wagner were performed sharing 1,992 performances, and Puccini was represented by nine productions, and a total of 1,874 performances. The works of Richard Strauss were popular, but received fewer performances, while Mozart, Gounod, Bizet, and Donizetti receive more performances. The total number of performances, and productions for each composer is certainly a reflection of their popularity with audiences, the availability of singers, and the costs of new productions when compared to their returns in terms of artistic accomplishment and box office receipts.

TABLE 11
MOST POPULAR CONTEMPORARY OPERAS IN
THE UNITED STATES, 1966–72

	Composer	Number of Performances
Amahl	Menotti	2,187
The Telephone	Menotti	894
The Medium	Menotti	669
Down in the Valley	Weill	444
Noye's Fludde	Britten	437
The Old Maid and the Thief	Menotti	388
Trouble in Tahiti	Bernstein	233

SOURCE: Central Opera Service, New York City, *Opera Repertory 1966–1972*, (New York: Central Opera Service Bulletin, 1972).

TABLE 12
NUMBER OF PERFORMANCES
AND PRODUCTIONS BY COMPOSER
METROPOLITAN OPERA 1883–1979

	#Perf.	#Prod.
Verdi	2,710	15
Wagner	1,992	10
Puccini	1,874	9
Mozart	742	4
Gounod	586	2
Bizet	521	1
Donizetti	472	5
R. Strauss	433	9
Mascagni	362	1
Leoncavallo	370	1
Rossini	283	3
Ponchielli	196	1
Bellini	182	3
Moussorgsky	180	1
Offenbach	142	2
Humperdinck	138	1
Beethoven	137	1
Saint Saens	111	1
Giordano	110	1
Debussy	73	1
Flotow	69	1
Gluck	69	1
Britten	51	3
Tchaikovsky	44	2
Cilea	36	1
Werther	33	1
Berg	30	2
Weber	26	1
Smetana	20	1
Poulenc	19	1
Meyerbeer	18	1
Massenet	17	1
Monteverdi	13	1
Janacek	12	1
Bartok	12	1
Berlioz	11	1
Levy	11	1
Barber	8	1

The most popular operas of the Metropolitan's Opera eighty-six year history included Puccini's "La Boheme," "Tosca," and "Madame Butterfly." Verdi's "Aida" was performed in all but two seasons since 1883. Other productions of Verdi included "La Traviata," "Rigoletto," and "Il Trovatore." Wagner's "Lohengrin," "Tristan und Isolde," and "Die Walkure," each had over 300 performances, and few seasons excluded Wagner since 1883. (see Table 13)

The New York City Opera Repertoire

The New York City Opera boasts a thirty-eight year history, in which eighty-nine composers were represented by 178 productions. Table 16 reveals that Verdi was the most popular with eleven of his works produced. The rank order of the other composers and their number of compositions produced were as follows: Menotti (10), Puccini (9), Mozart (9), Donizetti (7), Richard Strauss (5), Britten, Moore, Offen-

TABLE 13
MOST POPULAR OPERAS BY COMPOSER
METROPOLITAN OPERA 1883–1979

Composer	Performances	Seasons
Puccini		
La Bohème	676	74
Tosca	474	65
Madame Butterfly	433	63
Verdi		
Aida	648	84
La Traviata	477	76
Rigoletto	408	74
Il Trovatore	324	66
Bizet		
Carmen	521	69
Gounod		
Faust	412	68
Wagner		
Lohengrin	377	66
Tristan und Isolde	324	64
Die Walkure	324	68
Leoncavallo		
Pagliacci	370	64
Mascagni		
Cavalleria Rusticana	362	65

bach, Rossini, and Weill (4), Floyd, Ginastera, Monteverdi, J. Strauss, Gilbert & Sullivan, Hoiby, Orff and Stravinsky each shared 3 productions, while Bizet, Giannini, Lehar, Musgrave, Tchaikovsky, Wagner, Weisgall, Blitzstein, Janacek, Massenet, Prokofiev, Von Einem and Ward had 2 of their works performed the other composers listed in the table were represented by one performance of their compositions over the thirty-eight year history of this company. (see Table 14)

Undoubtedly, the total number of productions and composers has represented a diverse repertoire, which includes unfamiliar works of well-known composers, and more experimental and avant-garde productions of contemporary composers. Even with a shorter season than that of other companies, it has staged the works of a far greater number of composers.

The Seattle Opera Repertoire

The Seattle Opera's schedule spans a six-month period, in which thirty performances of approximately five composers are presented. Table 15 outlines a seventeen-year period (1964–80) of opera repertoire. Well-known nineteenth century operas are generally predominant, intermixed with a few unfamiliar or contemporary works. However, the majority of selections is derived from the repertoire of Verdi, Puccini, Donizetti, Wagner and Mozart. Verdi is represented every year except for 1964, while Puccini appears in twelve seasons, and Wagner, Donizetti and Mozart each share five seasonal appearances.

The San Francisco Opera Repertory

An analysis of a forty-nine year period (1923–72) was conducted for San Francisco Opera, (Table 16), and similar findings were found when compared to the other major companies. In rank order, the following composers were performed: Verdi, Puccini, Wagner, Mozart, Donizetti, Richard Strauss, Bizet, Gounod, Rossini, Massenet, Leoncavallo, Mascagni, Giordano, Beethoven, Montemezzi, Moussorgsky, Flotow, Saint Saens, etc.[4]

The Lyric Opera of Chicago

The Lyric Opera of Chicago has a three-month season from mid-September to mid-December, in which approximately fifty performances of seven composers are presented.[5] Table 17 lists the composers

TABLE 14
NUMBER OF PRODUCTIONS BY COMPOSER
NEW YORK CITY OPERA 1944–82

	Number of Productions
Verdi	11
Menotti	10
Puccini	9
Mozart	9
Donizetti	7
R. Strauss	5
Britten	4
Moore	4
Offenbach	4
Rossini	4
K. Weill	4
Floyd	3
Ginastera	3
Monteverdi	3
J. Strauss	3
Gilbert & Sullivan	3
Hoiby	3
Orff	3
Stravinsky	3
Bizet	2
Giannini	2
Lehar	2
Musgrave	2
Tchaikovsky	2
Wagner	
Weisgall	2
Blitzstein	2
Janacek	2
Massenet	2
Prokofiev	2
Von Einem	2
Ward	2

The following composers are each represented by one production: Argento Bach Bartok Beeson Belini Berg Bernstein Boito Borodin Bucci Charpentier Cherubini Copland DalloPiccola Debussy DeFalla Delius DelloJoio Egk Ellstein Gershwin Giordano Gounod Grief Handel Herbert Honneger Flotow Henze Humperdinck Kern Kirchner Korngold Kurka Leoncavallo Lieberman Martin Mascagni Montemezzi Morossi Moussorgsky Nicolai Pasatieri Purcell Ravel Rimsky-Korsakov Rorem Shostakovich Silverman Smetana Still Tal Tamkin Thomas VonWeber Walton Wolf-Ferrari

Verdi's productions appear more often than any other composer in American opera houses. The finale of the third act of "La Traviata," with (from left) Giorgio Giorgetti (Baron Douphol), Bernard Izzo (Marquis d'Obigny), Dorothy Krebill (Flora), Montserrat Caballe (Violetta), and David Cornell (Doctor Grenvil), performed at the Lyric Opera of Chicago (Lyric Opera of Chicago)

TABLE 15
FREQUENCY OF SEASONAL
APPEARANCE BY COMPOSER
SEATTLE OPERA 1964–80

	Seasonal Appearance
Verdi	16
Puccini	12
Donizetti	5
Mozart	5
Wagner	5
Gounod	4
Massenet	4
Bizet	3
R. Strauss	3
Rossini	3
Leoncavallo	2
Moussorgsky	2
Offenbach	2
Passatieri	2
Tchaikovsky	2
Beethoven	2
Floyd	2
Bellini	1
Boito	1
Delibes	1
Giordano	1
Mascagni	1
Saint Saens	1
J. Strauss	1
Ward	1

TABLE 16
SEASONAL APPEARANCE BY COMPOSER*
SAN FRANCISCO OPERA 1923–72

	1923–29	1930–36	1937–43	1944–50	1951–57	1958–64	1965–72
Verdi	15	19	22	23	28	23	
Puccini	21	15	12	15	23	18	
Wagner	1	16	6	11	6	14	
Mozart	0	2	5	8	12	13	
Donizetti	3	2	10	10	4	10	

*Five most popular composers.

TABLE 17
NUMBER OF PERFORMANCES & PRODUCTIONS
LYRIC OPERA OF CHICAGO, 1954–80

	Performances	Productions
Verdi	235	14
Puccini	168	8
Donizetti	83	6
Wagner	67	9
Mozart	65	4
Rossini	64	4
R. Strauss	42	4
Massenet	29	3
Mussorgsky	28	2
Bizet	27	2
Mascagni	22	1
Britten	20	2
Prokofiev	18	2
Gluck	17	1
Giordano	16	2
Bellini	15	2
Gounod	15	1
Penderecki	15	1
Stravinsky	14	1
Beethoven	13	1
Leoncavallo	13	1
Ponchielli	9	1
Berg	8	1
Saint-Saens	8	1
Boito	7	1
Bartok	6	1
Debussy	6	1
deFalla	6	1
Giannini	6	1
Monteverdi	6	1
Borodin	4	1
Orff	4	1
Ravel	4	1
Lehar	3	1
Cilea	2	1
DeBanfield	2	1
Janacek	2	1
Montemezzi	2	1
Thomas	2	1
Total	2,101	97

performed from its first season in 1954 to 1980. Once again, the popularity of Verdi-Puccini-Donizetti-Wagner-Mozart is evident throughout the twenty-six year history of this company. Fourteen productions
of Verdi were produced in 235 performances. Table 18 lists the most
popular operas of Puccini, Verdi, Rossini, Donizetti, and Mozart.
"La Boheme" had fifty-two performances. In fact, as the table reveals,
Puccini's operas ("La Boheme," "Madame Butterfly," and "Tosca")
were the three most produced operas. Other operas from the classical
repertoire have appeared with regularity and include Verdi's "La
Traviata," "Rigoletto," and "Un Ballo in Maschera," Rossini's "Il
Barbiere di Siviglia," Donizetti's "Don Pasquale," and Mozart's "Don
Giovanni."

Standardization of Repertoire

The repertoire of the five major companies in the United States shows
a dominance of Italian opera with a predominance of Verdi, Puccini,
and Rossini. Wagner and Mozart also appear with regularity. Generally, two to four new productions appear each year. During gala,
and anniversary years, companies show greater diversity in repertoire, and increase in the commissioning of new works, and greater
representation of works considered "adventurous." The budgets for
these years were supplemented by additional private contributions
and special funds. The rest of the repertoire is affected by these "new"
efforts. Some productions have had to be curtailed, both to reduce
overall costs and to allow for necessary extra rehearsal time for others.
The Metropolitan's 1973–74 season confirms this, since the monu-
mental and expensive production of "Les Troyens" caused the cancellation of a new "Don Giovanni," the June Festival, and the opera
in the parks.

The trend toward "standardization" — producing operas which
have survived a competitive selection over time — occurs with
greater consistency in the larger companies. The Metropolitan was
seen as more conservative than, for example, San Francisco or the
New York City Opera. The similarities between the Metropolitan and
Chicago, though of different size, makes one wonder whether the
significant factor in a "conservative" outlook is great reliance on contributions, the star system, or the support of longer seasons. Contributions for the Chicago Opera almost equaled income for some
years, while contributions for the Metropolitan represented only
about 30 percent of box office income. Besides Britten and Berg, no
composers from the "adventurous" repertoire were produced by

TABLE 18
MOST POPULAR OPERAS
LYRIC OPERA OF CHICAGO 1954–80

	Seasons	
Puccini		
La Bohème	52	11
Madame Butterfly	44	8
Tosca	41	10
Verdi		
La Traviata	38	7
Rigoletto	37	7
Un Ballo in Maschera	36	8
Rossini		
Il Barbiere di Siviglia	36	8
Donizetti		
Don Pasquale	27	5
Mozart		
Don Giovanni	27	6

Chicago or the Metropolitan, leading critics to accuse the two houses of being "stagnant."

The surprising inclusion of works from the contemporary repertoire and those of an experimental nature has been the result of deliberate, conscious commitments on the parts of the New York City Opera and the San Francisco Opera to present both familiar and unfamiliar works. Concomitantly, they have encouraged the production of traditional works and even support of the star system in an attempt to increase income at the box office to offset the cost of the "unpopular" compositions. The New York City Opera is distinguished from the Met both by this commitment and by the popularity of Beverly Sills.

From the beginning, and especially since it moved into the State Theatre, across the Plaza from the Metropolitan at Lincoln Center, the New York City Opera has had a marginal position in the New York Opera community. Since it could not compete with the Metropolitan's expensive and lavish productions of the old-time favorites, it was left to advance in the contemporary field. This has led to added newspaper publicity, and with strong foundation aid, it has at least in part satiated the hunger of a small but sophisticated, avant-garde audience in New York City.

At her American debut, Maria Callas as Norma during the
1954 Lyric Opera of Chicago production
(Lyric Opera of Chicago)

Among the Metropolitan's performances, hardly any contemporary works were presented, while the New York City Opera, with a smaller budget and in a much shorter time, presented many diverse productions and composers, including a number of contemporary composers.

In his annual review of the New York City Opera's 1972–73 season, Harold Schonberg wrote:

> the season just ended has maintained the ratio of familiar against unfamiliar works that sets his (Rudel's) company apart from all others. . . . The new productions brought whatever interest there was to the season (1973:17).

Henry Pleasants is more firm in his criticism of the repeated production of the classics.

> But the time has come to recognize that Carnegie Hall, Town Hall, and the Metropolitan Opera House, as well as their counterparts in other cities of America and Europe, are just as surely museums as The National Gallery and the Louvre. (1970:3)

This analysis of the repertoire systems of the Lyric Opera of Chicago, the Metropolitan, the New York City Opera, the Seattle Opera, and the San Francisco Opera was initiated to investigate whether a general musical trend exists in opera. It has been shown that a significant amount of the opera performed in the "commercial" companies has consisted of the "standard" repertoire and that the tendency is to rely more and more on "staples" offset by a few performances of rare and unfamiliar works. Both the Metropolitan and the Lyric Opera of Chicago, for example, due to their increased reliance on the box office, showed less variety and more productions of fewer works. In addition to this conservative trend, the opera house relies more and more on box office receipts as the budget rises. One can, therefore, conclude that the market has set particular constraints on opera and what ultimately is produced, without regard for what may be best by musical or artistic standards.

Operating in a relatively free society, politically and economically, opera is subject to the market mechanisms similar to those applied to nonartistic, or commercial products. What it can produce depends on what the public buys and on the funds acquired to supplement ticket sales. This trend seems to be intensified by the increased size of budgets.

This trend also affects the other performing arts — music, dance, and theatre. The box office successes are produced; they appear again and again, and receive private patronage. A closer examination of repertoire over a fifty-year period would support this thesis. This could be borne out by further comparison of the Metropolitan with other smaller companies connected with university departments, that have greater government subsidy, and by investigation of the increased standardization produced by the expansion of the organizational complex in the arts.

Increasing deficits have encouraged longer seasons, increased the total number of performances, lowered the diversity in repertoire, and, at worst, acceded to the demands of commercial interests. Artistic decisions with regard to repertoire, casting, and style are not independent of cost, or a production's ability to make a profit. Grandiose productions and the employment of superstars to sing established favorites insure full houses. These are the very things that motivate the public to buy tickets. Productions that don't sell are risky. Experimentation is too expensive. Rather than face destruction, managers have chosen the more secure productions. Given the time in which the standard repertoire becomes firmly established and the complex institutional matrix mobilized to support it (including publishers, recording industry, educational institutions, unions, mass media), repertoire trends are highly resistant to change. This trend has been consistent since the twenties or about the time when Puccini had his immediate success as a composer.

Since that time, classical repertoire has been performed to the virtual exclusion of contemporary repertoire. Such standardization is a manifestation of production values. The next two chapters will deal with the expression of this in the relationships between performers and managers who continue to argue over the technical aspects of productions. These come to be defined as artistic matters — matters which are part of the recreative process and involve the performance of dead composers.

In brief, the preceding has shown the effects the market has on the cultural "product." The consequences of such conditions on the roles of star performers will now be explored and the organization in which the performers work will be examined to try to determine the effects of traditions and standardization upon their roles and the meanings they give to their work. While standardization has allowed opera to achieve some of the advantages of mass production, it still has a high degree of individuality, singer specialization, and "prima donnaism." Opera, therefore, resolves the conflict between the collective (as expressed by the organization in a market situation), and the individual (as expressed by virtuosity and occupational specialization) relying on the star system which serves to present, paradoxically, both opera and the star's individuality.

Notes

[1]The general population has a perception that opera is the most snobbish and expensive form of performing art. The NCA Study (1974) revealed that opera attendance could increase substantially if it had less "class," requiring less formal dress, and less planning and preparation for attendance.

[2]See Alix Williamson, "Mass Music-Mindedness: A Problem in Promotion or the Private Relations of a Business in Publics," (unpublished); Gustle Breuer, "In the Beginning There Was Hope," *Opera News*, Part I, V. 37, #10, (January 13, 1973), p. 8 and Part II, V. 37, #1 (January 20, 1973), p. 10; Stephen Rubin, "Muscle Man Behind the Maestros, *The New York Times*, July 25, 1971, p. 15; and Joseph Lipman, "The Concert World: Where It's At," *Music and Artists*, April–May 1970.

[3]Rubin 1971:17. Since the publication of Rubin's book, Maestro Kubelik has resigned and given as his main reason the problem of "economics" in opera.

[4]All other composers had seasonal appearances of five times and less.

[5]The 1979 season of the Lyric Opera of Chicago represented its silver anniversary. Due to new productions, etc., it incurred a loss of $1 million above the norm. Consequently, the number of productions were curtailed during the following season.

Being well-prepared does not insure a major role. Brian Sullivan smiles happily after signing a contract with the Metropolitan's management, Rudolph Bing, after covering for another singer with laryngitis, 1952 (Metropolitan Opera Archives)

5 *The Social Organization of Opera: The Management*

Introduction

Studies in sociology treating the interaction between organizations and their environments (Hirsch 1975; Thompson 1967), analyses of non-profit administrations (Baldridge 1971; Kavolis 1973), and case studies which elaborate on how occupational ideologies reflect organizational structures and processes provide the theoretical boundary for this chapter. Weber's notion of "rationality" is crucial to the analysis. The Gerth and Mills' translation of the Weberian model of bureaucracy describes rational character as adhering to calculable rules, and maintaining efficiency by the evaluation of means and ends. The tendency is toward greater formalization of roles, and the objectification of the person. This chapter will explore the rationality in administrative behavior and its affect both on performers and on the organization itself.

    Other studies on music (Hirsch 1975), and film (Harvie 1970; Powdermaker 1950) reveal how audiences influence artistic content. While some studies on the administrator in the arts are emerging (ACA 1980), they do not concentrate on the artistic effects of managerial decision making. Baldridge (1971) and others concentrate on the conflicting role of the administrator in organizations which serve communal needs, and which function independently of economic considerations. Educators, social workers and health care professionals, for example, are caught in the ambivalence of serving community needs, and sustaining themselves and the organizations for which they work. Consequently, organizational goals often take precedence over the clients they are intended to serve. The client nature of artistic organizations offers an analogy. Unlike commercial rock music, non-mass culture art cannot sustain itself financially. However, its star system and the appeal it has to audiences function similarly in ensuring box office success. On the other hand, it is unique by vehemently adhering to Renaissance notions of the individual, the creative genius of the artist, and the notion that art stands above any practical and mundane circumstances of modern day life. It, therefore, refuses to admit audience demands and economic realities. With increased government support, the non-profit arts share with other "service" organizations the issue of accountability — public funds must reflect community interest. Along with the service orientation there is an increasing sense of professionalism which gets translated into an additional set of goals beyond the client, and includes the interests of the organization itself.

The interesting sociological question becomes one of a conflict of interests generated by the ambivalent nature of any public representative task. Public service occupations attempt to seize control over their work, and at the same time, profess to serve their clients. Who ultimately controls is determined by the prevailing economic system, and the nature of the task. For the arts, the situation is further complicated by the aesthetic definitions and requirements of the specific medium.

In opera, the person who defines his work by non-performing or extra-aesthetic criteria, is the manager of the opera company. In "boundary maintaining," the manager has to mediate the conflict between artistic standards and the public representative nature of the art. Given the increasing professionalization of the managerial role, ideologies evolve to legitimate the decision making and power in a work setting which constantly challenges, and whose traditions frequently contradict "rational" behavior. This chapter attempts to relate the performing arts organizational structure to the ideologies expressed by managers in their decision making with regard to repertoire, casting, and other policy.

The relationships between performing and non-performing opera personnel evolve as a result of the structure and nature of the organization in which opera is produced. In what ways, therefore, are the norms of relationships, values, and ethics contingent on both the organization's nonprofit structure and its nature as a performing art? The major musical issue — ensemble versus star — reflects the economic exigencies and structure of the market, which impinge on the interaction of performers. Many of the conflicts among and between performers and non-performers will be seen to revolve around these issues.

The specialization of performing artists and the increasing institutionalization of music has contributed to the formation of divergent occupational ethics for those involved in the performance, as well as for those involved with its administrative aspects. The latter, headed by the general manager, are committed to production values (that is, values which give precedence in decision making to cost, to what is popular, and to the hiring of performers on the basis of loyalty to the organization rather than on the basis of talent). In attempting to balance the budget, they yield to box office demands for certain operas and stars. As a result, the general manager has been criticized for denying the musical values and goals of a repertory theater, its ensemble nature, and its sense of experimentation. It is necessary to examine the roles of the general manager, and each of the specialized performing and nonperforming artists involved in opera, their interdependence, and the extent to which they represent either side of the issues mentioned above to fully understand these issues.

The repeated selection of the same works (the ABC of opera — "Aida," "La Boheme," and "Carmen") has met with much criticism; and the manager has been accused of lacking both musicianship and artistic integrity. Ironically, he would prefer an "ensemble" or repertory company that could ensure a more stable core of personnel, lower expenses and lessen reliance on the international talent market of superstars; this would free him from the restrictions of the box office as a measure of success. The "star — ensemble" debate is endless.

The following will focus on the general manager's attitudes towards his work, what he conceives his responsibility to be, and how he sees his relationships to singers, conductors, directors, and designers. The conflicts between the general manager and the performers reveal the norms of relationships governing occupational commitments, values, ethics, and rationales of musical style and interpretation.

Division of Labor Within the Opera Organization

There has been a deepening division of labor between performing artists, nonperforming artists, and ancillary personnel — including administrators, assistant managers, secretaries, and stagehands. "Performing" artists include conductors, singers and members of the chorus and ballet. The "nonperforming" artists include composers, stage directors, and stage designers.

Administrative duties have also been divided into "performance" and "nonperformance" categories which is perhaps an oversimplification. In most companies, however, this is considered the first line of the demarcation and definition of responsibilities. Administrative jobs have been designated as artistic, technical, stage and shop, financial, and stage management. The *artistic* category includes working with singers and performer's contracts and being a liaison with union representatives, chorus, ballet, orchestra and personal managers, as well as allocating time for rehearsals and the resolution of stylistic questions. The *technical* responsibilities include coordinating the activities of ushers and maintenance staff, and allocating space for rehearsals. *Stage and shop operations* cover working with stage crews, engineers, carpenters, hair and wig stylists, makeup artists, wardrobe, lighting, and film. *Financial* operations include analyzing budgets, overseeing the box office and gift shop, and preparing reports for the board. *Stage management* includes coordinating activities on stage, making sure artists are on time, escorting prima donnas, having the promptors and supernumeraries in place at the right time, and arranging for rehearsals and stage placements.

The board of directors also has committees, the number depending on the size of the organization. These committees reflect the major responsibilities of the board and may be divided into financial, artistic, production, planning, nominations, and fund-raising. This huge cadre of personnel is put into motion for each performance, and the general manager coordinates all of these activities.

The General Manager As Organization Man

Examining administrative activities provides a framework in which to investigate the meanings of work and the ways ideologies evolve; this will be accomplished by looking into the general manager's daily routine, and exploring the countless and often unforeseen exigencies of getting a schedule prepared and productions cast and produced. The general manager, as an organization man, is often in conflict with singers, conductors, and stage directors over such production and technical matters as rehearsal time and space, schedules, casting, and fees. Who's boss? Who has the say in matters of artistic and musical interpretations and conceptions? The audience, the critic, and the board member will also enter into the analysis since they play integral parts in the decision-making process. The public's tastes and musical preferences are taken into account, especially when deficits are on the rise and pressures from the board mount.

Opera has become so complex that it has increasingly required personnel assigned solely to coordinating its varied activities. In the historical section, it was noted that throughout the nineteenth century, composers produced and managed their own works — Wagner being the most famous. As opera companies grew, and audiences became larger, the financial aspects of opera management became too complex for the composer to handle. Composer-managers, however, did last into the early twentieth century. Opera houses and audiences became larger, staging and lighting more complex; consequently, the role of the composer was replaced by the conductor, and ultimately a musical director or manager by the early twentieth century.

The days of the single impresario in charge of finances, policy, planning, composing, repertoire scheduling, and casting are gone. Throughout its history, the management of the Metropolitan Opera House has symbolized this change. In 1908, Giulio Gatti-Casazza was appointed as manager. His father, while trained as a naval architect, had been musical director of the Municipal Theater at Ferrara, Italy. Gatti-Casazza was director of La Scala before entering the Metropolitan's management. He was succeeded by a singer, Edward Johnson, and in 1950, Rudolph Bing became manager after a career in concert and opera management in Europe. After twenty years of leadership, he was followed by Schuyler Chapin, another concert manager. At present, the Metropolitan is led by Anthony Bliss, a financial expert with no musical background. Below, careers of these men will be explored in an attempt to reveal the significance of this change and the political intrigue of the operatic world.[1]

One person usually dominates the scene; he is the general manager, musical director, or director. The nomenclature symbolizes the knowledge, reputation, and identification required rather than business-administrative expertise that is also necessary. Ideally, he is a rare combination of a trained artist and business administrator. He needs technical knowledge of music, a sense of organization, and a knowledge of the talent market — or at least a staff to supply him with expertise in these areas. His decisions often depend on the input of a corps of administrators and assistants. The extent to which top management formalizes the hierarchy and decision-making process has been a historical accident — a response to the size of the organization rather than an adherence to established musical traditions.

The organization's growth has required increasing specialization, but the "final say" has been the privilege of the general manager, supported in one way or another by the board. Musical advisors — including conductors, instrumentalists, and singers — have always been employed to help a manager in all phases of decision-making, especially if he lacks training in the performing arts. Directors of music organizations are well educated; 46 percent have master's degrees and 7 percent have doctorates. Administrators of performing arts centers tend to have had more administrative experience than most other arts administrators.[2]

The general manager has the overall responsibility for the company. It is he who is blamed for "poor musicianship," administrative inefficiency, "unventuresome repertoire," and miscasting. He acts as mediator in union negotiations, as amateur psychologist for performers, and as public relations man for the press and public. As if that were not enough, he must convince donors to give their financial support and maintain good relations with aristocratic families, board members, foundation directors, agents, scouts, critics, and superstars.

Since he has the sole responsibility for the selection of repertoire and casting, he is often seen as conservative and bourgeois by musicians and sophisticated audiences who are critical of his priorities, production, budget, and box office sales. Harold Schonberg of *The New York Times*, in reviewing Bing's regime and the 1972–73 Metropolitan season, wrote:

> And Mr. Bing's tastes are conventional, all the more in that he has made no secret of letting box office considerations dictate his repertory. . . . But many feel that the Metropolitan Opera repertory has been unadventurous and stagnant. And there have been constant complaints about the quality of musical preparation. Mr. Bing seems honestly insensitive to musical values. He always has been more concerned with production and administrative values (1973:13).

Such pressures have also been felt by the San Francisco Opera, and it was the aim of Kurt Herbert Adler, director since 1953, to mount new and contemporary repertoire. However, the following quote from Bloomfield's history of that opera company reveals his inability to do this.

> Most if not all of these events transpired during the regime of Kurt Herbert Adler, begun in 1953. In the 1960s his determined schedule of premieres slowed down slightly (first to balance the

These two superstars reflect their popularity by their sold-out performances! Joan Sutherland (left) and Marilyn Horne at the Lyric Opera of Chicago (Lyric Opera of Chicago)

Semiramide

repertoire, then the budget!) but this was a decade which saw a great crescendo in the number of new productions of standard repertoire (1972:309).

Critics accuse managers of an overrepresentation of the standard repertoire, of lavishness, miscasting, and flirting with the star system. This can be easily documented by the daily reviews. Managers, in turn, see these criticisms as unfair and beyond the function of "reporters." While managers often defer to creative personnel, they usually feel quite capable of evaluating vocal technique, design, and even musical interpretation. Their choices of composers, conductors, and designers determine musical interpretation. These choices are often challenged by singers, who resist the manager's "autocratic" authority and decisions which may conflict with personal career goals and commitments, and by conductors and directors who demand more expensive rehearsal time and equipment.

In New York, the audience usually supports the general manager when predominantly Italian operas are produced and superstars perform. Within the framework established by the board, the general manager, as leader of the organization, is in control of this internal drama, manipulating "safety valves," cliques, and loyalties, as well as dispensing rewards for "organization men." The general manager insists that he strives for the achievement of the best in musical and artistic standards; this, however, becomes synonymous with what is best for the house. He blames singers and unions for rising costs, holds mass tastes and business-minded boards responsible for lower standards, and insists that it is he who stands for the ultimate ideals of the performing art.

Anthony Bliss, the present general manager of the Metropolitan explained his solitary leadership:

> Planning and repertory have been a joint responsibility [with James Levine], but since this is a musical house, the primary selection of repertory and casting lies with Jimmy Levine. . . . I am involved only when the parties do not agree, or when certain policy or financial matters are concerned. I have made several changes in plans for the next two seasons, and I am now participating in determining whether designs submitted for new productions are acceptable (Boutwell) 1980:22).

Relations between managers and their conductors and directors depend on whether the manager is himself a musician or primarily an administrator. The source of conflict is usually the expense of particular conceptual and musical interpretations of a given compo-

sition, and the control over this aspect of production represents prestige and veneration. To avoid such controversies a principal conductor
or music director is often given sole responsibility, relinquishing authority on technical matters like scenery, costuming, and lighting,
but without losing sight of the need for conceptual harmony.

As one can easily see, the extent of shared responsibilities affects
the nature and style of the opera performed, and directly reflects the
organizational goals prescribed by the management. It is not merely
a matter of administrative style. In a performing arts organization,
administration becomes a significant factor in determining aesthetic
style and artistic standards. The repertoire and casting, an index of
musical trends, are influenced by management's values and the
requirements of the organization. The preceding analysis of the
repertoire systems of the five major opera companies confirms
this.

Carol Fox, of the Lyric Opera of Chicago, has commented on the
relationship between organizational structure and what it produces.
She ascribed a change in repertoire to the hiring of a "principal conductor," who shares in decision-making. A principal conductor functions as a stable "musical" representative. He usually lives in the city
of the opera house and devotes at least part of his activities to the
house in which he is director. "Since the advent of our present principal conductor, Bruno Bartoletti, we've begun to do a few works like
"Wozzeck" and "Angel of Fire" (Jenkins 1972:4).

The Adler administration, since 1953, at San Francisco Opera,
has had the help of conductors and the stage direction of Paul Hager.
The years are credited with expanded casting and scenic design.
Julius Rudel, when he was Musical Director of the New York City
Opera, was a conductor himself. In this company, his reign was
known for stressing ensemble singing, and improving on the orchestration.

Glynn Ross, as general manager of the Seattle Opera has selected
to produce the standard repertoire similar to the other major opera
companies. After an initial struggle to win support from his board,
and maintaining financial solvency, he chose to present well known
operas with popular singers. This, in turn, served to "legitimate" the
company. Bing summarized his organization by saying that a ". . .
theater must be a total democracy run by one man . . . [and he]
wasn't able to abdicate certain things which [he] felt were absolutely
vital to the standards of the house" (Bing 1971). Bliss is taking a
similiar approach, in saying, "when things aren't working out, I have
the responsibility to move in and see what can be done." (Boutwell
1980:22).

Artistic responsibilities are seen to be most important and the recipient high social position and prestige in the organization. An artistic administrator is next in line to the "general manager." It is he who works closely with singers, composers, conductors, directors and their personal managers, in negotiating contracts for the company. Because of its closeness to repertoire decisions, this artistic responsibility is least willingly relinquished. An assistant manager describes the subtle and complicated factors which enter into repertoire selections.

> That [selection of repertoire] is a very complicated thing. I would say that all the decisions of the company are made by the collective responsibility of the central core of administration — six or eight people. We have sat through stage committees, in which every aspect of the company is discussed at length and the resulting decisions are collective, not arbitrarily of any one individual. Certainly, if Mr. ———, who is co-director, wants to do something, they will do it and he has the right to do it. But I think they want to have a general consensus of the opinion of their staff in the process of their making a decision. The question of repertoire is discussed endlessly and what comes out is a distillation of all the major decisions.

The artistic director's responsibility for dealing with performers is the most difficult part of his job. He must, on the one hand, place organizational goals ahead of individual interests, and yet, on the other hand, satisfy the egos and interests of the individual artists. The difficulty of this job is aggravated by the fact that in opera, cultism is at its peak, and supports prima donnas. The artistic director is successful if he combines firmness with a subtlety and style that can charm egotistic personalities. One such administrator who is well liked is said to rule with a "Prussian hand in an Italian glove."

One technical administrator described his job as being ". . . responsible for everything that appears on stage but the people . . . but responsible for people backstage, the people who build the scenery, costumes . . . cleaning of the halls, and security." A financial director described his job as "one who runs trying to catch up."

Francis Robinson, a well-known public relations man, who dealt with critics and press representatives, and was concerned with the career aspirations of artists was described by a manager as, "having his head in the clouds and his feet in the box office."

In a company's daily activities, the artistic, technical, and financial responsibilities are not quite so distinct as they at first seem. The number of individuals required to cover each of these three areas of responsibility varies with the size of the organization. In addition, the nature of the performing arts organization causes activities to overlap and become shared, especially when deadlines approach, decisions are to be made, and budgets must be balanced. This prompted one manager to say:

> We tend to be a little more specialized so I devote most of my time with Mr. ——— in negotiating union contracts, negotiating individual contracts, to a certain extent with general financing, budget and that sort of thing. There are other departments that deal with the day-to-day operations of the company, rehearsals and that sort of thing. A person in my position in another company may have a broader area of responsibility. He may be much more directly involved in many things. My work is concerned with the future although, naturally, we always have a collective responsibility for what is going on, so when an emergency arises, we all go around making phone calls, etc., and try to pull the pieces together and get something done when the guidelines break down and the jobs become more hit or miss. But the general focus of my work is certainly much more oriented toward what will happen a year or two from now than it is on the moment.

The size of the organization, the specialization of activities, and the precarious nature of the company goals which are predicated on schedules, jet age artists, illnesses, indispositions, and equipment failures are "normal" for a performance setting and demand a deliberate and conscious attempt at coordination. The manager views himself as the chief integrator — putting things together, making final decisions, resolving conflicts, meeting schedules, enforcing rules, and encouraging commitments and loyalties to grow. A technical administrator spoke of the importance of coordination and meetings.

> There is a necessity of getting together regularly with the staff of the various departments. A necessary communication because we have so many employees and such varied activities in the theatre over the 52 weeks . . . . Without meetings and communication amongst ourselves and with our most responsible colleagues, I think we would grind to a halt.

The complexity of stage machinery and the huge and expensive maintenance problems of houses today prompted Bing to write:

> . . . one disaster after another [at the new house in Lincoln Center]. Even for me, enjoying crises and tight corners as I do, it came to be a little much. Krawitz, Gutman and I met in permanent

emergency sessions, with new and difficult and often painful decisions to make every day. (1972:307)

The manager, acting as confidant and psychologist for artists with personal and artistic problems and decisions, sees his rational and objective approach to things as a major contribution. An assistant manager emphasized his role in dealing with emotional problems which the artists, more than other employees, are prone to.

> In any situation where there are lots of people — in military organizations, hospitals, whatever it is, people have to come together. There are always the little things that go on. The special problem here is . . . that you have a greater cross-section of emotional range in people, people whose emotions tend to be at the surface.

And Bing wrote:

> With all this pressure, amid all these crises, with artists' losing their heads several times a day, a young man who kept his head could make a real contribution. . . . I adored it, I thrived on it. The more pressure on me, the more severe the crisis seemed to be around me, the more calm I felt. It was my task to be the stabilizing influence, and I was (1972:35–7).

Occupational Backgrounds of Managers

Opera administrators have come to opera from all fields of work both related and unrelated to music. Some have worked their way up the hierarchy; some have been recruited from other companies here and abroad. Others have been teachers, coaches, union experts, financial experts, instrumentalists, press agents, language experts, or conductors. Some musical background, at least on an amateur level, is required; not surprisingly, a musical background carries great prestige among administrative personnel. Other nonperformers within the musical community—personal managers, critics, public relations men — have also had some musical background.

One assistant manager, having had a great deal of experience in theatre groups, says: "At Harvard, they got involved in labor problems and I solved them rather successfully, so then I was known not only in producing theatre, but in labor and that's how I got to the opera." Another, in charge of finances, received an M.A. from Harvard Business School in 1936, did bank examining, worked in secu-

These two photographs represent the dramatic changes in stage technology. The upper photograph shows the switch board controlling all stage lighting, with its own glass-paneled room, in the rear of the auditorium of the Metro-politan Opera House. The lower photograph shows the light-board at the old Metropolitan Opera House on W. 39th Street (Metropolitan Opera Archives)

rities, at Standard Oil, and finally came to the world of opera. Another manager studied music, but ". . . . always wanted to go into some form of art administration in some performing art." Another says: "After student days, I worked on Wall Street . . . studied romance languages and music . . . worked in a banking and corporate trust company. . . ."

The majority of trained arts administrators have been hired within the last five to ten years as the demand for the services that they can provide in planning, financial analysis, budgeting, and development has grown. For the most part, they are predominantly white males, with master's degrees; over 60 percent are between the ages of forty and fifty-nine, and have come from liberal fine-arts or the performing arts. Chief executive salaries average $27,000, while assistants' salaries range from $16,000 to $20,000 according to a national study conducted by the American Council of the Arts (1980:52).

An analysis of the previous jobs held by administrators and artistic directors is shown in Tables 19 and 20. Table 19 deals with music organizations — rock, jazz, opera, choral, etc. — in New York State and attempts to see if former jobs vary with the sizes of the budgets. It appears that the highest percentage of administrative directors, 27 percent, previously held positions as producers, managers, or art administrators. Those who had been educators, make up 25 percent of current administrators, and former performing artists are the third largest group of today's administrators, 23 percent.

In comparing music organizations with all performing arts organizations, music groups more than dance, theater, and other presenters, have a tendency to employ art administrators, educators, and businessmen rather than musicians, composers or singers.

The most interesting revelations come with a comparison of previous positions and the sizes of the new affiliations, as measured by their annual budgets. Forty-three percent of the administrators in organizations with budgets over $250,000 had previous experiences as administrators, producers, or managers. The largest proportion of administrators in smaller organizations came from education and the arts. This is quite significant; it points to both the professionalization and bureaucratization of the arts. With the growth of their budgets, music organizations have employed men and women who have been trained as arts managers and administrators. The extent of university training in management or administration, as a standby occupation in the event of unsuccessful solo careers, facilitated this trend. Furthermore, small organizations are probably serving as training grounds and as sources for the recruitment, selection, and socialization of art administrators.

Table 20 lists the last jobs administrators held before they became artistic directors, in all the performing art organizations. The organizations with larger budgets more consistently hire artistic directors who were previously employed as arts administrators, producers, or managers. The sheer size and complexity of these organizations seems to dictate demands for specialized skills in management. Tables 19 and 20 indicate that "professional" art managers perfect their managerial skills in smaller companies before moving up to larger ones. These tables support the theory that the arts are becoming increasingly bureaucratized.

The fact that administrative directors are also members of boards, as Table 21 shows, could reflect the growing concern of the administrator over production and budgetary matters, as well as suggest that his authority is being shared by board members. Although all the performing arts organizations, including music, show the administrative director as a board member, this tendency seems to increase radically with the size of the organization. The figures next to the size of the budget, however, include both performing and visual arts organizations which seems to suggest that the latter organizations do not allow their directors to sit on their boards. This may imply a structural as well as an organizational difference between performing and visual arts organizations.

Repertoire and Casting Decisions

The ultimate responsibility of the general manager is his/her selection of what is to be produced and who is to perform in each production. His musical tastes as well as those of his staff and the public are reflected in his final decisions. Since the conductor claims his right to select, interpret, alter, and control all aspects of production, the appointment of one conductor over another determines the production's conceptual orientation. Financial and organizational pressures also enter into the decision-making process; the latter may be aggravated by the technical coordination, equipment, and space and time required by particular productions. Bing wrote of the numerous and complicated factors that went into his decisions:

> Planning the schedule is the opera manager's expertise. . . . The first step is to look at the two preceding seasons and decide which opera you wish to repeat and which you don't, considering primarily the success of the productions you need, which is partly a function of the works chosen if you have a

TABLE 19
JOB BEFORE BECOMING ADMINISTRATIVE DIRECTOR
OF NEW YORK STATE MUSIC ORGANIZATIONS 1971–1972

	Performing Arts		Size of Budgets*		
	Total %	Music %	$ 5,000 to $49,999	$50,000 to $249,999	$250,000 and over
Arts administrators, producers, managers	26*	27*	19*	24*	43*
The arts (directors, writer, composer, choreographer, painter, architect, etc.)	25	23	20	25	14
Education	18	25	22	15	18
Business	14	16	19	12	9
Administrator/executive of non-arts service organization	1	1	3	6	3
Professional	6	2	5	4	3
Government	2		2	4	3
Communications (TV, radio, newspapers)	1	1	2	3	2
Student	1	1	1	1	1
Housewife	1	1	2	1	
All others	5	3	5	5	4

SOURCE: National Council of the Arts, *A Study of the Non-Profit Arts and Cultural Industry in New York State*. (New York: Cranford Wood, Inc., 1973):31.
*Figure includes all visual and performing arts organizations.

"Pelleas et Melisande" or "Wozzeck" on the list, you know that
you cannot schedule twelve or fifteen performances of it, because
the public will not come. . . . Having chosen repertory, you must
decide where on the year's program to place each opera . . . You
must worry constantly about the subscribers . . . rehearsal schedule must be meshed with performances. . . . At the new house
in Lincoln Center the machinery is so complicated that whole
days must be reserved for its maintenance. . . . Union contracts
. . . become more burdensome with each renewal. . . . The prob-

TABLE 20
JOB BEFORE BECOMING ARTISTIC DIRECTOR
OF NEW YORK STATE MUSIC ORGANIZATIONS 1971

| | Performing Arts | | Size of 1970–1971 Budgets* | | |
	Total* (160)	Music* (68)	$ 5,000 to $49,999 (134)	$ 50,000 to $249,999 (48)	$250,000 and more (59)
			%	%	%
Music	29	61	22	20	21
Theatre	20	5	16	23	6
Arts administra-tors, produc-ers, managers	12	5	9	11	30
Education	11	15	16	7	4
Dance	16		10	11	9
Visual Arts	1		3	11	13
Student	4	5	9	7	4
Other arts			3		
Communication (radio, TV, newspapers)				4	
All other answers	4	7	9	4	9
Don't know	3	2	3	2	4

SOURCE: National Council of the Arts, *A Study of the Non-Profit Arts and Cultural Industry in New York State*. (New York: Cranford Wood, Inc., 1973):81–82.
*Figures based on organizations with separate artistic director and on total performing and visual arts organizations.

lem that grew ever more difficult was contemporary opera (1972:200–8).

Rudel, Music Director of the New York City Opera, answers the question of what determines repertoire.

There are so many ingredients that go into making these decisions, the question of whether you can do it, whether there will be enough interests for the public . . . whether we can do it well. If it fits into our repertoire, casted properly. These many, many questions go into making a program. The schedule is done more than two years in advance. It gets longer and longer. Of course, there is a long list of things I want to do, but you always are on the look-out, maybe I can do this and with whom . . . but this is a constant process of ready hand thinking, of experiencing and of seeing. New things always come to my attention, certain things we have commissioned that I am interested in, etc. There

TABLE 21
ADMINISTRATIVE DIRECTOR
AS A MEMBER OF THE BOARD

Arts Organization	Yes (%)	No(%)
Performing		
Music (101)	68	32
Theater (84)	71	29
Dance (53	60	40
Presenters (59)	60	40
Total (297)	66	34
*1970–1971 Budgets**		
$5,000 to $49,999 (293)	73	27
$50,000 to $249,999 (114)	44	56
$250,000 and over (90)	33	67

SOURCE: National Council of the Arts, *A Study of the Non-Profit Arts and Cultural Industry in New York State*, (New York: Cranford Wood, Inc., 1973): 99.
*Figures are based on 497 visual and performing arts organizations.

is no single process. It's a constant process. I guess a process of life.

The general manager must come to grips with the star system because of the star's mass appeal and the way audiences respond to virtuoso talents. The availability of singers and their preferences as to what they wish to sing often dictate repertoire selections. This is aggravated especially in a tight "star" market and in one in which role typing and a high degree of specialization prevail. The manager blames singers' fees and union scales for raising the costs of production and forcing him to concede to box office success. Because of the lack of alternatives in such a market, singers and other superstars, conductors and directors, reign supreme. Herman Krawitz said, "The basis for the schedule was individual artists and singers . . . . They started to sing more and more popular pieces, and so it was a conservative approach."

The manager of a company that boasts of its ensemble nature, but recently has been criticized for flirting with the star system, made the following statement.

> Well, I think from economic realities today, it is foolish not to take advantage of the stars one has . . . . The stars who have made their reputation in the company . . . we must find things to please all of them, to keep them with us. We have to give them new productions featuring them because this is important to them. They are not going to stay with the company if they are

going to do third Bohemes and fourth Traviatas and things like
that, and so the decisions as to repertoire relate to singers. We
have to look at the particular individual and things that would
be good for the company as a whole, things Mr. ——— wants
to conduct, things a stage director may want to direct, etc. Sometimes a new opera which may be of certain interest and could be
brought to New York may determine our decision of what to
produce. These are all weighed against one another. We generally
do three new things each season and rely on the repertoire we
have.

One journalist commented on the consequences of yielding to
the star system.

City Opera has hit the star system but the problem is that it has
only one star since Norman Triegle isn't singing. . . . Then they
have Beverly Sills, which is one level unto itself. Then go down
a level and you have people like ——— and ———, who aren't
really stars. They hit the star system because, once you have
someone like Sills, you have to start doing things for her. If
they're moving to a star system, they simply cannot afford it
because fees are so low. . . . They're trying to make their stars
happier. . . . They are paying more attention to them. . . . We
better give ——— something because she's very handy to have
and that sort of thing. Go down the list of first performances,
new productions, and you'll see for yourself.

Such "establishmentitis," as one director called it, reflects one
side of an old debate and the basis of different schools of musical
interpretation — the star system versus ensemble. "Ensemble" or the
"gesamkunstwerk" approach is usually thought of as ideal, for all art
forms — dance, music, voice, instrumentation, and theatre are integrated for a "total dramatic effect." The manager who subjects
himself to the politics of the star system in selecting repertoire and
in casting is sometimes accused of lowering standards by catering to
the pressures of a few top international artists and to the tastes of
audiences who "buy" not a particular musical composition, but the
star personality. By perpetuating this trend of the virtuoso and the
spectacular, the manager becomes a victim of it.
In the star system, planning and selection are determined by an
artist's availability, and decisions are made three to five years in
advance.
When Bing went to the Metropolitan, he wanted to undo the
emphasis on the singer and was committed to overhauling the chorus,
ballet, orchestra, and staging — the foundation, he claimed, for a

repertory company. Once again, however, a demand for the "spectacular," a desire for virtuoso techniques, and the visual aspects of
theatrical production prevailed. Bing then created more spectacular
and expensive productions by hiring star conductors, star designers,
and star directors. During a WQXR interview, Bing credits changing
stage technology with being a major influence on this shift in the
style of presentation.

> The move from painted productions to built productions, has
> many consequences quite apart from the purely artistic aspects.
> To begin with, it requires infinitely more storage, secondly, it
> requires more transportation and therefore expense, thirdly, it
> is more expensive to build than just paint a couple of backdrops,
> so it has meant economic consequences. . . . It was one of the
> most important changes I brought to the Metropolitan.

"Covering"' is an essential feature of an opera production and
becomes a serious problem in a star system. Each star has to have a
replacement, a cover, in case of cancellation due to sickness, errors
in scheduling, and the like. World or American premieres may even
require two backups. This becomes extremely difficult, especially
when highly individualized and specialized talents are engaged. They
cannot be duplicated. However, it is unrealistic to cancel a performance because of the absence of a star. Arranging for covers then
becomes the duty of the chief administrator, who must reward those
"organization-artists" who have been handy, loyal and reliable in
covering on previous occasions and on short notice. But how many
women could replace a Nilsson? A "near" star would have to be
engaged to match the caliber of the voice and demonstrate Nilsson's
ability to cope with her character roles. A singer with these qualifi-
cations will, however, not come to the Metropolitan solely as a
"cover." Inevitably, one has to offer other performances and at least
one prime role. (One also has to wonder why a star would voluntarily
"cover" for a competitor.)

A journalist recounts the problems of "covering" in the difficult,
long, and rare Wagnerian productions:

> The problem is that the Metropolitan is a repertory house. They
> must have coverage. Every performance must be covered if not
> once, twice. If you get Miss X, who is a big star at Covent Garden
> to cover Miss Nilsson in Siegfried, or Walkure, don't think she'll
> come here just to cover; she'll do at least one performance, maybe
> the last one. . . . It's a give and take, you come here, you cover,
> okay, and we'll give you a performance.

Some miscasting may well be due to management's awarding a particular role to a performer who has been especially cooperative. Some careers have been made this way, especially when the performer has spent most of a career in one major house. Bing described a case in point.

> In return for her courtesy in covering, she was entitled to whatever courtesies I could offer and when a role suited to her low-profile temperament came up in a new production — Ellen, the school teacher, in "Peter Grimes" — I felt obliged to assign it to her, even though George Solti, who was to conduct, had a rival candidate for the role and left our roster when Miss ——— was chosen. (1972:201)

An assistant manager spoke of the resentment against Bing expressed by many artists, who felt he was unfair to them.

> The way he covered, Miss ——— never forgave him. . . .It's a vocal art . . . artists who covered for other great artists were upset because he would place a Corelli with a Tucker. He did this constantly. He always wanted the best and we were willing to pay for it.

Carol Fox, General Manager of the Lyric Opera of Chicago, in reacting to criticisms of her bias in favor of hiring Europeans, blames the politics of covering in a star system:

> I offer you Cassio, ninety percent of the time, you refuse. You are a star, so now can you be publicized in a secondary role for the Metropolitan, or Chicago, or San Francisco when this is going to harm you in Houston, San Antonio, Montreal, Toronto, any place else? . . . . I can get a singer from La Scala or Covent Garden . . . to do less than major roles (Jenkins 1972:16).

We have seen the effects of the star system on covering, on miscasting, and on poor musical preparedness. One manager summarized the problems and tells of some attempts by management to avoid such consequences.

> Bad casting is a problem of major opera houses throughout the world. . . . I am a little more conscious of miscasting . . . young artists who do the supporting or compromario roles. This is the fault of management. I have seen many people who have had good voices come and go . . . just wither away . . . . Riecker, Kubelik, Chapin, and Levine are rehearsing second singers in

things that they choose to audition in. Change is occurring (Hawkins 1973).

A recent National Council of the Arts' study attempted to pinpoint the centers of power within performing arts organizations. Table 22 presents a summary of their findings. Fifty-four percent of the music organizations report that administrative directors are involved in budget decisions. Administrative directors are seen to play a larger role in larger companies — the figure jumps to 70 percent in organizations with the highest budgets. This aspect of decision-making appears to be shared significantly with board members. On the other hand, artistic directors contribute very little to budgetary decisions, but play a much larger role in programming decisions. However, as the size of the organization increased, administrative directors share programming decisions in greater proportion with artistic directors. Seventy-three percent of administrative directors are involved in programming decisions within the larger organizations.

The data confirms that a greater tendency toward administrative expertise and personnel is required in the larger organizations. Governance by board and administrative directors raises questions as to the shift in priorities and greater emphasis on financing in decision-making.

To a certain extent, a minimum number of productions is required for musical growth and to fulfill commitments to subscribers' series. How then, is this demand met and dealt with? Productions are often seen by the board as too expensive and lavish. The manager countervenes by saying that to do things economically may mean to do them "unartistically." At a place like the Metropolitan, these problems get solved by formulae since it is the "best" house and it has to strive for an expensive level. Fox, at Chicago, seems to imply that the board's tastes are synonymous with "what sells."

After a few years, we needed a great deal more money and more prestige people who would help bring money in, and we enlarged our board. Of course, the members are very interested in the monetary guidelines, but the most they might question a "Billy Budd" or a "Wozzeck" or anything else unusual they'll ask "Do you think it will sell?" They are cautious, but we have always met our debts and ended up in the black. Last year, we came again with 98.8% full house. So their basic control on the policy line is to make sure the public will support us to their ability to raise funds. (Jenkins: 16)

The manager internalizes organizational goals to the extent of interpreting "success" not in terms of artistic developments, but in

TABLE 22
WHO IS INVOLVED IN MAKING MAJOR DECISIONS
IN NEW YORK STATE MUSIC ORGANIZATIONS

	Budget Decisions					Programming Decisions				
	Perf. Arts Total %	Music %	1970–71 $5,000 to $49,999 %	Operating $50,000 to $249,999 %	Budget* $250,000 and Over %	Perf. Arts Total %	Music %	1970–71 $5,000 to $49,000 %	Operating $50,000 to $249,999 %	Budgets* $250,000 and Over %
Trustees, directors, executive committee	54	66	63	60	65	32	47	42	38	34
Administrative director	56	54	50	60	70	56	31	57	68	73
Artistic director	26	25	18	21	18	55	68	35	40	53
Administrative staff	16	15	15	12	26	15	14	14	23	26
Chairman of board	12	17	11	14	18	9	12	8	13	13
Other overseeing body	9	4	9	7	14	11	10	10	11	10
Outside consultants	4	4	5	2	3	5	3	6	7	8

SOURCE: National Council on the Arts, *A Study of the Non-Profit Arts and Cultural Industry in New York State*, (New York: Cranford Wood, Inc., 1973): 102–103.

*These figures are based on total performing arts organizations.

terms of balancing the budget or making as small a loss as possible. His main aim is to control costs, but, conversely, he claims "repertoire is purely an artistic matter!" Meetings between artistic and financial administrators are, however, continuous and the give and take make it difficult to distinguish these two responsibilities. Expenditures are made, watched weekly, and if they run too high, departments are told to cut costs. Rational planning includes daily supervision, analysis of box office receipts, weekly accounting procedures, and an extensive search for new sources of income.

The length of the seasons and the number of performances affect musical styles. European houses have government subsidies and can afford to risk time and money on a more diverse repertoire. In America, on the other hand, the lack of such diversity and innovation has been rationalized, and safe decisions on the part of the non-profit organization are defended. Donal Henahan of *The New York Times* in discussing the Metropolitan's forecast of the 1973 season, writes: "As part of [Chapin's] regime's overall strategy . . . the number of operas in next season's repertory will be reduced to twenty-two from twenty-seven this season." The Metropolitan justifies this decision by saying that "extra rehearsal time will be possible" (1972:29).

In addition, contemporary and/or experimental works are almost entirely excluded, and when included, they are done at a tremendous sacrifice to the rest of the repertory. Chicago had to cut "Lulu" for financial reasons; New York City Opera has had to sustain the losses on its first all-contemporary season at the new house over the past eight years. Expensive and lavish operas, such as "La Traviata" and "Rigoletto," may be produced because their fixed costs can be spread over a greater number of seasons since they are frequently repeated "favorites."

New productions, star roles, first performances, and broadcasts are the leverage with which a manager can manipulate the system of rewards. If one prima donna is given opening night, another prima donna will be given a broadcast; if one is given a new production, her rival could get one later in the season; so bargains are made and contracts signed. One journalist described the subtle and delicate circumstances which arise when rival divas are involved.

> Take Madame A; she's not singing this year. She has had two
> new productions. She is probably the reigning prima donna of
> the house. She had ——— and ——— (new productions). I hear,
> and this is gossip, she wanted to do ———, but Mr. Bing gave
> it to Madame B. And you could imagine Madame A was not very
> happy about that. This is a problem. Then you have Madame C.
> who sings every god damn first performance. They cannot run

the house without her. She sings repertory and there aren't that many voices around.

Conflicts constantly arise with regard to these issues and they are more than mere personality clashes. At times they are manifested in conceptual and musical interpretations; most arguments occur over matters of technique, rather than aesthetics and often over pay and other symbols of status. Bing wrote:

> In the normal course of events, most artists couldn't care less about new productions; they would just as soon not rehearse. But starring in a new production has become a status symbol and all artists fight for their roles. Indeed, they fight to have the first night in a revived older production, because the critics come to the first nights. Fortunately, we have two plums on the tree, because the broadcasts rate almost as highly as the premiere in the status conferred (1972:202).

Quite often, usually in private negotiating sessions, artists demand these symbols of status. There have been times, however, when these demands have been made publicly.

Managers and directors of opera companies have begun to see their role not only in terms of producing opera at the highest artistic level, but — like other organizational leaders — in terms of maintaining the stability of the company itself. A "service ideal" evolves, and managers see it as their function to provide a service to the community. Performers, not involved in this aspect of presenting opera, are viewed as lacking self-discipline, possessing emotional and egocentric personalities, and aspiring for personal gain. Sociologist Joseph Bensman, addresses the issue of conflicting individual and organizational goals within nonprofit organizations:

> As a result, in all non-profit work areas it is extremely difficult for the top officials to discipline, organize, and control the lower ranks. . . . Ideologists, from the standpoint of their bureaucratic bosses, thus become irresponsible, undisciplined, and disloyal officials. Wherever possible, high-level bureaucrats purge the ideologists. They do this in the primary use of ideological concerns, but only to develop a responsible, disciplined, loyal, and technically competent staff. At the same time, the bureaucratic elites will use existing ideologies . . . as means of advancing their respective organization. Thus to the bureaucratic elite, the partly acceptable ideologists among their staff are those that support organizational purposes at any given time. As a result the bureaucracy as a form attacks all individual ideologies and replaces

them by forms of ideological expediency. In addition, it worships competent, disciplined, self-controlled, and self-managed, technical virtuosity, nerve and an achievement motivation that is detached from the end or the values which the organization is set up to serve. The bureaucratic ideology tends to replace all other ideologies as bureaucratic forms of organization begin to predominate in business, government, universities, philanthropy, and other occupational areas. The bureaucrat's attack on independent ideologies takes the form of not hiring ideologists, firing them, retaining personnel to accept the bureaucratic ethos, and promoting those who do (1967:196–7.).

The organization's goal is directly in conflict with individual demands in relation to travel time, scheduling, covering and casting. Therefore, the general manager enforces rules, a sense of obligation, and responsibility, so that the company keeps functioning as a collective unit despite the wide range of differences among its artists, departments, and personnel. An assistant manager discussed some of the personal interests of the artists that interfere with the running of the organization.

> Difficulties are sometimes caused by artists over committing themselves. They say they will be in two places at once. We have to work out schedules. This wasn't so with Chagall; it was with Zeffirelli. With von Karajan, the problem was that his "Ring" was for a Festival stage and ours wasn't, so . . . sometimes difficulties arise between two artists, like von Karajan and Nilsson, and Bing had disagreements with them. Sometimes artists want to know who is the dominant one; the conductor or soprano. "Who do you love more? Me or him." I wish artists would never ask that question. My job was to prevent the asking of that question. When there is a showdown they want to know who is loved more. Who is the center of the production . . . Don't misunderstand me, we were used to it and in that sense one tries to minimize it.

Another manager stresses that clashes of interests are common among performing artists.

> Performers are as a class a rather emotional group of people, or their emotions are a little closer to the surface. And there are naturally lots of conflicting personalities, and we work upon and endeavor to keep the ship running. . . . I certainly never studied psychology specifically. . . . If someone comes and sits on this chair in my office with a problem, I simply try to solve it and the problems may be anywhere from having to deal with a direct

personality clash with another artist in a rehearsal to having been told by the management that they are not as good as they really think they are. Sometimes it's very difficult to tell people that they are not measuring up artistically . . . and sometimes lots of tears are shed and there is lots of unhappiness, but this is all part of life and we have to accept it. But the difference with the performers is that their livelihood is wrapped up in something that is somewhat more illusive than that of a butcher or baker who works and goes home at night. Their lives are so delicately tied up with other people and to the administration of opera companies.

Artists have conflicts with management over roles, debuts, fees, fringe benefits, and preferences for particular colleagues. Specific relationships are sometimes negotiated and become parts of contracts. Management, on the other hand, wants to guarantee a certain amount of rehearsal time with a number of performances thereafter, in repertoire needed by the company, restrict artists' engagements near the city in which the house is located, and insure their touring with the company.

The Board of Directors

The board determines the framework in which the opera company works by controlling finances, establishing general guidelines, making policy decisions, and allocating funds for new productions and advertising. In dealing with the board, the manager stands for the best in artistic excellence. The good board, in his view, is one who gives the money and says nothing about repertoire, casting, and production costs. Given the close working relationship between board members, and management, the board does influence repertoire and casting. However, the days of total control by the whims and erratic egotistical behavior of tycoons are gone. During the turn of the century, opera in New York was manipulated by a few individuals, who competed with each other, in an attempt to receive social status, recognition, and entrance into the social register by assuming control over opera companies. Opera, at that time, was a status granting institution, and opera halls were the showplaces for the rich (Teran 1974).

Since boards try to make up deficits, they are constantly searching for funds and new sources of income, including television and recording sales. Their preferences are the best sellers, those with the highest box office returns. Patrons too prefer the standard repertoire, they want their contributions to go toward the most popular works. Board members want to fulfill subscribers' wishes because they account for 50 to 60 percent of box office returns.

Some remarks of general managers and board members on the role of boards are helpful in defining the responsibilities of the boards. Sara Caldwell, renowned as a director, and artistic director of the Opera Company of Boston, remarked:

> But I think we have another responsibility, all of us together, to make this profession live in this country in a much more fortunate way than it is today. I think that the artistic personnel of opera companies in companionship with board members and heads of unions, all need to sit down together to try to find ways in which we can develop. Not just keeping stable what we have — because most of us with companies of various sizes have learned the art of survival in a particular manner. So hanging by our thumbs, we manage just to stay alive in a pattern that we have, more or less, fallen into (COS 1974).

John Ford, President of San Diego Opera Association, discusses his board as well as the role of the "production committee," a very important committee in opera associations and one vested with repertoire and programming decisions.

> Our professional staff, in its principal positions, was the original staff we had, and our board consists in the majority, of people who have worked long and hard in developing the program we now have. I believe we have worked hand in hand and I think our management has looked to us for the financing, but do not expect us to be just the fund raisers. They have presented all the plans and programs to us for approval, and I would say on many occasions, we have carried a rather strong weight in the artistic policy and the planning, particularly of productions. No matter how far you try to separate the two, the money to do a production affecting the artistic people comes from the board side. I would say the only places that we have had tension with our management is where either the board wanted to do a new production and the management was cautious about the funding, so that the board pushed and, in effect, took on the responsibility of raising that money; or management expected to do a new production and the board was very cautious — being afraid of the deficit situation that would be involved if we overextended ourselves.

Lowell Wadmond, Chairman of the Metropolitan Board was more specific in outlining the functions of the board, much to the approval of convention members at the National Central Opera Service Convention held in New York City, October 15, 1973.

> In the first instance, the responsibility and duty of the board of directors of any operatic organization is to see to it that the cash flow is sufficient to keep the enterprise alive. . . . Generally speaking, the functions of a board of directors of an opera association are pretty much akin to the responsibilities and duties of the Board of a general business corporation. . . . An opera association delegates to its general manager and his immediate associates the day to day responsibility of running and managing the opera company. The board of directors, on the other hand, has, in the first instance, the responsibility for selection of who its general manager should be, and in conjunction with the general manager, who the several top associates of the general manager should be. . . .
>
> When it comes to repertoire and new productions, again, quite naturally, that is for the general manager, in the first instance, to determine. But, in every well organized opera association, I would say that the board of directors has, as well as its financial and other committees, an able production committee, with which the general manager and his associates take counsel. . . . Even management problems as important as contract negotiations with the major unions are the responsibility of the general manager, in which the board and its officers should not interfere, except in crises, and when final decision must be made by the board.

While it is almost impossible to determine the extent of the board's influence, especially on repertoire and casting, the fact that they do exercise some authority cannot be questioned. A recently published report on the performing arts contains a profile of boards in music, dance, visual arts, and theatre. The "music" category includes opera, symphony, and both chamber and choral groups. The data become especially significant when compared with organization size. Table 23 confirms the relationship between the increasing size of an organization and a greater concern with business and administrative matters, as indicated by the occupations of the trustees. Business executives appear to predominate as trustees and board members in music organizations. Members of civic or non-arts social service organizations are the next most numerous, and they are followed by educators, then doctors or other professionals and members of art social service organizations. Although the second half of the table includes figures for all the performing arts in New York State, one can assume that the figures underestimate the percentages of

TABLE 23
OCCUPATIONS OF TRUSTEES IN
NEW YORK STATE-MUSIC ORGANIZATIONS

Occupations	Performing Arts Organizations Total % (497)	Music % (101)	Size of 1970–71 Budget* $5,000 to $49,999 (293)	$50,000 to $249,999 (114)	$250,000 and Over (90)
Business executives (1780)	18	20	18	19	30
Members of civic or non-arts social service organizations (1440)	13	14	18	13	17
Educators (1331)	15	14	19	15	8
Professional artists/present or former (960)	12	9	14	11	6
Lawyers (709)	7	9	8	7	10
Doctors or other professionals (671)	7	10	10	7	5
Bankers, accountants or financial experts (680)	7	7	7	6	12
Members of arts social service organization (602)	8	10	9	5	5
Arts administrators (576)	7	4	7	7	4
Retired (531)	5	7	7	5	6
Public office holders (354)	2	3	5	3	4
Students (168)	1	1	3	1	1
Union officials (158)	1	1	3	1	1

SOURCE: National Council of the Arts, *A Study of the Non-Profit Arts and Cultural Industry in New York State*, (New York: Cranford Wood, Inc., 1973): 93–94.
NOTE: The totals of these columns come to more than 100 because some trustees/directors qualified for more than one category.
*Based on total performing arts organizations.

business executives, lawyers, and bankers on the boards of music organizations. This assumption is substantiated by the fact that music organizations are the largest, the most "popular" and the most complex of the performing arts organizations. In the large organizations, 30 percent of the trustees are businessmen and 17 percent are members of civic or non-arts social service organizations. The larger the organization, the greater the proportion of businessmen on the board. By the same token, the number of board members who are educators or artists may be fairly significant in a small organization, but decreases sharply in the larger ones.

In order to get a clearer understanding of the role of the board, our analysis may be enhanced by investigating some recent findings on the reasons for selecting board members. Once again, the signif-

icant factor becomes the size of the organization. Table 24 indicates
that "experts in administrative areas" and "community leaders" are
the most sought after trustees in performing arts organizations of all
sizes. Other reasons for selection indicate the importance organizations give to their trustees' reputation in the community and their
ability to be good fundraisers. Community leaders presumably have
good contacts with financiers, and seem to be more willing to work
with the larger and more established performing arts organizations.
The National Council of the Arts' study asked administrative directors
about the importance to their organizations of their board members;
70 percent said "very important," 20 percent said "somewhat important," 8 percent said "slightly important," and only 2 percent said
"not at all." In organizations with budgets over $250,000, 72 percent
said "very important."

Most boards do not overtly acknowledge their control over or
influence on artistic affairs. However, Table 22 did indicate that trustees, directors, and the executive committees of music organizations
in New York State exert influence in 30 percent of programming
decisions, and in 65 percent of budgetary matters. In fact, the data
reveals that the chairman of the board and the artistic director have
equal say with regard to budgetary decisions. As in to the case of the
administrative director, the boards' power seems to increase with the
size of the organization. A publication by the Metropolitan put forth
suggestions by the board on how to lower costs:

> The longer the season and the greater the number of per-
> formances per season, the larger the box office revenues. On the
> other hand, the greater the number of productions per season,
> and in particular, the number of new productions per season, the
> larger the operating expenses. The Metropolitan Opera has been
> more cost-conscious than the West European countries under
> consideration. The length of season and number of performances
> per season are approximately the same for the Metropolitan as
> for the Vienna State Opera; the Hamburg has more than twice
> the current repertory than the Metropolitan.
>   This large repertory necessitates more costumes, sets, re-
> hearsal time and more personnel and thus adds to costs. . . . The
> conclusion of this examination is that the Metropolitan Opera
> probably more than other Western European Opera companies
> under consideration is trying to hold down its variable costs by,
> among other things, running productions for longer periods of
> time and employing fewer people who perform supportive roles.
> At the same time, the Metropolitan Opera has attempted to main-
> tain its advantage in generating box office income by keeping its
> house substantially full (1971:29).

TABLE 24
REASONS FOR SELECTION OF BOARD MEMBERS OF
NEW YORK STATE MUSIC ORGANIZATIONS

	Performing Arts		1970–71 Operating Budgets*		
	Total	Music	$ 5,000 to $49,999	$ 50,000 to $249,999	$250,000 and Over
	(297)	(101)	(293)	(114)	(90)
Experts in administrative areas of value to the organization	30%	34%	31%	30%	29%
Community leaders	21	22	25	19	26
Friends of board officers and/or board members, artistic director	17	21	15	18	12
Representatives of special interest groups in the community	14	13	16	15	11
Professional artists	14	10	14	12	5
Good fund raisers	12	13	7	8	18
Large contributors of funds or serve as security on loans and notes	7	9	4	7	14
Experienced arts administrators	7	6	8	7	4
Major collectors	2	2	4	2	3
Government officials	3	3	3	2	3
Professional historians/scientists	1	1	2	2	3

SOURCE: National Council of the Arts, *A Study of the Non-Profit Arts and Cultural Industry in New York State,* (New York: Cranford Wood, Inc., 1973): 95–96.
NOTE: Totals come to more than 100% because categories were chosen more than once.
*These figures are based on total visual and performing arts organizations.

Summary: The Rationality of Management

Due to the nature and structure of the performing arts organization, two perspectives exist — artistic goals and production priorities. Opera is an organization with two distinct orientations, each of which are legitimate and require an ideology for the people involved in implementing the goals. For the manager, what is best in musical standards became synonymous with what was needed for opera to "survive." Organizations on a smaller scale, or those receiving subsidy, have been less concerned with the efficiency and effectiveness of the organizations, and have taken more risks and involved more performers in decision-making processes.

The divergent nature of occupational identities and perspectives manifests itself in the constant disruption of the collective unit. Conductors, singers, stage directors, managers, and critics differ as to how they see themselves and each other in the general scheme of things. The production of opera, its ensemble nature and its repertoire goals often conflict with artists' musical interpretations and personal needs, and with budgetary limitations and box office demands. Ironically, all participants view themselves as "family" and as premieres approach, schedule pressures mount, and sicknesses and cancellations rise, everyone pitches in, work functions are shared, and conflicts are resolved in favor of the ultimate cause.

In general, opera companies, as non-profit organizations, provide a service to the community and see themselves as contributing to the vital and necessary cultural growth of the nation. These abstract and traditional ideals often serve as rewards for those who receive little pay. An ever-enlarging budget relies 50 to 60 percent on box office receipts, and on private philanthropy for the remainder. Considering the number who aspire to make careers in opera, the opportunities are few, but the rewards, prestige, and recognition for those who succeed are extremely high. With the reliance on a precarious instrument of the body, the voice, fear of failure is ever present. Work is very tense and emotional, given both the creative personality and the fact that an artist's talent must be constantly legitimated through performance.

The general manager approaches this art form somewhat ambivalently. Defensive of his identification with vulgar and practical issues of the budget, he stresses his interest in artistic standards, but he survives only if he maintains his ability to coordinate, integrate, plan, and pull things together. Musical and artistic goals, therefore, are supplemented by organizational goals. Repertoire is planned with an eye to box office returns (sales), and staging, lighting, and costuming are determined in terms of costs of production (net loss per production). Conductors and directors are evaluated according to how expensive they are and who they "draw."

The manager feels he represents the best in artistic excellence and ascribes financial troubles to fees, union demands, and unfair critics of his concession to box office demands. He views audiences with disdain, but realizes that they represent 50 to 60 percent of the sure income. He resents his subservience to superstars; the star system (and its effect on other dimensions of production, "covering," for example) is a situation which has always confounded financial officers. The traditional functions of the general manager have come to be shared, and at times dominated, by his board. One could argue, therefore, that repertoire is a reflection of public taste and of private contributors who together comprise the "market." Since they continue to support the "favorites," one can conclude that their tastes run in the same vein as those of mass audiences. Given the history of patronage in the United States, the upper class, first as owners, and now as board members, has done much to set styles for audiences to emulate.

The data presented here, concerning the jobs previously held by administrators and the roles of administrators and board members within the arts organization, all point to the increased professionalization and bureaucratization of the arts. The "careers" of arts managers, and their probable shifts from smaller to larger companies, seem to indicate an increasing professionalization. Along with status and specialized expertise, they acquire a sense of production values. There is no doubt that smaller organizations seem to function as the recruiters and socializers of arts managers, whose roles alter according to the size of the organization: the larger the organization, the greater the emphasis there is on production costs. More and more managers are needed to organize the large houses, and to take care of rehearsal time, room allotments, schedules, casting, cancellations, and the like.

It is true, as Baumol and Bowen suggested, that the economic dilemma in the arts lies in its inability to meet increasing costs with increased productivity or increased income. Income rises at a much smaller rate and may even have reached its maximum. This book's analysis, however, shows that the bureaucratization of the arts — the need for additional income to cover the costs of the huge administrative machinery required to maintain the large art centers — has aggravated this situation and created a most "irrational" form of organization. Maintenance costs are stupendous even though "production" has increased. Many organizations have extended their seasons and increased their number of performances, but dare not diversify their repertoire.

The analysis experiences related above indicate that this occupational ideology promotes the "rationalization of production." "Accountability" and "organizational survival" served to legitimate managerial decisions when artistic standards or repertoire innovation were at stake. The future effects on the arts of this managerial role will certainly not result in bold new repertoire. In fact, throughout the last two chapters, it has been shown how "rationality" in management resulted in the standardization of repertoire, and the objectification of artistry.[3]

Government subsidization, momentarily on the rise, is related to accountability — an issue which most individuals do not associate with artistic integrity and freedom, but rather with a public service "outreach". Ironically, government funding was initially intended to loosen the constraints created by the market. It seems instead to have intensified those constraints. Organizational complexity and government funding will continue to contribute to the formalization of roles with the inevitable effect of lessening the autonomy of artists. It is reasonable to suppose that the conflict will be sustained by the occupational structure itself, in the training and recruitment of business-oriented arts administrators.

Notes

[1] For a discussion of impresarios of the past (e.g. Hammerstein Mapleson, Gatti-Casazza, Kahn and others), see Gatti-Casazza, 1941; Bing, 1972; Kolodin,1954; Fitzgerald and Jacobson, *One Hundred Years at the Metropolitan* (forthcoming).

[2] National Council of the Arts, *A Study of the Non-Profit Arts and Cultural Industry in New York State.* New York: Cranford Wood, Inc., 1973, p. 64. More and more, managers are hired for their skills in management rather than in music. This varies with the size and philosophy of the organization, and is worthy of a comparative study.

[3] See Rosanne Martorella, "Rationality in the Artistic Management of Performing Arts Organizations," in Kamerman and Martorella, *Performers and Performances: The Social Organization of Artistic Work* (forthcoming).

6 *The Social Organization of Opera: The Star Performers*

Introduction

Since producing "grand" opera involves a huge organizational complex of diverse talents, skills, and knowledge, a performer must often cope not only with another's interpretation of a composition, but with the organizational demands which act to integrate all the different elements of a production. Both these elements focus on a different goal, each one legitimate and each one requiring a separate ideology for the people involved in implementing these goals. Performers often find themselves in conflict with other artists' musical interpretations, with managerial controls over repertoire, casting, fees and schedules, with boards, and with a public-sponsored "Kulture." The success of each performance and each career is contingent, however, upon numerous rehearsals which serve to integrate these interdependent activities. Performers work in a constantly changing, ill-defined, and economically unstable situation. By focusing on the conflict in this artistic subculture, it is possible to expose the norms which govern the relationships in it, and the foundation of their human exchange.

All performing artists have expectations of themselves and their careers; their socialization as performers does not adequately prepare them, however, to assume roles in organizations. For the most part, operatic performers are highly motivated, critical of themselves, and individualistic, and they dislike routine and identification with work they consider mediocre or mass-oriented. Their involvement with "serious" music commits them to a life of performances that are educational rather than entertaining. Consequently, they view publicity and other demands from the mass media with disdain. Unlike other artists, their work is measured by the "performance" so that pressures from schedules, premieres, and rehearsals are unparalleled in other cultural products such as architecture, painting or poetry. Although music is institutionally affiliated with universities, conservatories, workshops, unions, and publishers, it remains highly individual in nature. Vocal training and coaching serve to emphasize the "solo" character of the work. The training is self-centered and requires strong egos. All of these factors contribute to the feeling of alienation and the sense of conflict performers confront when they join organizations. A performance which involves interpreting a composer's work, while taking cues from a conductor, director, and designer, is central to the everyday dynamics of opera production, and yet it is the source of conflict between the individual artist and the organization in which she works.

The organization's ultimate aim is to develop an art form of a high musical and artistic level at a "realistic" cost. The organization sets itself particular goals but, to attain those goals, it must employ individuals with intensely self-centered interests and values. What are the accommodations which develop to meet the conflict between internalized personal goals, which can only be realized in a commercially-oriented organization, and that organization's own collective goal? Becker's work on jazz musicians and Coffman's study of rock musicians are especially enlightening on this very point. Coffman wrote:

> Artists develop their own expectations and needs as individual performers for autonomy, privacy and the right to apply their own standards when judging their performance. Naturally, this attitude produced a conflict in roles which require them nevertheless to meet audience expectations, and forces a number of devices of accommodations to meet this dilemma . . . based on conceptions of embodying unique qualities that set them apart from not only commercially-oriented representatives but also from other audiences — their publishers, upon whom they ultimately depend (Hirsch 1969:268).

The similarity among artists in many fields is revealed here. A high degree of individuality and creativity is in direct opposition to the artist's dependence on managers, producers, publishers, and other performers. Opera is even more difficult because of its reliance on many kinds of performance skills. Viewing opera as a recreative, virtuoso, and interpretive art form, each performer sees himself or herself as the most important element of a production. Conflicts over relative consequence are the basis of most disputes among colleagues. Possession of a rare and unusual talent, cult-like followings, and the adulation and respect bestowed on artists by members of all social strata are significant factors, used by artists to show that they are justified in viewing the organization as a means to achieve their personal career goals. This theory was shown to be applicable to other "nonprofit" organizations by Joseph Bensman. He argued that ideologies of service and high ideals

> constitute the basis of the self-definition of the group and of the personal and occupational pride, security, and motivation of its members. The strength and tradition of the ideological legitimation of the high-minded professional give them a peculiar source of inner security . . . . The ideology of the nonprofit organization stresses higher purposes, nobler ends, and ultimate ideals . . . . These purposes are legitimated and sanctified by age old traditions, beliefs, and dogmas (1967:74).

Specific and diverse talents converge in the nonprofit performing arts organizations. The ideology adopted by performers is worked out in the context in which opera is produced. It describes performers as involved in an important artistic endeavor, and their specific role as the most important in the aesthetic interpretation of opera.

Productions grow from talk about future programming to actual decisions by the board and administrative staff. The general manager or the artistic director casts major roles and comprimarios. Meetings begin with the conductor, director, and designer and later include the chorus master and directors of other departments. Sets are built, costumes designed, and lighting rehearsals held. Rooms, schedules, and covers must all be accounted for and integrated with the rest of the season's repertoire. Piano rehearsals involving one or two singers, stressing diction and some acting preparations, advance to ensemble pieces with comprimarios and chorus. Indeed, a climactic moment occurs during the "Sitzprobe" (sit-down rehearsal), when voices and instruments are first combined. This leads to rehearsals on stage, working run-throughs, and finally to full dress rehearsals with costumes and make-up. The latter are kept to a minimum due to their costs and are very similar to actual performances.

Opera, as mixed media, requires a dynamic exchange between singer, composer, and director (Lyric Opera of Chicago)

Vickers & Brouwenstijn
Walküre I

The Composer

Since the majority of operas performed by large companies are taken from the classical repertoire, the function of integrating the different aspects of production and providing a musical interpretation is delegated not to the composer but to the conductor. If present, however, either as an executant of his own work or as a conductor, the composer is considered the most prestigious member of the musical community. His celebrity is due more than likely to his success as a conductor, especially given the ability of audiences to understand this role more than composing skills. In fact, most famous contemporary opera and symphonic conductor-composers (for example, Leinsdorf, von Karajan, Schippers, Kubelik, Bernstein, Boulez, and others) have made their reputations from conducting, not composing.

In the historical chapter, the importance of the system of patronage, and the musical preferences of audiences regarding the role of the composer and his position in society were stressed. Audiences who preferred instrumental music were shown to respect composers over performers. The reign of composer-performers was seen as a transitory stage in the development and supremacy of the virtuoso performer. Once opera companies were established with impresarios or managers acting as producers, composers were forced even further into the background. It was noted, however, that while some operatic composers (such as Rossini) made fortunes during their lifetimes (throughout the nineteenth century), by the end of the century, the situation had changed:

> The growing repertory of favorite old operas provided more and more competition for the newcomer's work. As opera companies learned to get along nicely with the works of Mozart, Wagner, Puccini, and other old reliables, they began to turn a more and more jaundiced eye on new compositions. Why spend money on new scenery and extra time on learning and rehearsing unfamiliar arts for a new work that might be a total failure. (Samachson 1962:74)

Prior to this time, the composer had created, produced, and performed his own works, maintaining control over the entire process. His role has been taken over by managers, stage directors, conductors and performers. Musicologists and sociologists both contend that this is a major reason for the widening gap between the composer and his patron-audience.

Today, there are probably very few composers who can live solely on their commissions. Performing rights, board and trustee appointments, teaching, and publishing often provide the necessary additional resources. Composers William Schumann, Aaron Copland, and Quincy Porter are also teachers; Leonard Bernstein and Leopold Stokowsky are conductors; Henry Cowell is a publisher; Virgil Thomson is a writer and critic; and Marc Blitzstein is an author. Films, radio, and the recording industry have supplemented the incomes of others. But these "rent payers" are accepted as a compromise with the current situation. The universities have played a tremendous role in engaging composers as performers and teachers and in commissioning their works. They have played a crucial role in creating a market for contemporary repertoire. "But despite a large group of awards and commissions the composer's livelihood is solely dependent upon royalties and is still one of the most perilously earned in all the field of art."[1]

The highly informal and precarious patronage system makes the composer dependent on those willing to commission works, but such support is in the hands of a very few individuals and foundations. William Schumann, in a radio interview, spoke of the composer's dependence on mass audiences and patrons:

> The reason that it [writing only popular works that would have performances] never affected me is that I determined at a very early age that I was going to be my own patron. I made up my mind that I wasn't going to rely on patronage from any source . . . because I wouldn't want to be influenced in what I chose to compose by what its commercial destiny might be, and I followed that all my life and that's why I started teaching and taking other posts as they developed throughout my life. It was because I wanted to be absolutely free as a composer. I write exactly what I want to write and that's only possible because I have supported myself and my family by other things.

Table 1 revealed that the standard repertoire had 5,482 performances in 1980, while the contemporary repertoire had 3,361 performances. While there has been a continuous increase in productions of contemporary works, for the most part, these performances take place in university workshops, conservatories, summer theatres, and other experimental groups that have been supported by grants from foundations and state university education funds. There is a great disparity between the size of the audiences in large opera houses where classical works are performed and the size of the audiences in small university workshops where contemporary works are included along with the classics. The most popular contemporary works are those of Menotti, Weill, Britten and Bernstein.

Gian Carlo Menotti described some of the modern composer's dilemmas:

> "The first need of every composer is the need for money" . . . . More orchestra rehearsals . . . . Mr. Menotti hastened to add that one cannot expect this from all opera companies, or they would all be bankrupt. But he strenuously objected to the one orchestra rehearsal followed by the general dress rehearsal, which then inevitably must still be a working rehearsal . . . He made a plea for all contemporary composers when he said that modern operas, whether a success or failure, must not be dropped immediately after one season . . . . "It is discouraging because our operas are like orphans that never find a home, are never invited back. Some time ago producing a contemporary work was considered a dangerous adventure, — now it is considered a grim duty . . . In spite of the long run of some of these . . . they are not big money makers, and because of the expenses involved, it is almost impossible to find a producer . . . ." He [Menotti] does not intend to write an opera in the near future because of the difficulties of production. (COS 1963:11)

Given the expenses of commissioning, rehearsing, and producing a new work, and the probable losses at the box office, companies that rely on ticket sales and private support do not see producing works that aren't popular as their responsibility. Grants from the National Endowment of the Arts and university aid have assumed this responsibility. The New York State Council on the Arts has begun an unprecedented commissioning program involving sixty-nine American composers in orchestral, choral, jazz, chamber, and electronic compositions. The composers have had to rely on commissions from public sources; tastes and audience preferences have not entered into today's creative process. Much modern music is beyond the comprehension of the lay public. Peter Rosenfeld writes of Schoenberg's music:

> For with him, with the famous orchestra and nine piano pieces, we seem to be entering the arctic zone of musical art. None of the old beacons, none of the old stars, can guide us longer in these foreign waters. Strange, menacing forms surround us, and the line is bleak and chill with faint (1971:233).

The modern composer's education and training reinforce particular compositional styles and serve to widen the gap between him and his audience. They strengthen his commitment to a musical subculture with elitist values. A closed system of relationships evolves. The composer, no longer "needing" a public, creates and performs for other musicians. Paul Hindemith described this new process:

> Thus a solitary, esoteric style will be the result, the well-known kind of secret language understandable only to the initiated, removed from any music desires of an ordinary music lover and thriving under hothouse conductors. No wonder, then, that clashes occur whenever a piece of this kind appears in our concert life. That the situation is created which was described earlier in this book: the so-called modernist composer and the ordinary concert-goer, each following his own line of interest and totally disregarding the other's considerations, are drifting apart and the gap between them is widening with each further performance of an obscure piece (1953:293).

Leon Kirchner, an American composer who studied at Harvard, remarked, "At that time I really didn't understand what he [Stravinsky] meant, but now. . . , well, I'm ambivalent . . . . Boulez was right about that. It's a place where composers write for one another and lose sight of the outer community." (Henahan 1973:15) It appears that universities serve to perpetuate the development of musical subcultures, thus insulating the composer from a potential public.

The opposite side of this coin is that the public itself may serve to inhibit composer experimentation. When audiences are no longer receptive, the composer turns inward and writes for other composers in esoteric and avant-garde styles that do not communicate with present day audiences, as the above statements reveal. The university, in becoming the home of experimentation in opera, has facilitated the composer's withdrawal from the production of operas for large houses.

Henry Pleasants supports the important role of audiences.

> It is his failure to meet contemporary requirements that distinguishes the contemporary composer from composers of any earlier epoch . . . . If modern music had any real vitality, it would take its place normally within the framework of contemporary musical life and make its own way. It would not need special promotion to obtain grudging performances and tolerant attention . . . . In modern music, popular success has ceased to be a circumvention. All that counts is the word of the professional — conductor, composer, and critic — none of whom gives a damn what the public thinks (1973:4).

Having taken the composer to task, Pleasants locates the problem in a "cultural lag" of aesthetic norms and values.

> The serious composer has lost touch with the currents of popular taste. The traditional forms to which he is committed — operas, cantatas, symphonies, sonatas, and chamber music — are unrelated to modern society. They originated and spoke for small aristrocratic and bourgeois communities that had as yet not come with our mass communities of today . . . . In free societies he is assumed to be responsible only to his art, as supported by what he calls his own artistic integrity . . . . This concept of the composer as the servant of a vague identity known as Art has encouraged society to take for granted the present widening gulf between new serious music and the community of serious music lovers. The result is disaster. It separates artistic evolution from social evolution. In other words, our view of the composer as independent of the law of supply and demand is of very recent origin. Previously the composer was regarded as a working professional. (1973)

Julius Rudel, former Director of New York City Opera, in an article in *The New York Times*, places the issue of producing contemporary works in historical perspective. He feels that not all operas are destined to reappear and gain stability over time. Throughout history, a small number of operas have succeeded and taken their places alongside the classics. He contends that inadequate box office receipts and a 2,800 house capacity at New York City Opera are to blame for their not commissioning works.

The bias manifested by audience preferences for European repertoire and for star performers also accounts for the lack of popular American compositions. The bicentennial celebration may have served to generate new commissions for American composers, but the Lyric Opera of Chicago decided to commission Krzystof Penderecki to write an opera for the celebration. Henahan, a *New York Times* critic, commented on this decision.

> The inevitable assumption is that someone in authority in Chicago — no doubt the general manager, Carol Fox — believes that 200 years have been insufficient to produce an American artist capable of measuring up to Chicago's standards. To be fair about it, Chicago's opera company has a record of enterprise in older repertory that few can match. American music just happened to be a blind spot (1973:9).

The difficulty of atonal music for both the ear and voice is often given as a reason for not producing American music. Rudel seems to feel, however, that, "Perhaps what this tells us is that most operagoers are not ready for the more avant-garde works (which, of course, in some quarters are already being called "dated"), but that as we continue to perform them, they will gain greater acceptability." The technical demands on the singer have encouraged most to shun experimental pieces. In a radio interview, Bob Sherman of WQXR asked Irene Gubrud, a soprano, about the necessary changes of "approach" (including the method of producing a tone, size of voice, etc.). She replied:

> I think there is a certain amount of difference simply because for the things like Mozart and Haydn it necessitates for me a lightening of the voice and the texture of the voice as opposed to singing larger things like Schoenberg which requires today more sound. But, on the whole, I don't change too much. It's not even the musical approach, maybe it's the emotional approach. It depends on what you're trying to say, what the music is communicating. I do find that I am shying away a little bit from contemporary music . . . . I don't want to be labeled as a contemporary singer because there is too much that is rewarding in the earlier periods . . . . I think that it is possible, however, if you do any one kind of music too much you are hurting yourself because the voice is like any other muscle, it needs to be exercised and used in all ways it could possibly be used. Any one style could be bad for it. However, it is true that the more Mozart and Haydn I sing, I realize how fabulously they wrote and you almost cannot sing badly because they wrote so naturally for the instrument (1973).

On the other hand, some singers have been most adaptable; they do not find the musical requirements of contemporary repertoire dangerous. Henahan wrote of Jan DeGaetani:

> But if her intellectual grasp of, and sympathy for, the works of living composers have made her their dream girl, she also sings Bach, Schubert, Ravel — you name it. Her recent recordings have included not only individual songs but an album of Stephen Foster songs (1973).

Audience tastes, the expense of new works in rehearsal time and in losses at the box office, and the difficulty of "atonal" music for the voice and ear all account for the continued dominance of the classical repertoire and the present position of the American composer.

The Conductor

The star conductor is at the pinnacle of the prestige scale. Adored by audiences, envied by stage directors, and resented by singers, he

views himself as the chief coordinator of a performance, the setter
of musical standards, and the sole authority on interpretation. Conductors, except for the unique von Karajan, are accused of knowing
little about the voice or the techniques of theatrical production. Singers and directors resent the conductor's directorship and charge him
with deviating from the composer's intentions while he claims a legitimate right to select, interpret, alter, and control all aspects of
production.

Although most star conductors now limit themselves to short
periods as directors of large houses, guest conducting has become a
life-style. Opera houses must share the conductor's artistry. Abbado,
for example, was appointed by La Scala and the Vienna Philharmonic,
was principal guest conductor of the London Symphony, and was
a leader much sought after by other ensembles. Leif Segerstom, a
guest conductor at the Metropolitan Opera, was music director of the
Royal Stockholm Opera, and chief conductor of the Deutsche Opera.
Boulez, Rudel, Downes, Thomas, and Kubelik have similar multiple
commitments. Like singers of comparable fame and status, conductors are booked two to three years in advance. A success in one house
creates a demand for additional performances at other major houses.

If a major conductor is also the music director of an opera company, he occupies the most influential position, making production
decisions and engaging the instrumentalists, soloists, and chorus.
These responsibilities have, in fact, been reserved for maestros Kubelik and Levine as music director and principal conductor of the
Metropolitan. The music director's responsibilities are varied, ranging
from a concern with box office and administrative problems, to a
responsibility for resolving feuds among artists, and the necessity of
familiarizing himself with the availability of talent. He must maintain
the respect of almost one hundred competent and well-trained musicians and possess the musical and personal leadership qualities
necessary to command the respect of the chorus, ballet, technicians,
soloists, audiences, and critics.

Playing a key role in determining repertoire trends, he must
make the most efficient use of limited resources, and is inevitably
under attack. An eminent sociologist-musician, the late John Mueller,
wrote about the conductor's vulnerability:

> [His] prestige and authority seem to be reflected in repertoire
> policy. In fact, it is a classic complaint that the repertoire doesn't
> represent the "taste" of the audience, but rather that of the con-
> ductor who constructs the programs and whose aesthetic ideol-
> ogy determines his presence. With a kind of parental solicitude
> he is said to apportion the musical diet, not according to what

> is "good for it" . . . even the most obstinate conductor dare not, as if he would, flaunt his own eccentricities and ignore the basic communal repertoire that resides in the habits and expectations of the public. (1959:397)

Very often, conductors have to be familiar with the costs of production. An impresario-conductor of a small but well-known touring company talked about the importance of knowing not only the musical and artistic talent at hand, but also how that talent could work within the economic limitations of the company.

> You have a variety of problems that you have to somewhere deal with because of the conditions and facilities available to you which are faulty and incomplete. Oh yes, you cannot just say it has to be that. Money is always important and you have to deal with what you have. . . . Opera is endlessly expensive. . . . Nobody knows how to handle it so as to receive the best results under existing monetary conditions, under existing talent conditions, facilities, and time availability.

Conductor and singers seem most at odds with each other because of the former's dominance in musical matters. The popularity of the singer prevailed throughout the Metropolitan's early years and some feel that the singer still retains the "overruling" position. The decline of the singer's supremacy in performance undoubtedly contributed to the rise of the conductor's status. A greater emphasis on total theater in opera, as well as the decline of a singer's identification with a single house, have enhanced the role of the conductor. In fact, Bing thought that the most important debuts of his years of management were those of conductors. But, in his history of the Metropolitan, Kolodin wrote: "As for conductors, it was Grau's convinced opinion that, 'No one ever paid a nickel to see a man's back' " (1966:178).

Audiences have always been accused of worshipping singers without regard for the music. One journalist feels that the less sophisticated audiences of today have transferred their preferences to the conductor — the new performing virtuoso of opera. One music-journalist feels that the supremacy of the conductor or singer is often dictated by the score itself, and remarks in an interview:

> Well, from a musical standpoint the conductor is it! From the dramatic standpoint the director is it! Sure, again, we're trying to make it much too black and white. With "Falstaff," it's black and white. Either you have a great conductor, or you cannot do "Falstaff". You could do "Traviata." . . . It's purely an ensemble

work. There isn't an aria in the piece; it's constant flow of probably the most beautiful music ever written. Purely an ensemble. . . . "Cosi Fan Tutte" is another one like "Falstaff." . . . It
must have ensemble. You don't want stars.

The elevation of the conductor was greatly influenced by Berlioz's
"L'Art du Chef d'Orchestre" (1856) and Wagner's celebrated writings
especially "Uber das Dirigieren" (1869), viewing the orchestra as a
unified instrument. The chapter on opera history in the latter volume
recalls the importance of the concept of "gesamtkuntswerk" in establishing the supremacy of the conductor — a person capable of
integrating music, drama, song, instruments, and dance. With recent
developments in staging and production, the conductor's control has
been extended to include some administrative aspects of a production.

Today conducting is respected as an art of "interpretation." The
conductor's ultimate and sole responsibility, one that no one dare
challenge, is in determining the tempo of a particular composition.
This has been the root of many disputes among conductors, and
problems often arise when a conductor takes on an already established production. Donal Henahan dealt with the subtle and difficult
requirements of musical "interpretation" in writing about Michael
Tilson Thomas.

> Experienced orchestra men, while happy to talk about the
> measurable, weighable elements in a conductor's make-up (dex-
> terity, rhythmic precision, sharpness of ear, and so on) find them-
> selves unable to pinpoint what makes one competent leader better
> than another. "The whole duty of a conductor is comprised in
> his ability always to indicate the right tempo," [Richard Wagner]
> wrote, in a much quoted but usually hopelessly misunderstood
> simplification . . . . [And Berlioz wrote] of "other almost inde-
> finable gifts without which an invisible link cannot establish itself
> between him and those he directs" (1971:44)

James Levine, a well-liked, young and articulate conductor of the
Metropolitan, has described the process of subordinating his biases
to those of the composer.

> Well, I would say that it begins by accepting the responsi-
> bility of trying to produce a performance as faithful to the com-
> poser's intentions as possible. That is a complicated goal, for it
> requires much more than literal fidelity to another musician's
> notated instructions. It means somehow fathoming the depth,
> breadth, and complexity of the most imaginative impulses of

men, many of whom lived hundred of years ago, retaining the essence of their conceptions yet making it valid for our time. To approach this goal, the conductor must study thoroughly the score he is performing, but he must steep himself also in a number of other things — as much of that composer's output as possible, as well as the language, culture, human experience, psychology, and performance practice of the period. (1972:29)

Conductors who give individualistic interpretations of a score are considered flippant and egotistic. Placing individual interests above the composer's aims — which may take the form of indulging in vocal displays, shortening the score, or emphasizing techniques at the expense of overall musical interpretation — is considered vulgar, mediocre, and unmusical. This debate was previously encountered with regard to the *castrati* and in the current dispute over ensemble versus the star system. The "entertainment" aspect of "serious" music — the emphasis on the virtuoso, usually identified with mass tastes — is considered vulgar. A journalist described the popular conductor, Kostelanetz, this way:

He is loathed by highbrows, who disdainfully dismiss him as nothing but a cheap popularizer. They say he will stop at nothing to attract audiences. They are right. He shocked them in the thirties when, on the radio, he had the audacity to create a medley out of themes from "Tchaikovsky's Fourth Symphony and the pop tune, 'Alabama Bound'." (Rubin 1973:17)

The ability to capture the stylistic nuances of the composer remains the mark of the truly great conductor. This has become especially evident since Toscanini's arrival on the scene. He did much to encourage fidelity to the score. Schonberg seemed to favor virtuoso display when he said, "The composer is now exalted, and the performer is supposed to keep himself and his nasty ego as far as possible from the composer's message." (Schonberg 1967:62) While some may disagree with Schonberg, the composer is undoubtedly respected. Many different schools of interpretation have, however, evolved. They range from the literal reading to looking at the double meanings of the libretto and score as frameworks within which the conductor and director "create." Some conductors attempt to achieve authenticity through studying not only the score but other writings of the composer — letters, history notations — as well.

Particular styles have prevailed at different times. During the latter part of the nineteenth century and into the twentieth century, the singer held center stage. More recently, "musicianship" has come to mean acting and ensemble singing. These elements, together with the goals of total theatre in opera, have enhanced the prestige of the conductor.

The role assigned to conductors has simultaneously raised the prestige of the stage director and designer; it is the combined efforts of all three that evolve into a particular "concept." The "verismo" of Tavernia's stage directing and Rolf Gerara's setting and costuming of "La Boheme" seems to enhance Puccini's score; the lustful Camille of Corsaro's imaginative direction of "La Traviata," and Gentele's concept of Don Jose as a killer, juxtaposed with the Svoboda sets, combine in an integrated interpretation. Undoubtedly, the musical score, its tempo, its climactic moments, and the use of instruments prescribe staging so that the dramatic and musical counterparts compliment each other.

This is not to say, however, that composer-performers and conductor-directors are never at odds in this area. The Metropolitan's 1972–73 production of "Carmen" attempted to achieve such integration with a union between conductor, director, and designer. Prior to his tragic death, Gentele had collaborated with both the conductor and designer. The stark, modern Svoboda sets and the black and white costuming heightened the sensuous, and southern Spanish feeling of Bizet's score and reflected the interpretation that Don Jose was both a lover and a killer. Bodo Igesz, who assumed Gentele's responsibilities as director, spoke of the difficulties inherent in blending drama and music.

> The production had to seem organic, as if sets, costumes, and direction had evolved together. In order to achieve my goal, I had to discard some of Gentele's conception. For instance, he had called for a ballet in the fourth act. The costumes for it were finished. But since we were not using the old interpolated music of the Arlésienne suite, which has always been dreadful, I didn't know why he called for choreography . . . . As for the dialogue, I cut it down quite a bit. (1973)

A "concept" cannot be credited simply to one person, for it evolves over time, and takes on character with the passage of many performances. Usually about eighteen months prior to a new production, the designer, director, and conductor meet, sometimes calling on solo singers to sit with them. Ideas may have been developing in the artist's mind for years; prior experiences and previous performances will also affect his or her final interpretations.

The conductor's major concerns are with the technical, dramatic, and musical aspects of a production. Disputes with soloists, directors, and other conductors are not uncommon. The conductor may feel that the director is being too gimmicky or that s/he clutters the stage. She often finds that dramatic requirements force a tone and color in the voice contrary to his interpretation. Although she should have a knowledge of the voice — its colors, possibilities, tones — singers complain, often justly, of his or her failure to allot time for breathing and proper tempo, especially in holding high C's or in other color-atura passages. In turn, the conductor thinks singers are egotistic and unmusical, for their training often does not include knowledge of an instrument, musical theory, or note reading. This she believes to be the cause of their infidelity to the score. The conductor must also have the diplomacy to handle long feuds and intense jealousies.

His or her right to intervene in all matters of a production from specific technical details to major issues of style and interpretation is dramatized in Harvey Phillips' account of a "Carmen" production conducted by Leonard Bernstein.

> and McCracken (Don José) continued his experimenting with positions, attitudes, and business, but all in terms of the Bernstein interpretation — the fiery entr'acte to act four. The maestro did not stint in his detailed directions, even asking the tambourine to modulate its piano dynamic marking and the strings to "rip your skin off on those pizzicati. More flamenco nonsense." He had devised a wild accelerando and crescendo in the middle, where the piece becomes most markedly Spanish in flavor. "I may kill all this, but that's what rehearsals are for." Nevertheless, he found the effect "sensational" and kept it.

For Carmen's character, he suggested to Marilyn Horne:

> [Y]ou should not be surprised that José is there. It's just part of fate. It's like Carmen doesn't even have to look, maybe just the slightest look, to confirm what you already know, that this is the day of your death. You're dressed to the nines, and you've come out with your new trick to die. You knew all about this in act one when you threw the flower. You're always reading the cards, not just in act three. It's fate. You're like Dido, in Jocasta. (88–90)

James McCracken, in the main tenor role of Don José, spoke to Director Igesz:

> "It's just a suggestion," explained the tenor. "We could start our scene together on the small side of the stage, then build it out to the larger playing area on the left. I see we're in trouble with what we have, so I'm making a suggestion." Igesz agreed to try

this, but Bernstein ended his retreat and in a way, reiterating his lecture to Horne, told them that Carmen's action was to stand still, to remain inflexible in the biggest possible space where these two forces could face each other, to let José come closer and closer, and not to move until the first roar of the crowd was heard. Otherwise she should be dead cold. "I hope I haven't thrown in a monkey wrench," the maestro added. "It's a good monkey wrench," the director acknowledged. Bernstein, now having accomplished the delivery of his thought, departed.

Probably the most severe and most frequent complaint of the conductor is the lack of rehearsal time. For economic reasons, rehearsals are shortened and scheduled with caution; a dress rehearsal is a singular luxury. A new production, which demands many rehearsals is compensated for by standard works which need little or no rehearsal time. The "stagione" system — or at least a version of it — lowers overall costs by reducing the rehearsal time needed for productions. It enables companies to produce an opera on consecutive nights for a given time.

For the conductor, rehearsals are a must; it is there that he works out the rhythms, dynamics, and overall style of the composition. Most conductors feel that these have to be worked out fully, but leave a little to chance so a degree of spontaneity might occur at a performance. Henry Lewis, conductor of the New Jersey Orchestra, and guest conductor at the Metropolitan, confronts the problems created by the lack of rehearsals:

> But the rehearsal problem! And the changing of casts like musical chairs. Under such conditions you simply can't accomplish what you'd like to. You can't do anything untraditional; you get to where you take the safe course. Rehearsals, rehearsals, and more rehearsals are the only solution. But then there is a danger of too much: you can rehearse through the performance. (Eaten 1973:23)

Boris Goldovsky seems to feel that many conflicts stem from the extent of specialization of functions today. Conductors of the past who were also stage directors did not have to contend with the meeting of the minds that famous teams presently do.

> It so happens in my own company, I conduct a performance and stage direct them both. . . . He (Richard Wagner) conducted the performance and had them conducted very much to his liking. He stage directed the performance himself. This was a unit. Since he was boss, he was in a position to more or less get what he wanted. . . . The same was true for a very great man in the field,

Gustav Mahler . . . . At one time, it was the rule that the composer produced the piece; he controlled the orchestra and the staging, conducted the first big performance, and then it was set and somebody else took it over. What we normally have today, since these things become complicated, is a man conducts, a very fine conductor, and an expert stage director, and that is a very tricky situation because the conductor has no interest often except to their sensitivities. The stage director doesn't understand enough the musical problem . . . so that it becomes a question of who's boss, who's more important and who is famous. . . . There have been many such couples or teams that have worked well together. . . . At times, they forget about each other and stage the problem as theirs alone. (1973)

Because of the star system, conflicts are decided according to star rating and the ability of stars to sell tickets. One conductor remarked that, "Even a Reiner would bow, but to a Stravinsky." An additional factor often enters into and is a by-product of the star system, which is that "reliable" artists are given contracts which bind management to give them particular privileges generally reserved for superstars.

The Director and the Designer

The nature of stage directing and stage design in opera has been greatly influenced by theatrical trends and the development of stage technology. The latter, in turn, has been affected by changes in architecture and sculpture. The realistic settings and conventional furniture, props, and scenery, of the traditional theatre are increasingly being replaced by impressionistic settings and the imaginative use of lighting and space. New York City Opera's 1972 production of Delius' "A Village Romeo and Juliet" experimented with the use of still and motion picture sequences. Schonberg wrote that, "After the 1972 'Romeo and Juliet' in Washington, it was apparent that a new era in stagecraft had arrived. No longer are bulky, expensive sets and props needed. Any company can use this kind of projected production." (1973:15)

In the 1973–74 production of Berlioz's "Les Troyens," the Metropolitan used film to portray the invasion of Troy by the Greek army and to project fiery-red blazes of light to symbolize Cassandra's premonition of the devastation and bloodshed to follow.

The use of modern material is spreading. The recent construction of stages, warehouses, and other facilities makes it possible to in-

corporate the most modern theatrical technology in lighting, architecture, and film. The Metropolitan's famous "revolving" stage
encourages the creative use of props and scenery changes. In addition, an audience willing and able to support its preference for spectacle facilitated the employment of such non-opera directors and
designer-artists as Zeffirelli, Berman, Guthrie, Chagall, Graf, Caldwell, and Corsaro. Coming as they do from other fields, they have
contributed much to opera through their particular expertise and
experience in painting, cinema, theatre and television.

Chagall's set designs for the Metropolitan's "The Magic Flute"
and Zeffirelli's staging and designing of "Cavalleria Rusticana" are
excellent examples. On the other hand, criticisms abound when the
transfer from one medium to the other is awkward. Zeffirelli's unfortunate attempt at directing and designing Samuel Barber's "Anthony and Cleopatra," which was thought to be too massive, busy,
and overpowering for the opera stage, is a case in point.

Samachson in *The Fabulous World of Opera* wrote of the frustration
felt by directors who come from a non-operatic tradition:

> The staging of opera turned out to offer less room for novelty
> than most stage people supposed . . . . The director was over-
> whelmed with difficulties resulting from insufficient rehearsal
> time and the interference of the conductor, members of the cast,
> and the management . . . . The director of a stage play is often
> revered as a genius — the single person who can make an oth-
> erwise dead play come alive. No one in this country ascribes such
> magical powers to the power of the director of an opera. (1978:118)

Directing as a specialty in opera has been encouraged by the
emphasis placed on achieving "total" theater or "ensemble" singing.
The works of Wagner, together with Shaw's outstanding writings,
did much to establish this trend. Until recently, the conductor and/or
composer took charge of staging. An important aria brought the
singer center-stage in the traditional pose of bent knee, pointed toes,
and hands at mid-waist. Today such gestures are viewed as unmusical
and egotistic. Singers perform while they are sitting, walking, or
lying, and even with their backs to the audience, thus enhancing the
dramatic quality of the production. In the past, the managements of
Grau, Gatti-Casazza, Johnson, and even Bing, placed singers in the
supreme position. Both Johnson and Bing assumed their leadership
with the hope of revitalizing the staging, lighting, and scenery of the
old Metropolitan Opera House. Bing, however, soon found he had
to compete with superstar directors, conductors, and designers.

In his biography, Herbert Graf describes how staging has changed over the past fifty years. He recalls that he enrolled in three different schools in preparation for a career in directing.

> But when I started out on my career, the director was not a star. In fact, he hardly existed at all. The conductor ran the show . . . they were more like acting coaches and stage managers than the czar producers of today. As luck would have it, my professional life runs parallel to the emergence of the director as prime mover of the production. (Rizzo 1972:25)

And staging and dramatic requirements were far from what is considered acceptable today. He says:

> The first thing to remember is that there was a terrible scarcity of money. New productions, in the sense of new costumes and scenery, were very rare indeed. And rehearsal time onstage was strictly limited. Most of the staging was done on the roof stage, where scheduling was no great problem, but the net result was that the singers didn't get to work on the set until the last moment; and given the general shabbiness of the physical production, the total effect was a good deal less than theatrical. Then the lighting was a great problem. Not that the equipment wasn't there, but we were defeated by the repertory system. With seven performances of as many operas in any given week, it was impossible to hang and light each production except in the most generalized way. (Rizzo 1972:15)

Like star conductors and singers, the stage director is now able to limit his engagements, charge higher fees, and make more decisions regarding the production's total musical conception. One general manager says: "We used to put up with the director rehearsing set scenes once with the piano in rehearsal, then with orchestra, and then the dress. Now no stage director we hire will accept this."

The stage director employs the voice and body to portray emotions and character in the drama; he uses color, lighting, costuming, and scenery to complement musical ideas. The director must resolve the inherent problem of pacing dramatic action along with musical beat. Most often, his creativity and novelty are not accepted as they are in the world of the theater, where he is directing new works and more than likely working along with the author and producer from the inception of a play. Historical sources, and original librettos, novels, and short stories on which an opera may have been based, provide accurate information about life-style, costuming and other details of interest to the director/designer. Journalist and critic, Harris Green

Margherita Wallman, the great stage director of European opera, is seen here during rehearsal of the Lyric Opera of Chicago's production of "Carmen," in 1959
(Lyric Opera of Chicago)

evaluates the Metropolitan's Graf-Berman production of "Don Giovanni," and reveals how this director/designer team was able to capture the "drama giocoso" of Mozart and his librettist Da Ponte, by costumes, scenery, and the physical movement of the singers.

> And how did Berman and Graf meet this challenge of reconciling opposites? . . . [They did it with] sets that delight the eye without overwhelming the music; costumes that characterize their wearers while brightening the stage (the marauding Don enters in scarlet, the metallic Donna Anna has an underskirt of gold gleaming through her mourning garb); staging that is neither too farcical for the drama nor too naturalistic for the opera stage; a close collaboration between designer and director that brings intimate arias and ensembles forward, before the forecurtain.(1972:11)

The director sees himself as a revitalizing force, exploring new dimensions within the standard repertoire. For some, this involves incorporating the latest innovation in experimental theater. Such a director is the least likely to view the libretto and score as sacrosanct, urging instead the unfolding of the drama with the full integration of the performing arts, instrumentation, and voice. Given this commitment, he clashes most with conductors and singers who deviate from his interpretation or resent his insistence on dramatic requirements which may interfere with the orchestral and vocal aspects of the score.

The score and libretto are the basic materials with which a director and designer must work; the liberties they take in interpreting the composer's work often reflect the fashion of the composer's day. *Bel canto* has encouraged baroque scenery, costuming, and gesturing; Verdi seems to call for a dramatic realism, while the New York City Opera's production of Handel's "Julius Caesar" was highly stylized. Some director-designers, however, have imposed more avant-garde approaches on the classical repertoire, as in the multi-media staging of New York City Opera's "The Makropoulos Case," or Svoboda's "Carmen" for the Metropolitan with its modern geometric sets, or Corsaro's "La Traviata" and "Don Giovanni" for New York City Opera.

Performers and critics alike feel the stage director's recently acquired autonomy threatens opera. They argue that he misinterprets score, adds a modernized, often political theme, and incorporates action that distracts from the impact of the music. Frank Corsaro, a highly respected director, argues in favor of his profession, and feels it has been stage directors who have given new life to the works of both living and dead composers. In defense, he writes:

I have never forgotten the impact of the triumphal scene (while listening to a broadcast of Aida conducted by Arturo Toscanini). Only until I became privy to tapes of Toscanini's rehearsals, later on, could I at last understand some reasons behind that special magic. In his cranky, cajoling way, Toscanini spoke to his orchestra like a stage director. I paraphrase: " You have been traveling on foot for miles. You are dusty, parched, and feel you will never see home. Suddenly someone shouts! Then another shout! The gates of the great city have come into sight. Home at last! You place your cracked lips to your instrument and shout your joy." All that was in the brasses, a blare of raucous majesty such as I've not heard since (Corsaro 1981:7).

Frank Corsaro has been known since the 1960s for his unusual and off-beat interpretations. Music critic Donal Henahan questions Corsaro's identification with the music.

This is the director, you may remember, whose past City Opera stagings have featured a near rape in "Rigoletto," a "Madame Butterfly" with Cio-Cio-San in Western dress, nude films in "The Makropoulos Affair," and a Marguerite who goes to the scaffold at the end of "Faust" instead of being levitated to heaven in a shower of rose petals. (1972:44)

Other critics of Corsaro have been horrified, "because he directs opera in a manner that is "murderous." He "discards music and libretto and acts to gratify his Actors Studio appetite for 'method' effects" (Zachary 1972:16). Corsaro addressed these criticisms in a WQXR radio interview:

And by the way when you get into those areas, you get into the fantastic areas of what it is to produce an opera today. Primarily you are dealing with libretti, who had literally censure problems of their day. Curiously, the opera, "Don Giovanni," is about rape and shows the man at a period when seduction is not able to be carried out . . . . Therefore, what has become literally what was the dictate of the time has become a philosophic point of view of our time. (1972)

Today's director is committed to the belief that the libretto is not sancrosanct and he delves into memoirs and historical records to explore the subtle meanings of a composition. Director-designer teams view it as their mission to make opera come alive even if this requires placing it in a contemporary framework. They value "ensemble" singing and theater and feel they can best fulfill this function by emphasizing stagecraft.

So far, the discussion has focused on the roles of the conductor, composer, and stage director, showing how their status is expressed within the structure of the work setting. The social organization of opera, including the inter-relationships of these roles, are circumstantial to the structure of the market. Musical issues of star versus ensemble, conductor versus director, staging versus tempo, etc., are manifestations of the concern over finances and audience preference.

The Solo Singers

Singers are as preoccupied with the deterioration of the body as dancers and athletes. They strive for stronger voices, and like athletes work for informal rewards, lobby for better contracts, and compete for job opportunities. In the past, many decisions were made according to the whims and fancies of prima donnas, but with the rise in importance of the conductor, singers no longer hold dominant positions on the prestige scale.

Singers maintain an informal code regarding bowing, upstaging, covering performances, holding and releasing, but it must be understood that these devices for attracting attention, support their artistic independence from audiences and managers. This section will discuss the star system and the norms which govern star performers and their relationships with management. In the past twenty years there has been greater cooperation among star performers, and conflicts — when they arise — are more common between singers and conductors, managers or directors.

The increased specialization of the singer confirms the historical precedence of this role. Opera has traditionally been defined as a singer's art, encompassing all the climactic elements, virtuosity, skills, and ostentations displayed on and off stage by prima donnas. But long gone are the days of the singer's domination of the musical stage as witnessed in the nineteenth century. That period, however, gave the voice a supremacy which lasted almost two hundred years, established musical principles of vocal technique which are still part of theory today, and produced infinite operatic folklore, including myths and superstitions about singers and their vocal chords. The celebrated opera houses that make up the international circuit are viewed as career stepping-stones for the few who have achieved the special status of prima donna. This is a group of highly emotional, egocentric, and gifted individuals who must conform to the routines and conditions of work set forth by operatic organizations, who must face the limitations established by an inflexible, and insecure market, and who must contend with the rigors of a highly respected but extremely difficult technique. Considering these factors, one cannot be surprised by the demands or occasionally erratic behavior of the superstars.

A noted soprano, Evelyn Lear, succinctly and intelligently summarizes the making of an operatic career:

> There are four ingredients for a career. The first one, and the least important, is the talent — the voice, musicality, charisma, any ability you have. The second quality is hard work. You've gotta really work your ass off. Don't put that — it's true, but it's vulgar, and I should be a proper diva. The third thing is timing and luck, as in any profession. The fourth point is the most important: it's having sheer unmitigated gall and the skin of an elephant on the outside and the heart of a dandelion on the inside — vulnerability with a hard shell. That's what it takes to make a career. (Wadsworth 1980:11)

Biographical accounts of singing careers all describe long and arduous years of study of musical scales to technically develop the voice. It is not unusual for a single note to take a singer three or more years to perfect. Of the thousands of singers that venture into an operatic career, only a few are successful, and a handful achieve international acclaim. To the opera performer, reliance on the voice means a precarious existence, wrought with anxiety. Pavarotti writes in his autobiography: "Suddenly I saw that I had conquered all my goals. There were no more obstacles, only the chance of failure." This led to a depression, which, fortunately, he overcame. The loneliness of success, and of self-consciousness — which is heightened for performers — are ever-present, though not often mentioned.

Singers are constantly on their guard against selecting roles which are inadequate for their vocal type. Some singers, especially in this jet age, sing artistically diverse roles in too short a time span. A diva of our time, Beverly Sills, having celebrated her retirement as a singer and assumed the administrative leadership of the New York City Opera, recalls how particular roles shortened her career, and led to the decline of her voice.

> I pushed my voice. "Devereux" shortened my career by three or four years, and I knew it when I picked it. But I would still go back to having those ten exciting years . . . . "Puritani" was medicine for my voice, like Handel was, but I wouldn't trade those "Normas" with Sarah Caldwell for anything else in my career. I paid the price, but I love the score. It was worth the

wear and tear on my voice. I don't regret those decisions (Jacobson 1980:10).

The star system is perpetuated by the artists, their managers, and their fans; critics and musical directors tend to express contempt for its vulgarity, its resulting vocal ostentation, and its financial costs. Critics and managers yearn for a true ensemble company in which music and drama seem perfectly interwined, without recourse to individual displays. Sills describes the atmosphere of the New York City Opera during her early days there:

> When I made my debut with the New York City Opera in 1955, it was a repertory company. That meant that everybody had to do everything — sometimes that were not appropriate at all. We had to act, because our roles were so often unsuited to our voices. But that was part of the job. When you're a utility singer, you don't have much choice. You sing everything they ask you to. Now it's altogether different. They pick the opera to go with the voice. (Sargeant 1973:99)

The star plays hard to get, demands and receives the highest fees, and is in a position to bargain for particular roles, time schedules, and final say over vocal and other artistic matters. He combines the ultimate in vocal technique, musicianship, and "personality." Bargaining power is contingent on his drawing power at the box office. Since there are only a handful of superstars, they are booked by houses around the world and scheduled two to three years in advance.

The symbols of status in the opera community include the extent of vocal range, the number of roles in a singer's repertoire, debuts at important opera houses around the world, extent of musicianship, technique, and style, community recognition, fees per performance and number of recordings. Singers who hold contracts with La Scala, the Metropolitan, and Covent Garden and who do private concert work and record, rate extremely high while those who rely on tour companies, annual contracts, opera workshops, and summer festivals do not have comparable prestige.

Luciano Pavarotti, in his autobiography, wrote of the importance of having successful debuts at San Francisco, Chicago's Lyric, and New York's Metropolitan.

> It is impossible to overestimate the importance of a success at the Met in the career of anyone hoping to reach the top of the operatic profession. Put most simply, it is almost impossible for a singer to have an important international career without making a resounding success at the Met (Pavarotti 1981).

Interaction among singers is inhibited by the rigors and schedules of their work. They view themselves as "professional," but the individual nature of the work and personal goals seem to negate collective goals and identification vis-à-vis each other. Goals are stated in terms of their own specific career goals, and in terms of the art form itself. Their informal codes, training, rivalry, etc., do constitute a subculture, but, unlike other occupational subcultures, it is unique in its sense of individuality and virtuosity.

The managers of opera houses dispense the symbols of status among the superstars and reward divas by casting them in new productions with top fees, first nights, premieres, and broadcasts, while excluding them from mundane travels, rehearsals, and other organizational routines. These rights and exemptions become the indicators of a singer's status and are vigorously sought after. The allocation of such status and prestige by management functions to control performers and reduce the conflict with management over the conditions of their employment, but it heightens disputes among the stars. Soloists rely on agents to negotiate their contracts with management, but in day-to-day relationships, management deals directly with the stars.

Singer Jess Thomas, commenting on his success and what it means to his personal career, wrote about those symbols that reflect a performer's status.

> One never arrives where he really wants to be, but I'm close now. I'm getting top fees at every house I appear in. I can afford to limit myself to about forty performances per year; that way I am good to the voice. It took a while to get here — I want to say [about seventeen years] (Klein 1971:17).

While the singer requires opera companies to produce operas, the organization is seen as a mere vehicle for advancing his or her own career. Singers see themselves as the most important part of the production. Since it is the singer's art form, it should produce works which are best suited to the singer's vocal range and abilities. The company, on the other hand, feels it provides high monetary and social remuneration, cult following, and great international prestige. These "external" rewards find meaning in the light of the unusually intense satisfaction derived from the activity itself. The singer's unwavering commitment to the art form functions to suppress some individual conflict. This, however, seems more appropriate for the comprimario, dancer, chorus member, instrumentalist, and administrative worker whose greater reward is the social identification with the organization instead of high payment. The long, intense and arduous training, vocal technique, nerve, skill, and personality seem to justify the demands for the high fees and glamour that superstars are accustomed to. They want to sing more popular works. Pleasing the fans seems to solve, for the singer, the "music for the masses" issue.

In a "star-oriented" society, the ideology of "service" and "high ideal" seems to work for the superstar only up to a point. After that the singer's demands seem justified because of management's reliance on the box office returns the star brings in. The nonprofit ideology is contradicted by the fact that artists view patrons as rich corporate executives rather than as middle class citizens who buy tickets.

While the manager supports the star system, he would generally prefer an ensemble or repertory company so as not to feel the constraints imposed by individual career choices, personal privileges, and the inflexibility generated by reliance on a handful of stars. The circumstances created by an almost slavish dependence on the star system in a society that must rely on the box office for its survival are inevitably, limiting. It is at the point when a singer's ability to sell tickets becomes evident, and management begins to provide symbols of status, that artists bargain with managers. One singer spoke of the situation in the following way:

> It's one thing to feel you're overpaying somebody and it's another thing to know that when you put that person on the roster the house will be sold out. This is very important . . . . Yeh what's the alternative. To kick Franco Corelli out, Birgit Nilsson, and Joan Sutherland. You're going to kick them out of the company to have ensemble. Then who's going to come to the Met! You've got to deal with all of these terms in a very practical way.

Fees are probably the most important and the most secret status symbol. Hearsay is that stars average about $6,000 per performance with a major company. Some figures reportedly exceed this amount. Fees reflect the artists' reputations and are justified by their ability to sell tickets. Covent Garden, for example, has more or less come to terms with the star system by engaging "guest artists" and raising ticket prices accordingly. Standard prices are maintained for performances by company artists who are not members of the international star circuit.

The manager makes repertoire and casting decisions as he bargains with stars. His choices are severely limited with regard to the superstars, on whom he must rely, since audiences come to hear "names" rather than an unusual interpretation of a rarely performed composition. Managers, therefore, program and schedule around these stars; new productions, premieres, galas, etc., are most certainly built on the availability, preferences, and vocal adaptability of available stars for the particular repertoire. Sills and Sutherland dominate the *bel canto* repertoire, while Nilsson delights the Wagnerites.

In a desperate attempt to routinize some aspects of the market, some opera companies have instituted the "stagione system," but jet travel has almost defeated such attempts. The stagione system goes hand in hand with "homeguard" favoritism in the casting of "utility" singers. These performers are able to cover, to go on tours on short notice, and are "dependable." This availability obligates management to cast them in major roles later in the season. Managers need to have such singers on hand.

A character tenor at the Metropolitan, explains the politics of casting and the ensuing rivalry among prima donnas.

> Then, of course, you have to combine all of these elements and create seasons out of them and without offending anybody, giving "La Traviata" to Madame A without offending Madame B, and to placate Madame B by giving her "La Boheme" and say to Madame C "I don't have enough "Bohemes" now but later in February, I'll give you a couple of "Butterflies." And then everybody is happy. This is, of course, a star house. All the divas and divos, and there are divos, get a little hard to handle.

With increasing prestige and notability, singers are able to demand particular roles and at convenient times to fit with their own engagements and concert work. One singer explains:

> As your reputation and prestige grow so does your ability to go in and bargain, saying, "I would like to sign with you next year but it would be nice if I had a new production of something . . . . " I think what determines what's going to be done is a handful of superstars who decide what they want to do.

He also comments on the importance of public tastes in determining what singers get to sing.

> Well, it all gets down to the public. If the star wants a specific opera, and the public wouldn't buy or won't go to it why then it doesn't make any difference what the star wants . . . ." Julius Caesar," . . . was really something avant-garde. . . . It really doesn't make sense, and, they're probably right, but Beverly Sills and Treigle wanted it. We were completely unprepared for the kind of response we got. It seems as though the public was starved for this kind of music so it was a big success.

Most singers are content with what they sing especially if they are given "popular" works that promote their personal recognition and public appeal. Horne said that, "The part [Elisabeth in "Tannhauser"] suits me, and I think it's marvelous, but it doesn't turn people on, so I'm glad it's going to be 'Carmen.' " Renata Scotto, on the other hand, resented being given less popular productions and angrily complained that, "For next year, they give me "Butterfly." I don't want to sing "Butterfly"! I know the public. They like me and want me in something different, something new." A superstar able to demand a particular singing partner beamed as she remarked, "The moment had arrived that I was waiting for. I could ask for "Puritani' in New Orleans . . . . Pavarotti will sing 'Puritani' or I won't sing. I made a deal for a choice of three tenors."

Singers control repertoire if they are in positions of power. There remains, however, another important dimension peculiar to the singer. Unique and individual styles are established not only by vocal ranges but also by particular artists. Callas revived the *bel canto* tradition, her present-day contemporaries being Sutherland and Sills. Their coloratura technique is undoubtedly rare and most admired by audiences who make comparisons with the "golden age" of singers. Such talent is rare, in great demand, and gives the possessor undisputed power in the game of opera politics. Price's "lyric-spinto" quality and Arroyo's more dramatic color are in great demand, especially for the Verdi repertoire, a favorite among audiences. One singer outlines the status hierarchy based on vocal range:

> If you're a dramatic tenor, you're in great demand. There are very few today. There always have been very few dramatic tenors so they're in demand all the time. If you happen to be a dramatic tenor who's 6'2" and handsome it makes you much more in demand . . . . The hierarchy would be the coloratura sopranos, the superstars, then the dramatic soprano, dramatic tenor, being able to draw people, having following, demand bigger fees; after dramatic tenors, you may come to spinto tenors. The lower voices generally are lower on the hierarchy, basses, and baritones and mezzos certainly don't mix with them. There are exceptions like Marilyn Horne who broke the rules . . . and Milnes as baritone, but generally this is the way the hierarchy is set up. [Why?] People hear coloratura doing vocal gymnastics and they're suddenly impressed even non-knowledgeable people in opera . . . . It's more spectacle, more showy.

Rivalry, feuding and jealousy between prima donnas must be understood in the light of the organizational setting. They are engaged in a struggle for prestige in a highly competitive system where top positions are scarce. Sudden indispositions, walk-outs, refusals to sign contracts, or disagreements over technical issues are symptoms of an individual quest for supremacy. These eruptions are not manifestations of whim or insignificant temper tantrums, but are a revealing aspect of the musical subculture. In reconfirming their superstar identity, stars maintain the traditions, folklore, myths, and values which are so much a part of the opera community and which set them apart from "outsiders." Economic conditions perpetuate a need for stars so that rivalry becomes a by-product of a tight, yet flexible, market.

The norms that condition the system of interrelationships and allow for the resolution of conflicts operate within the work context of the nonprofit structure and the performing art activity. Particular codes, informal rules, and professional ethics govern conflicts among colleagues. It is an unspoken rule that feuds and jealousies are not to be brought into the public domain, although they are disseminated through the musical subculture of fans, publicists, and sycophants in the form of idle rumor. The stars fear that the media will expose conflicts to the disadvantage of their careers or opera companies. The notoriety of the Bing-Callas controversy undoubtedly left many managers with the feeling that "no publicity is better than bad publicity."

Most artists also agree that conflicts over aesthetic interpretations should never appear to be resolved on the basis of self-interest. The score and text usually dictate what is best for the total production. This allows for maximum flexibility in the performing arts organization. Intense, intimate and competitive work conditions foster a kinship setting within which gossip flourishes but where there is also an unusually high regard to secrecy. Fees, contracts, and other colleagues are not publicly discussed and a performer remains neutral in discussions concerning colleagues. In spite of the intimate nature of the work setting, close friendships are rare.

Memoirs and folklore show prima donnas to be temperamental and opinionated, especially when roles which are unsuited to their voices are being considered. Disagreements appear to take place over technical and superficial issues such as dressing rooms, hotel suites, and, years ago, over railroad cars. Today, we hear of more disputes with other singers, conductors, directors, and managers over particular production techniques and interpretations. The greatest hostility is toward the management of major opera houses, because of schedules, time demands, and role assignment. Leontyne Price describes one situation which almost inevitably leads to disagreement between a singer and management.

> Relations between singers and impresarios of opera houses are
> always strained. They really don't like each other. They act like

sulky children. This is because the impresario is primarily concerned with getting the show on the road, regardless of the strain
that might be involved for any particular artist. Often the artist
feels that he has been singing too much, or that he would prefer
not to sing a certain role in the shape his voice is in. And the
manager overrules him. That doesn't make for absolutely smooth
relationships (Sargeant 1973:159).

Marilyn Horne addresses another difficulty, the particular vocal
requirements of certain parts.

The tessitura of the part [Carmen] is somewhat disruptive vocally.
It is low and it can't keep the high vocal range oiled. It is necessary
to keep using the voice, so one can keep it in good shape . . . . If
you don't use it for a while, you get nervous about it . . . . The
trick is to leave it for a while . . . . While Rossini is medicine for
the voice (WQXR 1973).

Rivalry has helped some careers especially due to the publicity
it creates and the added role that fans and sycophants play in supporting and perpetuating such rivalry. One is reminded of the Leh-
mann and Jeritza dispute in Vienna and Tebaldi's famous statement:
"I was lucky I had the greatest press agent in the world — Callas!"
One of Callas' more adoring biographers comments that the greater
the artist and her success, the more bitter her rivals.

The more successful she was, the more resentful her rivals became. The public itself, almost ready to enjoy such rivalries, helps
much in creating them . . . . As both prima donnas were now
appearing consecutively during the season at La Scala, the public
took it for granted that they were bitter rivals. Sections of the
public would on many occasions show their preferences for one
or the other singers (Galatopoulos 1973).

Sargeant wrote of Nilsson that she doesn't speak of or mingle with
Sutherland, probably because she's her only competitor as top prima
donna in the world.

Those who support the star system often claim that this is what
opera is all about and that memorable performances are those in
which singers are compared and perform unusually well. In an interesting article entitled, "The Star System: Curse or Coup," Gilson
followed this argument.

If, in performance, a part is more exciting than the performer,
the enthusiastic opera lover will find it preferable to listen to

records . . . . Conductors and singers can and do mold and change a work. One cannot talk or write of it without considering the performers. To the opera-goer who knows the music of a work he is to see, it is the performance that will make the difference between a routine evening and one that becomes history (1972:20).

By examining the organizational structure of opera, the relative merits of the star system and the ensemble company can be better understood in terms of interrelationships among performers. Conflict arises because the singer believes in vocal virtuosity, which takes the form of holding notes, inserting different tempos and coloratura passages, and altering staging and other dramatic specifics — all contrary to the goals of the director, manager, or conductor.

Joan Sutherland, a singer, comments on noteholding characteristic of the *bel canto* style.

> I think there were a lot of vulgarities that crept in, I don't mean holding notes too long and that sort of thing — I'm a great noteholder myself, and I don't think I'm vulgar — but some ornamentation of the golden age was excessive. People walked in and out of the registers of the voice. There was a lot of indiscriminate gear changing. (Sargeant 1973:45)

Yet another soprano, Irene Gubrand, views her freedom in this area as due to the demands made by particular audiences: During a radio interview, she remarked:

> It depends what the audience expects of you . . . go to D flat in "Medea" . . . . I was expected to in Mexico City. The first thing that I was asked because Callas did it. . . . I try to follow the conductor's lead. I will not go against the conductor . . . or if it's not musical. Certainly, I will not do it in New York . . . . We're at the age where the conductor and stage director dictate everything and the singer follows into a mold and you have a certain sameness sometimes creeping in . . . . If it's going to make that much of a controversy, the conductor is still the one you have to go with. I mean he is in control. You are the singer and without you there's no opera, that's true . . . . It does cause excitement, [noteholding], if I felt it was right, I would do it . . . . You do have a certain significant part of the public that are opera going people and they know what they want. And the performer . . . if you have, you should sometimes exploit it.

Nevertheless, a singer who is known solely for vocal display is regarded as lacking in musicianship and is frowned upon. Pavarotti,

The photographs on these pages represent the impact stage choreography has had on the singer. The photograph on the facing page shows Olive Fremstad as Salome in a 1907 production at the Met. Over seventy years later, obvious changes in acting, costuming, and scenery have occurred. Shown above in Strauss's "Salome" is Grace Bumbry (Metropolitan Opera Archives)

a leading tenor, reacts to a favorable review of his Tonio in "La Fille du Regiment."

> I was happy that Harold Schonberg of the *Times* praised my lyrical second-act aria more than the first-act one with the high C's. I want to be known as a tenor of line, not a tenor of the top. That is what I work for (Phillips 1973:24).

Disputes with conductors over the importance of tempo arise when singers feel conductors rush the music, making it difficult to progress from one phrase to another, or when they make the music too slow, causing a shortness of breath, or when playing too loud overshadows the singer by fortissimos. Sutherland commented on a dispute she had over tempos.

> "There was one of those little squabbles that shouldn't get into the papers," she said. "It was a question of tempos. I wanted the tempo of Maestro Serafin, with whom I had sung the part. The Fenice conductor wanted it different. I still maintain that he was wrong. He was very rude to me — he said, 'Madame, I am the conductor here' — and he was very rude to the chorus master also. A bad match." Miss Sutherland walked out after this occurrence and has never sung with that conductor again. She was insisting on a prerogative dating from the *bel canto* period — that a singer must set his own tempos according to his breathing capacity and his current feeling about his agility in fioritura, and that it is the conductor's duty to follow. (Sargeant 1973:31)

Robert Merrill felt that a good conductor and director:

> . . . should understand the artists. Know singers' capabilities. How far can he go. Know voice limitations and work around it. A good musical director and conductor must let the artist do what comes naturally first, then comment and help . . . , shouldn't say do this and that . . . , because you will not get that far with artists. We are all different . . . we're built differently.

Alternatives were discussed in interviews regarding the resolutions of conflicts. To some extent they vary with individuals and, more importantly, with the status of the individual. A disputing party may either try to convince the other person "amiably," as co-workers, or they may refuse to work with the person. Depending upon the status and popularity of the complainant, a manager may engage another conductor to work with Nilsson or Sutherland or another singer to work with Zeffirelli. The star system, the star's relative position in the market, the availability of vocal range, and specific opera house requirements, may play a part in resolving disputes. One tenor confirms this.

> Certain directors like Visconti, Zeffirelli, De Sica, or Ustinov and not with giants as Karajan would get their way. . . . It's a matter of personality. Who has more weight. Sometimes the singer. You can't force Nilsson to do anything she doesn't want to do. Even if it is Zeffirelli or Karajan. He doesn't use Nilsson anymore . . . . She told Karajan to go. She doesn't need him.

A conflict between the designer Josef Svoboda and Marilyn Horne was over the extensive amount of carpeting used to cover the stage floor as scenery. Fearing the carpeting would absorb the sound, and demanding that the prompter's box (which was covered up by the carpet) be reinstated, the singer became furious, and the artistic director had to intervene. Phillips writes of this disruption:

> The previous day's mini-explosion had two direct results: (1) a prompter's box (dubbed, by the less reverent, the "Marilyn Horne Memorial Prompter's Box") was assured and the necessary scissors work was done on the carpet; (2) all observers were barred from attending rehearsals for the next three days. It was decided that since an outsider had been privy to a scene of relatively high tension, it would be wiser for him to keep a low profile. Also pushed into exile were all photographers and anyone else of a remotely journalistic stripe. (1973:64)

The performing aspect of this type of organization creates demands on its personnel that account for the not uncommon high level of anxiety among artists. Recurrent changes in programs and already hectic schedules are the norm. Routine for the creative personnel is almost nonexistent. Individuals who consciously encourage and nurture individuality and are aware of themselves as vanguards, pose particular problems for the organization. In a real sense, conflict functions to fulfill narcissistic needs and allows the organization its necessary on-going development. Conflict functions to maintain superstar identity. It is an integral part of the "creative" environment and deeply embedded in subcultural norms. The organization has to allow, even foster, competition, without forfeiting musicianship. There is constant give and take while diverse ideas are integrated so that a given "conception" cannot be seen as the contribution of a single individual, but as the product of both front and backstage personnel, *performing and nonperforming.*

Marilyn Horne, in discussing her "Carmen," during a radio interview, points to the difficulty of crediting specific individuals with certain aspects of a production.

> That becomes difficult to say because somebody may throw out an idea and by the time you grasp it, and you decide that you'll do it, it's almost by then instinctive. It's very difficult to say. I told you before that I'm an instinctive actress and a lot of times it doesn't work. There is something about opera that is terribly important and that is, you are reacting to what people say around you and if you could constantly listen and have a fresh approach . . . that keeps your performance fresh . . . . Its changed a lot since opening night [of "Carmen"].

Sargeant in his biography of five reigning divas recounts a petty argument that Sills had with a costume mistress. It is enlightening in that it reveals the respect she gained by her defiance, an act which, by the way, was considered appropriate.

> Thenceforth, Miss Sills was regarded with awe backstage, as well as on the other side of the footlights. She was recognized as a true diva, and, needless to say, she got her silver costume. When the performance of "The Siege of Corinth" was over, she had become what in operatic circles is called a superstar. She immediately tripled her fees and started the superstar's formula . . . of limiting her future engagements. No longer could Beverly Sills be expected to sing in places like Shreveport or Garden City. Only the world's greatest opera houses would be worthy of her, and they would want her in the roles for which she was most famous . . . . The display of temper during the rehearsal at La Scala was, of course, not the real source of her climb to superstardom. But, in a way, it symbolized the achievement. (1973:79)

Habitual display of temperament can be further understood, given the nature of the art form. The unique career patterns of soloists today, the precarious conditions of the market, and the reliance on the physical good health of the human body cause the "stage fright" syndrome, superstition, and anxiety among performers. Training is long; commitment is "vocational;" success is won by luck and preparedness. This calls for personal defenses which rivalries and temperament manifest. Setbacks and failures are inevitable and feuds may well serve as rhetoric for such failures. Misfortunes are superstitiously accounted for by the "evil eye" of competitors. Artists, in addition, develop an unusual ability for self-evaluation, often becom-

Puccini's "Tosca" has had 474 performances by the Met since 1883!
Dorothy Kirsten astounded audiences by singing the famous
aria, "Vissi d'arte," in this dramatic position, 1964
(Metropolitan Opera Archives)

ing their own critics. This aggravates their anxiety and further sets them apart from "outsiders."

Although we have seen that the conductor and director have assumed the position of authority, we have implicitly assumed that their supremacy was facilitated by the declining influence of the composer in opera houses which continue to perform the works of past composers. However, the view that the musical score is sancrosanct, and that the diverse elements should strive towards some form of "gesamtkuntswerk" has served, on an aesthetic level, to provide a framework for discussion of artistic matters.

The Star System and the Resolution of Conflict

The attitudes of the major artists — composer, conductor, director, designer, and singer — toward their work govern the system of relationships and affect the integration of the various aspects of production. The discord between the operatic subculture and the organizational structure stems from the fact that the power structure within the organization is based on the character of organizational tasks. These tasks reflect the performance requirements of opera. It has been shown how long established traditions (and feuds) affect the process of the production from rehearsal to a performance. The nature of the art form itself (whether perceived as a singer's art form, or as total musical theater), determines the status of one performer over another. The status of the artist is reflected in organizational tasks, and becomes the basis for resolving conflicts among each other, or with management.

Opera has always been a battleground for different elements of music, but these battles are resolved within the framework of programming where economic forces dominate. Disputes among major soloists over musical interpretation, drama and voice, and orchestration and staging are expressions of the personal goals of those who must rely on a commercially-oriented organization. The star system, with its inherent rivalries sustains the superstar status and distinguishes the individual artist from "outsiders," i.e., managers, audiences, and publicists who are regarded ambivalently.

Rivalries, feuds, and conflicts in this highly competitive system are not mere idiosyncracies of creative temperament. They reflect the importance placed on colleague evaluations and the need for self-respect. Were it not for such conflicts, superstar identity could not be maintained. In a competitive system, where rewards are great but granted to few, conflicts are used to assert supremacy. Defying authority, breaking contracts, and ignoring technical demands of peers and administrators is a form of resistance to formal controls. To some extent, these conflicts are tolerated in order to insure the evolving nature of the performing arts organization.

The display of temperament by prima donnas — be they singers, conductors, composers, or directors — has been encouraged by the history of opera. Rumor and folklore have contributed to the mystery of the "diva." This seems to prevail more in opera than in other professional circles. In a subculture which lacks routinized rules of succession, in which status is individually and precariously held, and which boasts no leadership, conflicts are inevitable.[2]

The star performer confronts the organization in encounters with the impresario-manager of major opera houses who need superstars for box office successes. Artists who realize their position are able to bargain for "rewards" which reflect their status in the international circuit. Singers, conductors, directors, and composers view themselves as embodying and fulfilling the highest ideals of a performing art, creativity and individuality. The managers say they also strive for these goals, but they are faced with increasing production costs and an income source which has reached its optimum. They must concern themselves with maintaining the organization. Clashes among artists have been kept to a minimum in recent years through the interpretation of opera as "ensemble" or "gesamtkuntswerk." The individual with virtuoso talent has been devalued, and the prestige of conductors and directors has increased. Perhaps the "seniority" system, the recruitment process, and rehearsals have prevented further conflicts.

Superstars do not concern themselves with administrative functions; and do not need the economic and occupational security that identification with the organization could provide. They remain above such mundane matters. They possess something that only a handful of individuals has and which top opera houses around the world compete for. They have come to terms with the organization by maintaining their identity through the rivalry system, while the organization fulfills the "recreative" goals.

Notes

[1]Reis 1947:203. See also, Nash 1952; Bensman and Gerver 1958; Pleasants 1970; and Henahan 1973.

[2]For a discussion of operatic feuds at the turn of the century, see: Wagner 1961; Alda 1937; Gatti-Casazza 1941.

In 1962, the Lyric Opera of Chicago successfully ventured
into the Russian repertoire. Borodin's
"Prince Igor" featured bass Boris Christoff,
dancers Sonia Arova and Rudolph Nureyev,
and conductor Oskar Danon
(Lyric Opera of Chicago)

7 The Structure of the Market and the Social Organization of Opera

This study concludes by assembling the arguments and inferences made throughout the earlier chapters and re-examining the thesis stated in the introduction, as to the socio-economic effects on the style, organization, and content of opera, on the role of performers, and the nature of the social organization which results from the structure of opera.

The "bureaucratization" of the arts was brought about through increasing specialization, unionization of artists, an international market of performers, the construction of huge art centers, and a shift from private to public philanthropy. All of these forces have contributed to the consolidation of opera into two major categories: a few large "commercial" companies supported by mass audiences, and university departments devoted to training and the performance of experimental and avant-garde works. Since the large companies are dependent on box office returns and private patronage, they cannot afford the losses that would be incurred in producing "unpopular" works.

Opera has indeed become a grandiose economic phenomenon involving a complex web of relationships between the artist, his work, and his public. The performer is, in effect, a member of a number of organizations besides the company that engages him, including publishing houses, recording companies, unions, and public relations firms. The significant individuals in his career are his colleagues, coaches, teachers, managers, conductors, and critics. This study has been concerned with these elements of opera only insofar as they affect the producing companies.

Opera companies, like other organizations, function through the interaction of the various elements of their institutional environment whenever decisions must be made, and this environment affects organizational structure and effectiveness. (Hirsch 1975:327) The opera organization's nonprofit base entails high risk and uncertainties which must be dealt with. Institutional mechanisms of the environment, which affect opera organizations, and over which they have no control, include inflation, union demands and a generally conservative opera public. Administrators reduce the threat of instability, and attempt to establish organizational stability, by lessening the constraints created by the institutional environment. Organizations in this situation attempt to seek alternatives for both internal and external resources. By gaining prestige, for example, an opera company can be placed in a more powerful position vis-á-vis their environments. (Thompson 1967)

Consequently, at the organizational level, "effectiveness" is achieved by controlling the uncertainties of the market (which include the costs of production and box office receipts). This is best accomplished by selecting casts and repertoire that fill the house (new repertoire is rarely introduced), developing a "covering" system of "ensemble" singers which insures good replacements for absent superstars, and persuading government agencies and private individuals to fund the arts and expand their support.

The opera organization has been affected by the constraints imposed by its environment, and as a result companies which produce opera have attempted to adapt to such market mechanisms. There is no doubt that the prestige and societal importance of art, and the performance of artistic expression, are of paramount importance, in maintaining effectiveness. The organizations, looked at in this study, are the largest and most prestigious within the United States, and, therefore, monopolize its limited resources and whatever national commitment there may be to this art form. While the Metropolitan is the largest, possessing a deficit equal to the combined budgets of the other companies, its sheer size and prestige enable it to attract more government funds, launch more extensive advertising campaigns, and maintain a higher level of legitimacy.

This discussion cannot be concluded without arguing that the pervasiveness of "rationality" is the sole basis for decision making. Internal effectiveness means accomplishing goals — in this case, producing opera at the highest possible artistic level. The organizational hierarchy, its tasks and its internal effectiveness are governed by this goal. Star performers occupy powerful positions, in contrast to "organization" men, who function to make the organization more stable and on-going. The respected manager is one who can generate creativity in the delegation of organizational tasks and achieve organizational effectiveness by a high performance level.

In the nineteenth century, music and the arts were characterized by virtuosity and individualism; the twentieth century is marked by the increasing influence of the collective over the individual. The socio-economic conditions of the market facilitated professionalization — the growth of specialties from composer-performer, singer, conductor, stage director and art administrator.

As opera became a part of a large organizational complex, managers with technical expertise in coordinating, administering, and maintaining the fiscal balance of these organizations became an essential part of opera production. The increased influence of art managers and board members is in direct proportion to the size of the organization. Large middle class audiences and a private system of patronage have produced changes in the status and roles of artists and in the content and styles of opera. As audiences came to revere the virtuoso performer, the position of the composer declined, and operas that allowed the expression of virtuosity became part of the standard repertoire. The works of Verdi, Puccini, Rossini, and Wagner came to be performed excessively in the leading houses.

The New York City Opera has attempted to produce a greater variety of works by presenting more works less frequently, but even there the tendency in the last few years has been to present more and more works from the "standard" repertoire. Economic conditions seem to be the dominant force in determining repertoire selections.

Since there is little diversity in the selection of repertoire and little commissioning of new works, the way operas are produced becomes most important. Staging, lighting, orchestration, and acting have become the tools for recreating and reinterpreting works of the past. With this development, the conductor and stage director gained both prestige and authority. Audiences come to hear singers, while stage directors and conductors provide dramatic changes in the old standards. A taste for the spectacular and the modernization of stage technology have facilitated this trend, performance has come to mean creative interpretation.

Since stars mean greater box office returns, their bargaining power is high, and a wide range of behavior is tolerated and even expected. The artists use the star system to define and confirm their identities and as a device to fight the "system." The structure of the musical subculture sustains self-definitions which may conflict with the management of the opera organization. The development of air travel made opera international. Competition among stars takes the form of vying for particular roles that they have sung around the world. Engaging a singer for a season or for several years was a phenomenon of the first quarter of the twentieth century. Small companies and municipal opera companies in Europe do not compete on an international level with the major opera houses of the world.

In addition to conflicts between artists and management, there are aesthetic struggles between the various elements in opera — between libretto and score, voice and instrument, conductor and singer, musical line and orchestration.

Wagner argued for a total integration of the score, music, voice, and orchestra. Yet, in the past, it was the emphasis on the orchestral score over all other elements that dominated and determined musicianship and excellence in artistic standards. Today the emphasis is on total effect, but the major effort is in staging to provide a total sensation for the audience. The music is devalued. Changes are introduced to keep the same audiences returning to see the same operas season after season.

At present, however, all energy seems to go toward incorporating new developments in lighting and stagecraft and developing few experiences for the audience. These innovations are not innovations in opera as a musical form; they are undertaken primarily with reference to the restaging and redesigning of "dead" opera. Wagner's total opera was a creation in music in all its elements. The "total" opera of the present is only an innovation in staging. Genuinely creative work in the development of the opera is done outside the major opera companies. This limits the development of opera that is creative in its essential forms.

The battle among opera's various components continues but, unlike the past, the battle is primarily over reproduction or recreation. Because of economic conditions, creativity in opera is hidden away at the universities. Communication between contemporary opera and an audience is limited. The world of the opera has split in two. One is a world of virtuoso production and the other a world of living but sometimes uncommunicative creation. These two worlds do not form a basis for opera as a living force presenting new ideas to an audience.

Future Research

With the design of the Great Society cast in the 1960s, the arts expanded. However, like their counterparts in the social services, the arts have not been able to fulfill the rising level of expectations. Its non-profit base has left companies so economically unstable that they are incapable of absorbing any errors from risky, innovative, or experimental productions. Although public funding for the arts has increased, it has reached its maximum, and continues to be the smallest source of income. Unfortunately, the rise of neo-conservatism in the United States, in affecting all public funding, will be consequential to the arts as well.

The economic crisis of opera has led its supporters to emphasize the social utility of opera and social utility is often defined in extra-artistic, extra-cultural, extra-aesthetic terms. Opera, music, and the other arts have proven that no such justification is necessary. If the justifications force the producers of opera to devalue that which is intrinsic to an on-going living opera, then government subsidies do not guarantee a living operatic tradition. Opera can be usable today only if the eighteenth and nineteenth century traditions of creating and producing opera, that are directly meaningful to on-going audiences, can be revived. Otherwise, opera will remain a museum to the art of the nineteenth century, or an aesthetic cult anxious to belong to a very small elite.

Few sociologists have analyzed the role of the creative person in an organization, and so we must look to the development of mechanisms that foster creativity and innovation. Udy (1962), for example, suggests that rationality declines as organizations become more socially involved, and when patterns of stratification reflect occupational-professional prerequisites rather than organizational hierarchy. Guetzkow (1965) dedicates his research to the analysis of the creative person within industry. Among the mechanisms he addresses are explanations of how industry decentralizes authority and decision-making; opens channels of communication; stimulates ideas, research, experimentation, and brainstorming; creates hetereogeneous personnel policies; assigns non-specialists to problems; takes risks; and ensures organizational security and autonomy. Artistic organizations should exemplify such mechanisms, and, rather than seek them, assume them and take them for granted.

In a very real sense, we are once again reminded of the consequence of the "disenchantment of the world." Art, along with mystery and magic, is disappearing. Certainly, modern man is less concerned with value, symbolic meaning, and artistic expression and creation. On a less philosophical level, we can investigate practical means of inhibiting the rationalization process in the arts. Greater analysis and understanding of the non-profit structure can, it is hoped, create the organizational security in which greater freedom, alternatives and risks can exist. We must also look to the recruitment of artists and performers as administrators, and we must build such structural vehicles into occupational recruitment and socialization.

Appendix A

Methods

Historical Material

Historical and current material related to operas and opera production, personal documents, opera company records, press releases, editorials, criticisms, and biographies were searched for evidence of the attitudes and issues of debate within the musical community. While I am aware of the disadvantages of the use of personal documents, such material lent itself not only to descriptive analysis but to the content and nature of this research. It was helpful in gaining familiarity with the area, in focusing on a research problem, and in formulating and validating interview material and findings. In the field of music it is necessary to understand past virtuosos and traditions since they are so much a part of the present folklore and vocabulary. Given the paucity of sociological studies in this field, it became necessary to rely heavily on journalistic material.

The Interview and Participant-Observation

Interviews and participant-observation were the techniques found most suitable considering the nature of the study and the subjects involved. They have been the most time-consuming and yet the most valuable source of information.

The specific duration of observation could not be determined at the outset. At times, I felt saturated with data, and resorted to interviews and other research. Participant-observation included work as a supernumerary and in an administrative department at one of the major opera houses. Observations proved essential especially in the preliminary stages of this investigation, and were supplemented by intermittent questions and interview collecting.

The Sample

The names below represent many of the elite of the New York and international musical community. The criteria for selection have been based on celebrity, specialty, career patterns, and vocal range. Their availability became a determining factor in who became part of the final sample. (See bibliography for the date and time of each interview.)

Managers and Directors:

Boris Goldovsky, Goldovsky Opera Company
John Gutman, Metropolitan Opera Association
Sol Hubay, Metropolitan Opera Association
Herman Krawitz, Director, Davis Performing Arts Center, City
    University of New York
Mary Peltz, Metropolitan Opera Archives
Maria Rich, Central Opera Service
Francis Robinson, Metropolitan Opera Association
Daniel Rule, New York City Opera

Conductor:

Kurt Adler, Metropolitan Opera Association

Critics and Journalists:

Harriet Johnson, *New York Post*
Stephen Rubin, *The New York Times*, Stereo Review
Harold C. Schonberg, *The New York Times*

Personal Representatives and Managers:

Peter Gravina
Joseph Lippman
Alix Williamson

Singers:

Nico Castel
Dominic Cossa
Clara Friedman
Robert Merrill
Thelma Altman

Interview material broadcast on the radio, appearing in newspapers, and taped at seminars and gatherings of singers was utilized
as a source of data and represents the secondary interview material
cited throughout this study. The following artists have been included:

Sopranos

   Maria Callas
   Phyllis Curtin
   Reri Grist
   Evelyn Lear
   Leontyne Price
   Beverly Sills
   Joan Sutherland
   Renata Tebaldi

Mezzo-Sopranos:

   Marilyn Horne
   Christa Ludwig

Baritones:

   Ezio Flagello
   Norman Treigle

Conductors:
   Leonard Bernstein
   Piere Boulez
   Rafael Kubelik
   James Levine
   Michael Tilson Thomas

Tenors

   Franco Corelli
   Guiseppe diStefano
   Placido Domingo
   Nicolai Gedda
   James McCracken
   Barry Morell
   Luciano Pavarotti
   Jan Pierce
   George Shirley
   Richard Tucker

Managers and Directors:

   Kurt Herbert Adler
   Amyas Ames
   Rudolph Bing
   Schuyler Chapin
   Julius Rudel

Composers:

   Aaron Copland
   Gian Carlo Menotti
   Virgil Thomson

Interview Questions

The following questions were utilized and varied depending on the
person being interviewed. They became guidelines for discussion and
were not necessarily strictly adhered to. Both the time available and
the status of the respondent made each interview situation unique
and different. In no way do they reflect the order in which they were
asked. They include questions on working conditions, relationships
with colleagues, career contingencies, training, biographies, and the
determination of aesthetic norms.

Singers:

Career questions: How did you enter the field of music? What was the best advice given you along the way? Is there a specific event which was most important in your career?

What are the most important characteristics for singer/ conductor/director/ and manager of a large opera house?

What kinds of things are negotiated in a contract?

On the Company: How do working conditions at the ——— compare to those in other countries? How did you prepare for the ———? Did you have any problems or difficult adjustment? Give examples. Are there particular roles you would like to perform and sing? How would you go about getting them? Who decides what you sing? How are relations between general manager and director being defined?

Basis of conflicts: How do the ensemble and star approaches to opera differ? What are the trends in opera today? Who and what determines them? How are ideas worked out? How do you feel about the stage director's role today? Chapin's quote on the Met as a repertory theater means what to you? What does ensemble mean?

Can you describe the different roles of the manager, the director, and the conductor?

How is a given interpretation arrived at? Who and what contributes toward making a concept? What is the worst thing that a conductor, or director, or manager could impose on you?

Are there conflicts? Over what issues do they usually arise? How are the different segments of opera enmeshed and worked out in a production? How are the conflicts resolved? Who has final say? Give examples.

Does the fact that there are so many elements, which must be coordinated and organized in a company, itself affect opera and the style? What factors, circumstances, management, production, etc. affect style?

How important is promotion and publicity? How does this affect one's career? Is a star chosen at the expense of musical standards in that they stress individual talent and virtuosity over "ensemble"?

Do you think opera is important in America today?

Who or what is the most important element in a production and why?

Which singers, conductors, critics, managers, and directors have you admired in the past and why? Who has affected your career most and in what ways?

Is the audience reaction important to you and why? Are fans different today than they were in the past? How? Do you feel they set artistic standards?

Are there any do's and don'ts in your profession?

Are you satisfied with your working conditions?

What does a working ensemble mean to you or to a repertory company?

What do you think about bowing rules? New casting rules and the stagione system?

How is the balance between the drama and song arrived at? How do the conductor, singer, director and manager, affect your interpretation of this? Are there major differences between you and any of them? What is the difference between German, Viennese, and Italian styles?

Is there a star system? Who would you say is at the top within the opera community? What is the basis for the position? Who determines stardom, the audience, fans, critics, or managers? Is the star system important today and why?

Do you feel that opera has become standardized into something that is the business of tastemakers — managers, press, critics — rather than the artists? If so, to what extent and in what ways? Give examples.

What changes would you make, if any, in your profession?

How did you become a recognized singer? What does success include?

Do you think opera stresses individual talents?

Is the star system the antithesis of musical standards? How does it conflict with production goals?

Once you have become a star, do you always have to live up to that standard?

How have mass communications affected your career? What role does publicity play in opera and what for the artist today?

What are the essential qualities of a star, other than voice? Do artists feel overwhelmed by scenery, singers, costumes and staging?

Managers:

With what aspects of opera have you been most concerned? Innovations, goals, priorities, repertoire?

What are the advantages of the stagione system? Can it happen in America today?

Kolodin wrote that Bing had created an administration that could function regardless of who was in command. What is your reaction to this analysis of the Bing regime?

Has the deficit affected repertoire and casting decisions? If so, in what ways?

What are you doing to improve relationships between management and the staff?

It has been said that, in order to survive, any organization in America must succumb to rigors of routinization and bureaucratization. How does this affect artistic goals?

Why are opera companies criticized for not being adventuresome? What causes this?

How do you cope with personal feelings and emotions when they arise?

How do you define a good administrative leader in the arts' field?

Is there a channel for the flow of ideas in the opera organization? How does it work?

What aspects of opera production interest you most? How did you enter the field of opera?

What are the essential qualities for singers, conductors, directors and managers?

What works would you personally like to produce?

Have you participated in the commissioning of new works? How does this work?

Why is there such an emphasis on ensemble and theater today? What factors contribute to this?

Have you ever tried to resolve conflicts? Give examples.

How is a given interpretation arrived at? What determines aesthetic norm? Who contributes to it? Do you find that your interpretation differs from artists?

How do all the components, personalities, management, decision-making, finances, techniques, styles, and casting, affect a production?

How do boards make their decisions?

Is it easier to coordinate activity for companies committed to ensemble and, if so, why?

Critics:

Is there a difference between reporting, journalism and music criticism?

Who is your audience?

In a recent article, Scotto said————. What is your reaction to this?

The recent discussion over the problems confronted with the "Siegfried" production reflects conflicts over musical interpretation, casting, etc. Do you agree?

I would also like you to comment on the "acting" approach in opera and the recent debate on Corsaro's method and approach.

Henahan said regarding the paying of prima donnas ————. Do you agree or not?

To what extent do the boards support the star system and repertoire?

What is the most essential quality of a singer, conductor, director, manager or critic? Who is your ideal in each category? Can you say what characterizes the most famous of these?

Personal Managers and Press Agents:

How would you define your function and job in the musical world today? What do you do in a typical day? How does your job differ from that of a press representative? What led you to this specialization?

What are the essential qualities for a manager, for a star?

In what areas are you most helpful to your client? What factors are important in negotiating a contract?

What do singers want stipulated in their contracts? What is the difference between a star's contract and a comprimario's?

Which factors determine a successful booking?

Have particular critics made and broken careers? Give examples.

Do you think opera has been standardized?

What is the relationship between the press, the manager, and the individual artist?

What changes would you make in your profession? Has it changed over the past twenty years? How?

Both Wilford and Henahan have commented that artists are overpaid. What is your opinion?

How has your job been affected by the mass media? And by the organizations of managers?

How does the serious artist fit into today's glamour-oriented musical and entertaining world?

Interviews

Personal:

Adler, Kurt Herbert, November 1, 1972. 8–9:30 p.m.
Altman, Thelma, March 16, 1981, 11:00 a.m.–12 p.m.
Castel, Nico, December 28, 1972. 9:15–10:30 p.m.
Cossa, Dominic, January 4, 1973. 12:30–1:30 p.m.
Friedman, Clara, November 27, 1971. 10:30–12:15 a.m.
Goldovsky, Boris, January 12, 1973. 11:00 a.m.–12:00 p.m.
Gravina, Peter, April 15, 1973. 2:00–2:45 p.m.
Gutman, John, July 31, 1973. 11:30–12:30 a.m.
Hadley, William, March 17, 1973. 1:00–2:00 p.m. and July 18, 1973. 10:30–11:15 a.m.
Hubay, Alfred, August 7, 1973. 11:00 a.m.–12:00 p.m.
Johnson, Harriet, January, 1973. 5:00–7:00 p.m.
Krawitz, Herman, March 19, 1973. 11:00 a.m.–12:00 p.m.

Lippman, Joseph, February 15, 1973. 3:30–5:00 p.m.
Merrill, Robert, August 2, 1973.
Peltz, Mary, December 8, 1971. 11:00 a.m.–12:30 p.m.
Rich, Maria, April 15, 1973. 1:00–2:30 p.m. and March 12, 1981 11 a.m.–12 p.m.
Robinson, Francis, December 3, 1971. 3:00–4:30 p.m.
Rubin, Stephen, November 27, 1973. 2:15–4:15 p.m. and December 7, 1971. 12:00–1:30 p.m.
Rule, Daniel, March 6, 1973. 10:00–11:00 a.m.
Schonberg, Harold, November, 1972. 4:00–5:15 p.m.
Williamson, Alix, December 27, 1972. 4:00–5:15 p.m.
Yellin, Florence, August 18, 1971. 3:00–5:00 p.m.

Radio:

Adler, Kurt Herbert, WQXR, February 7, 1974.
Bing, Rudolph, WQXR, December 31, 1971.
Bokey, Collette, WQXR, December 1, 1972.
Boulez, Pierre, WQXR, June 11, 1973.
Foss, Lucas, WQXR, January 4, 1973.
Chapin, Schuyler, WQXR, "Opera News On The Air", December 9, 1972 (with C. Riecker, W. Hadley, F. Robinson and M. Bronson.)
Corsaro, Frank, WQXR, (with G. Tozzi), November 16, 1972.
Forrester, Judith, WQXR, January 10, 1973; April, 1973.
Galvany, Marisa, WQXR, June 19, 1973.
Gubrand, Irene, WQXR, November 13, 1972.
Hawkins, Stanley, WQXR, February 3, 1973.
Horne, Marilyn, WQXR, July 6, 1973; July 11, 1973; July 12, 1973.
Jellinick, George, WQXR, February 5, 1973.
Levine, James and Gedda, Nicolai, WQXR, April 11, 1973.
von Stade, Federica, WQXR, February 5, 1973.
Merrill, Robert, and Richard Tucker, WNYC, June 25, 1973.
Milnes, Sherrill, WQXR, June 12, 1972.
Moffo, Anna, WQXR, August 12, 1971.
Williamson, Alix, WQXR, January 14, 1973.
Pavarotti, Luciano, WQXR, January 5, 1972.
Price, Leontyne, WQXR, December 20, 1971.
Rudel, Julius, WQXR, June 20, 1973.
Schuman, William, WQXR, April 18, 1973.
Tebaldi, Renata, WNYC, October 1, 1972.
Thomas, Virgil, WQXR, November 23, 1971, and February 7, 1973.
Verdy, Violette, WQXR, May, 1973.
Verett, Shirley, WQXR, March 8, 1973.

Seminar (Conducted at New York University):

Boulez, Pierre, Spring 1971.
Copland, Aaron, March 7, 1973.
Curtin, Phyllis, October 13, 1971.
MacCracken, James, October 27, 1971.
Merrill, Robert, November 3, 1971.
Peerce, Jan, October 20, 1971.
Sills, Beverly, November 12, 1971.
Warfield, Sandra, October 2, 1971.

Television:

Pavarotti, Luciano, March 2, 1981.

Appendix B

Opera Related Groups

Opera Companies With Budgets Not Less Than $150,000*

Arizona Opera
Artpark
Baltimore Opera Company
Canadian Opera Company
Central City Opera
Charlotte Opera
Chautauqua Opera
Cincinnati Opera
Civic Opera of the Palm Beaches
Connecticut Opera
Dallas Civic Opera
Edmonton Opera
Festival Ottawa Opera
Florentine Opera of Milwaukee
Fort Worth Opera
Greater Miami Opera
Hawaii Opera Theatre
Houston Grand Opera
Kentucky Opera
Lake George Opera Festival
Lyric Opera of Chicago
Lyric Opera of Kansas City
Metropolitan Opera
Michigan Opera Theatre
Minnesota Opera

Nevada Opera
New Orleans Opera
New York City Opera
Opera Company of Boston
Ope Company of Philadel-
    phia
Opera Memphis
Opera/Omaha
Opera Metropolitana, A.C.
Opera Theatre of Saint Louis
Opera Theatre of Syracuse
Pittsburgh Opera
Portland Opera
San Antonio Symphony/Opera
San Diego Opera
San Francisco Opera
Santa Fe Opera
Seattle Opera
Southern Alberta Opera
Tri-Cities Opera
Tulsa Opera
Vancouver Opera
Virginia Opera
The Washington Opera
Western Spring Opera
The Wolf Trap Company

*Source: Central Opera Service

Opera Companies With Budgets Not Less Than $25,000*

Anchorage Civic Opera
Arkansas
Anchorage Civic Opera
Arkansas Opera Theatre
Augusta Opera
Chattanooga Opera
Chicago Opera Theater
Cleveland Opera
Colorado Opera Festival
Co-Opera Theatre
Fargo Moorhead Civic Opera
Glimmerglass Opera Theatre
Greater Utica Opera
Hinsdale Opera Theatre
Indianapolis Opera Company
Louisiana Opera Theatre

Mississippi Opera
Mobile Opera Guild
New Jersey State Opera
Opera Company of Greater
  Lansing
Opera Company of Jacksonville
Opera Midwest
Opera Theatre of Rochester
Pennsylvania Opera Theater
San Jose Symphony/Opera
The Scholar Opera
Shreveport Opera
Stamford State Opera
Utah Opera Company
Viennese Operetta Company of
  N.Y.

List of Opera Companies and Workshops Cited

Lyric Opera of Chicago, Carol Fox, General Manager, Chicago, Illinois
Metropolitan Opera Association, Anthony Bliss, General Manager,
    New York City, New York
New York City Opera, Beverly Sills, Musical Director, New York
San Francisco Opera, Kurt Herbert Adler, General Director, California
Seattle Opera Association, Glynn Ross, General Director, Washington

Arts Councils**

American Council for the Arts
American Guild of Music Artists
Associated Council for the Arts
Business Committee for the Arts
Center for Arts Information, Inc.
Concert Artists Guild
Council of National Arts Organization Executives

*Source: Central Opera Service
**Source: Opera America

The Ford Foundation, Arts Program
Martha Baird Rockefeller Fund for Music
Metropolitan Opera Guild, Inc.
Metropolitan Opera Archives
Metropolitan Opera National Council
National Endowment for the Arts
National Federation of Music Clubs
National Opera Association
National Opera Institute
National Research Center for the Arts (Louis Harris Associates)
New York City Dept. of Parks, Recreation and Cultural Affairs
Opera America, Inc.
Partnership for the Arts
Performing Arts and Educational Facilities

Bibliography

BOOKS

Adorno, Theodor. *The Philosphy of Modern Music.* Trans. Anne G. Mitchell and Wesley V. Blomster. New York: The Seabury Press, 1973.

Albrecht, Milton C., Barnett, James H., Griff, Mason, eds. *The Sociology of Art and Literature.* New York: Praeger Publishing Company, 1970.

Alda, Frances. *Men, Women and Tenors.* New York: Librarian Press, 1937.

Angel, Juvenal. *Careers in Music.* New York: World Trade Academy Press, Inc., 1960.

Antal, Frederick. *Florentine Painting and Its Social Background.* London: Kegan, Paul, Trench, Tribner and Co., Ltd., 1948.

Arian, Edward. *Bach, Beethoven and Bureaucracy: The Case of the Philadelphia Orchestra.* Alabama: University of Alabama, 1971.

Benedict Stephen, and Linda C. Coe, *Arts Management: An Annotated Bibliography.* Rev. edition. New York City: Center for Arts Information, Inc., 1980.

Bensman, Joseph. *Dollars and Sense: Ideology, Ethics and the Meaning of Work in Profit and Nonprofit Organizations.* New York: Macmillan and Company, 1967.

Bensman, Joseph, Lilienfeld, Robert. *Craft and Consciousness.* New York: John Wiley and Sons, 1973.

Bing, Rudolph. *Five Thousand Nights At The Opera.* New York: Doubleday and Company, 1972.

———. "Learn to Manage." In *The Bing Years, The Metropolitan Opera Association.* New York: Metropolitan Opera Association, 1972.

Blackman, Clarence. *Behind the Baton.* New York: Charos Enterprises, Inc., 1964.

Blau, Peter M., Scott, Richard W. *Formal Organizations.* New York: Doubleday and Company, 1962.

Baldridge, J. Victor. *Power and Conflict in the University.* New York: John Wiley & Sons, 1971.

Baumol, William J., Bowen, William G. *The Performing Arts — The Economic Dilemma.* New York: Twentieth Century Fund, 1966.

Becker, Howard S.: *Boys In White.* Illinois: University of Chicago Press, 1961.

———. *The Outsiders.* New York: Free Press, 1963.

Bowra, Cecil M. *Primitive Song.* New York: The World Publishing Company, 1962.

Brockway, Wallace and Weinstock, Herbert. *The Opera: A History of Its Creation and Performance (1600–1940).* New York: Simon and Schuster, 1941.

———. *Men of Music*. New York: Simon and Schuster, 1958.

Bruno, Nettl. *Music in Primitive Culture*. Cambridge: Harvard University Press, 1956.

Bukofzer, Manfred. *Music in the Baroque Era: From Monteverdi to Bach*. New York: W. W. Norton and Company, 1947.

Cantor, Muriel G. *The Hollywood Producer: His Work and His Audience*. New York: Basic Books, 1971.

Carr-Saunders, Alexander M. and Wilson, P.A. *The Professions*. London: P.A. Wilson, 1964.

Chagy, G. ed. *Business and the Arts*, New York: Paul E. Erikson, Inc., 1970.

Chasins, Abram. *Music at the Crossroads*. New York: Macmillan and Company, 1973.

Coser, Lewis. *The Functions of Conflict*. New York: Free Press, 1956.

Dent, Edward. *The Rise of Romantic Opera*. Boston: Cambridge University Press, 1976.

———. *The Foundations of English Opera*. New York: DaCapo Press, 1965.

Dovan, Frederic. *The History of Music in Performance*. New York: W. W. Norton and Company, 1942.

Dreitzel, Peter H. *Recent Sociology, Number 2*. New York: Macmillan and Company, 1970.

Durkheim, Emile. *The Division of Labor in Society*. Trans. by G. Simpson. Glencoe: Free Press, 1947.

Dyer, Frederick C., Dyer, John M. *Bureaucracy and Creativity*. Florida: University of Miami, 1965.

Elkin, Richard. *Careers in Music*. London: Novello and Company, 1960.

Eells, Richard. *The Corporation and the Arts*. New York: Macmillan and Company, 1967.

Einstein, Alfred. *A Short History of Music*. New York: Alfred A. Knopf, 1954.

Faulkner, Robert R. *Hollywood Studio Musicians: Their Work and Careers in the Recording Industry*. Chicago: Aldine Publishing Company, 1971.

Flaherty, Gloria. *Opera in the Development of Critical Thought*. New Jersey: Princeton U. Press, 1978.

Finck, Henry T. *Success in Music and How It Is Won*. New York: Charles Scribner and Sons, 1909.

Galatoupoulos, Stelios. *Callas-Le Divina*. New York: London House and Maxwell, 1970.

Gatti-Casazza, Giulio. *Memories of Opera*. New York: Charles Scribner and Sons, 1941.

Gingrich, A. ed. *Business and the Arts*. New York: Paul E. Erikson, Inc., 1969.

Goddard, Joseph. *The Rise and Development of Opera*. London: William Reeves, 1911.

Goldin, Milton, *The Music Merchants*. New York: Macmillan and Company, 1969.

Goldovsky, Boris. *Bringing Opera to Life*. New York: Doubleday and Company, 1959.

Goffman, Erving. *Presentation of Self in Everyday Life.* New York: Doubleday and Company, 1959.

Graf, Max. *Composer and Critic: Two Hundred Years of Musicians Critics.* New York: W. W. Norton and Company, 1946.

Greer, William, J. "The Artist as a Member of a Formal Organization." Ph.D. dissertation, University of Minnesota, 1969.

Grout, Donald. *A Brief History of Opera.* New York: Columbia University Press, 1965.

Habenstein, Robert. "A Sociological Study of An Occupation (Categories and Descriptions of Analysis)." Missouri: University of Missouri, 1970 (Mimeographed).

Hauser, Arnold. *The Social History of Art,* Vol. 3: *The Roccoco, Classicism and Romanticism.* New York: Vintage Books, 1951

Henderson, William J. *Early History of Singing.* New York: Amsterdam Press, 1921.

_____. *The Art of Singing.* New York: The Dial Press, 1938.

Hindemith, Paul. *A Composer's World – Horizons and Limitations.* Massachusetts: Harvard University Press, 1969.

Hirsch, Paul. *The Structure of the Popular Music Industry.* Michigan: University of Michigan Press, 1969.

Hitchcock, H. Wiley. *Music in the United States: An Historical Introduction.* Englewood Cliffs: Prentice-Hall, 1969.

Honigsheim, Paul. *Music and Society.* Edited by K. Peter Etzkorn. New York: John Wiley and Sons, 1973.

Kagan, Steven. *On Studying Singing.* New York: Holt Rinehart and Winston, 1950.

Kamerman, Jack and Rosanne Martorella. *Performers and Performances: The Sociology Organization of Artistic Work.* Massachusetts: J. F. Bergin Publishers, Inc. (In press).

Kolodin, Irving. *The Metropolitan Opera 1883–1966: A Candid History.* New York: A. A. Knopf. 1954.

Lang, Paul Henry. *Music in Western Civilization.* New York: W. W. Norton and Company, 1941.

Loft, Abram. "Musician's Guild and Union: A Consideration of the Evolution of Protective Organizations Among Musicians." Ph.D. dissertation, Columbia University, 1950.

Marcello, Benedetto. *Teatro Allo Modo* ("The Fashion in Theatre"). In *Source Readings in Music History,* edited by Oliver Strunk, pp 518–31. New York: W. W. Norton and Company, 1950.

Martens, Frederic Herman. *The Art of the Prima Donna.* New York: Appleton and Company, 1923.

Martin, George. *Verdi, His Music, Life and Times.* New York: Stein and Day, 1973.

Martindale, Andrew. *The Rise of the Artist in the Middle Ages and the Early Renaissance.* New York: McGraw Hill Company, 1972.

Matz, Mary Jane. *Opera Stars in the Sun.* New York: Farrar Strauss and Cudby, 1955.

216 THE SOCIOLOGY OF OPERA

Merriam, Alan P. *The Anthropology of Music.* Chicago: Northwestern University Press, 1964.
Mordden, Ethan. *The Splendid Art of Opera.* New York: Metheun, 1980.
Mueller, John H. *The American Symphony Orchestra: A Social History of Musical Taste.* Indianapolis: University of Indiana Press, 1951.
Nelson, Charles A. and Frederick J. Turk. *Financial Management in Arts.* New York, 1975.
Nettl, Bruno, *Music in Primitive Culture.* Cambridge: Harvard University Press, 1956.
Netzer, Dick. *The Subsidized Muse: Public Support for Arts in the U.S.* New York: Cambridge University Press, 1978.
Newman, William S. *Understanding Music.* 2nd ed. New York: Harper and Row, 1961.
Nielsen, Waldemar A. *The Big Foundations.* New York: Columbia University Press, 1972.
Nosow, Sigmund and Form, William H. *Man, Work and Society.* New York: Basic Books, Inc., 1962.
Orrey, Leslie. *Concise History of Opera.* New York: Scribner and Sons, 1972.
Pahlen, Kurt. *Great Singers from the Seventh Century to the Present.* New York: Stein & Day, 1974.
Pavalko, Ronald. *Occupations and Professions.* Florida: Florida State University Press, 1971.
Pavarotti, Luciano. *Pavarotti: My Own Story.* New York: Doubleday & Company, 1981.
Powdermaker, Hortense. *Hollywood: The Dream Factory.* Boston: Little, Brown, 1950.
Peyser, Ethel Rose, and Bauer, Marion. *How Opera Grew.* New York: G. P. Putnam and Sons, 1925, 1956.
Phillips, Harvey E. *The Carmen Chronicle.* New York: Stein and Day, 1973.
Pincherele, Marc. *The World of the Virtuoso.* New York: W. W. Norton and Company, 1963.
Pleasants, Henry. *The Great Singers.* New York: Simon and Schuster, 1966.
——. *The Agony of Modern Music.* New York: Clarion Press, 1970.
Raynor, Henry. *A Social History of Music: From Middle Ages to Beethoven.* New York: Schocken Books, 1972.
Reich, R. *The Voice.* New York: Dodd, Mead and Company, 1971.
Reis, Claire Rafael. *Composers in America: Biographical Sketches of Contemporary Composers With A Record of Their Works.* New York: Macmillan and Company, 1947.
Riley, Matilda, ed., *Sociological Research.* New York: Harcourt, Brace and World, 1963.
Rolland, Romain. *Some Musicians of Former Days.* New York: Books for Libraries Press, 1922.
——. *A Musical Tour.* Trans. Bernard Miall. New York: Books for Libraries Press, 1922.
——. *Musicians of Today.* Trans. Mary Blaiklock. New York: H. Holt and Company, 1915.

Rosenfeld, Peter. *Musical Portraits: Interpretation of Twenty Modern Composers.* New York: Books for Libraries Press, 1971.

Rosenthal, Paul. *The Great Sopranos and Singers of Today.* London: Golder and Boyart Ltd., 1966.

Rushmore, Robert. *The Singing Voice.* New York: Dodd, Mead and Company, 1971.

Ruzabelow, Allan S. "Music and Social Groups: An Interactionist Approach to the Sociology of Music." Ph.D. dissertation, University of Minnesota, 1968.

Samachson, Dorothy & Joseph. *The Fabulous World of Opera.* New York: Rand McNally & Company, 1962.

Sargeant, Winthrop. *Divas.* New York: Coward, McCann and Geognegan, 1973.

Schonberg, Harold C. *The Great Conductors.* New York: Simon and Schuster, 1967.

———. *The Lives of Great Composers.* New York: W. W. Norton and Company, 1970.

Sessions, Roger. *The Musical Experience of Composer, Performer, Listener.* Princeton: University of Princeton Press, 1950.

Simmel, George. *The Sociology of George Simmel.* Edited by Wolff, Kurt. New York: Free Press, 1950.

———. *George Simmel 1858–1918: A Collection of Essays.* Translated by Kurt H. Wolff. Columbus: The Ohio University Press, 1959.

Stevens, Denis. *A History of Music.* London: Cassel, 1961.

Strunk, Oliver. *Source Readings in Music History, Vol. I: Antiquity and the Middle Ages,* Vol. II: *Classical Era* and Vol. III: *Renaissance.* New York: W. W. Norton and Company, 1950.

Teran, Jay. *The New York Opera Audience: 1890–1974.* Ph.D. Dissertation, New York University, 1974.

Thompson, James D. *Organizations in Action.* McGraw-Hill, New York, 1967.

Thomson, Virgil. *The State of Music.* New York: Vintage Books, 1939.

Toffler, Alvin C. *The Culture Consumers.* New York: St. Martin's Press, 1964.

Twentieth Century Fund Report. *On Performing Arts – Bricks, Mortar and The Performing Arts.* New York: Twentieth Century Fund, 1970.

Udy, Stanley H., Jr., *Organization of Work: A Comparative Analysis of Production Among Non-industrial Peoples.* New York: File Press, Human Relations Area, 1967.

Volbach, Walter R. *Problems of Opera Production.* Texas: Texas Christian University Press, 1953.

Vollmar, Howard M. and Mills, D. L. *Professionalization.* Englewood Cliffs, Prentice-Hall, 1968.

Wagner, Alan. *Prima Donna and Other Wild Beasts.* New York: Argonaut Books, 1961.

Wagner, Susan. *A Guide to Corporate Giving in the Arts.* New York: Association Council of the Arts, 1980, 1981.

Watkins, May F. *Behind the Scenes at the Opera*. New York: F. A. Stokes and Company, 1925.
Weber, Max. *Rational Foundations of Music*. Edited and trans. Martindale, Don, Neuwirth and Riedl. Illinois: University of Southern Illinois Press, 1954.
Westrup, Jack. *An Introduction to Musical History*. London: Hutchinson University Library, 1955.
Wilson, Robert N. *The Arts in Society*. Englewood Cliffs, Prentice-Hall, 1964.
Yorke-Lang, Alan. *Music at Court*. London: Weidenfeld and Nicholson, 1954.

ARTICLES

Albrecht, Milton C. "The Arts in Market Systems." August 27, 1973. (Mimeographed.)
_____. "The Art as an Institution." *American Sociological Review* 33 (June 1968): 383–97.
Baldwin, James. "Mass Culture and the Creative Arts: Some Personal Ideas." *Baudalus* 89, sec. 2 (Spring 1960): 373–76.
Barnard, Chester. "The Function of Status Systems." In *Reader in Bureaucracy*, edited by Robert K. Merton. New York: Free Press, 1952.
Barnes, Clive. "Dance: Killing the Joffrey With Alibis." *The New York Times*, March 25, 1973, p. 20
_____. "May Critics Say 'Stop the Money'?" *The New York Times*, April 15, 1973, p. 31.
Barnett, James H., "Research Areas in the Sociology of Art." *Sociology and Social Research* 42 (July–August 1958): pp 401–05. Printed in Milton Albrecht, James H. Barnett, and Mason Griff. *The Sociology of Art and Literature*. New York: Praeger Publishing Company, 1970, and printed in *Sociology Today*. Robert Merton, Leonard K. Broom, and Leonard S. Cottroll. New York: Basic Books, Inc., 1959.
Becker, Howard S. "Some Contingencies in the Dance Musician in Chicago." *The Outsiders*. New York: Free Press, 1963.
_____. "The Development of Identification Within An Occupation." *American Journal of Sociology* 61 (January 1954). Printed in *Symbolic Interaction; A Reader in Social Psychology*. Manis, Jerome G., and Meltzer, Bernard N., Boston: Allyn and Bacon, 1967.
_____. "The Musician's Career." *Human Organization* 12 (1953): 22–26. Bensman, Joseph. "The Future of Cultural Services." *Journal of Aesthetic Education* 7, No. 4 (October 1973): 81–96.
_____. "Status Communities In An Urban Society." 1970 (Mimeographed.)
_____. "Classical Music and the Status Game." 1970 (Mimeographed.)
Bensman, Joseph and Robert Lilienfeld, "A Phenomenological Model of the Attitude of the Performing Artist." Journal of Aesthetic Education 4, No. 2 (April 1970).

Bensman, Joseph and Israel Gerver, "Art and Mass Society," *Social Problems* 6, No. 1 (Summer, 1958).

Berger, David, G. "Status Attribution and Self-Perception Among Musical Specialties," *Sociological Quarterly,* 12 (Spring 1971): 259–65.

Bernheimer, Martin and Hume, Paul. "Critics Compare Opinions." *Music and Artists.* (March 1972): 14–15.

Bing, Rudolph. "Nobody Knows the Traubels I've Seen." *The New York Times,* April 26, 1972, p. 13.

Blasi, Anthony, J. "Phenomonology and the Sociology of Grand Opera." Presented at the Annual Meeting of the Midwest Sociological Association, Minneapolis, Minnesota, April, 1977.

Boutwell, Jane. "Turning the Tide: Men of the Met." *Opera News,* New York: September, 1980, p. 18.

Bruer, Gustl. "In the Beginning There Was Hope." *Opera News* January 13, 1973, pp 8–15, and January 20, 1973, pp 10–13.

Buckley, Thomas. "The Cost of Putting Footprints in Sands of Time." *The New York Times,* October 17, 1973, p. 49.

Cicourel, Aaron. "Basic and Normative Roles in the Negotiation of Status." In *Recent Sociology,* No. 2. Hans P. Dreitzel. New York: Macmillan and Company, 1970.

Corsaro, Frank. "Malinscentation" *Opera News,* March 7, 1981, p. 9.

DiMaggio, Paul and Michael Useem. "Social Class and Arts Consumption." *Theory and Society* 5 (1978): 141–61.

Eaton, Quintance. "Introducing Henry Lewis." *Opera News,* January 20, 1973, pp 22–23.

Ericson, Raymond. "A 'Midwife' For Composers." *The New York Times.*

_____. "New Director Road Scheme." *The New York Times,* May 27, 1973, pp 13–21.

_____. "Rudel Looks Ahead, *"The New York Times,* March 25, 1973, p. 17.

_____. "At Twenty-Nine, An Impresario", *The New York Times,* February 11, 1973.

_____. "Adieux Now (Bing) and The (Gatti)", *The New York Times,* April 16, 1972, p. 13.

Etzkorn, Peter K. "George Simmel and The Sociology of Music." *Social Forces* 43 (May 1964):101–107.

Ferretti, Fred, "Endowment Points Up Fiscal Crises at the Components of Lincoln Center," *The New York Times,* September 21, 1973, p. 50.

Festinger, Leon and Aronson, E. "The Arousal and Reduction of Dissonance in Social Contests." In *Group Dynamics Research Theory,* edited by Doram et al., 2nd ed. New York: Row Peterson Company, 1960.

Foote, Nelson N. "Identity as the Basis for a Theory of Motives." In *Symbolic Interaction: A Reader in Social Psychology,* edited by Jerome G. Manis and Bernard Meltzer. Boston: Allyn and Bacon, 2nd ed., 1972.

Forsyth, Sondra and Kolenda, Pauline M. "Competition, Cooperation and Group Cohesion in the Ballet Company." Printed in *The Sociology of Art and Literature* Milton Albrecht, James H. Barnett, and Mason Griff. New York: Praeger Publishing Company, 1970.

Getzels, J. W. and Czikszentimikalzi, M. "On the Roles, Values and Performance of Future Artists: A Conceptual and Empirical Exploration." *Social Problems* 9, No. 4 (Autumn 1968): 516–18.

Gilson, Estelle: "The Star System: Curse or Coup?." *Music Journal*, October, 1972: 20–23.

Green, Harris. "If You Want Them to Love the Classics." *The New York Times*, April, 1973.

_____. "Don't Send the Don to Hades." *The New York Times*, November 26, 1972, p. 11.

Gouldner, Alvin. "Cosmopolitan and Locals: Toward an Analysis of Latent Social Roles" *Sociological Quarterly* (February 1957): 287–306.

Griff, Mason. "The Commercial Artist: A Study in Role Conflict." Printed in *Identity and Anxiety*. Maurice Stein, Arthur Vidich, and White. New York: Free Press, 1960.

_____. "The Alienation of the Artist." *The Arts in Society*, edited by Robert N. Wilson, New Jersey: Prentice-Hall, 1952.

Gruen, John. "I'm a Very Normal Human Being." *The New York Times*, October 31, 1971, pp. 15 and 28.

Gussow, Melvin. "City Center Cuts Funds to Joffrey." *The New York Times*, March 14, 1973, p. 29.

_____. "Ford Foundation Lending Million to the City Center." *The New York Times*, March 19, 1973, p. 46.

Henahan, Donald. "What Price Peace at the Metropolitan?" *The New York Times*, December 7, 1980, p. 1.

_____. "Labor Trouble at the Met in Perspective." *The New York Times*, October 12, 1980, p. 49.

_____. Who Supports the Arts Today? And Who Tomorrow?", *The New York Times*, November 2, 1980, p. 19.

_____. "American Composers: The Insulted and the Injured?", *New York Times*, July 22, 1973, p. 9.

_____. "Two Orchestras–Can They Live?" *The New York Times*, July 15, 1973, p. 11.

_____. "An Orchestra Tries Self-Government," *The New York Times*, July 11, 1973, p. 46.

_____. "Can Musicians Cope With Age, Sex and Stress?". *The New York Times*, June 24, 1973, p. 17.

_____. "Do We Dare Help the Artist Who Dares?", *New York Times*, June 10, 1973, p. 17 and 37.

_____. "Will Congress Pass the Comedy and Drama to the People," *The New York Times*, June 17, 1973, p. 17.

_____. "So Lie Down and Face the Music." *The New York Times*, June 10, 1973.

_____. "Met Will Sing Its First 'Troyen' in Fall," *The New York Times*, March 14, 1973, p. 26.

_____. "If He Had Taken Stravinsky's Advice, *The New York Times*, March 11, 1973.

_____. "What A Sock in the Midriff Did For Jan," *The New York Times,* January 14, 1973, p. 15.

_____. "When the Stage Director Takes On at the Opera," *The New York Times Magazine,* November 12, 1972, p. 44.

_____. "Are Opera Stars Worth Every Cent They Are Overpaid?", *The New York Times,* September 17, 1972, p. 15.

_____. "A New Way of Looking at the New–and the Old", *The New York Times,* July 16, 1972, p. 11.

_____. "Happiness? It's Verdi," *The New York Times,* June 4, 1972.

_____. "Gentele's Dream — and Awakening," *The New York Times,* March 14, 1972, p. 15.

_____. "Is Toscanini or Boulez the Better Conductor?", *The New York Times,* January 9, 1972, p. 15.

_____. " 'He Reminds Me of Me at That Age', Says Leonard Bernstein," *The New York Times Magazine,* October 24, 1971, p. 36.

Heyworth, Peter.: "What is Boulez Up to With the Philharmonic?" *The New York Times,* November 14, 1971, pp. 17 and 35.

_____. "Will Paris Opera Become the Greatest?" *The New York Times,* March 25, 1971.

Horowitz, Louis I. "Consensus, Conflict and Cooperation: A Sociological Inventory," *Social Forces,* 41 (1962): 177–188.

Hughes, Everett C. "Personality Types and the Division of Labor." *American Journal of Sociology,* 33 (1928): 754–768.

Jacobson, Robert. "Miss American Superstar." *Opera News.* October, 1980, p. 9.

_____. "New Means for New Music." *Sociological Review* 28 (September 1968): 57–9.

Jenkins, Speight. "Carol and Company." *Opera News,* November 1972, pp 14–19.

_____. "Chapin and Kubelik, News of the Met's 1973–1974 Season." *Opera News,* April 1973, p. 9.

Kadushin, Charles. "The Professional Self-Concept of Music Students." *Opera News,* April 1973, p. 9.

Kavolis, Vytautas. "The Institutional Structure of Cultural Services." *Journal of Aesthetic Education.* 7, #4 (October) 1973.

Klein, Howard. "Tristan is a Tenor Named Thomas." *The New York Times,* December 12, 1971, pp 17 and 22.

_____. "Do We Dare Help the Artist Who Dares?" *The New York Times,* June 10, 1973, pp 17 and 22.

Levine, James. ". . . Which Brings Me To." *Opera News,* December 9, 1972, p. 28.

Litwak, Eugene, "Models of Bureaucracy which Permit Conflict," *American Journal of Sociology,* 67 (September 1961) 177–184.

Malinowski, Bronislaw. "Complex and Myth in Mother-Right." *Psyche* 5 (1925): 194–216.

Marek, George. "Malinscenation? Yes!" *Opera News,* March 7, 1981, p. 8.

Mayer, Martin. "Horne Aplenty." *Opera News,* March 18, 1973.

_____. "The Economics of Opera Recording.", *Opera News,* December 9, 1972, pp 12–15.

_____. "Hey, Who Pinched My Libretto?" *The New York Times,* March 19, 1972, p. 15.

_____. "Managing Orchestra is Fine Art Too." *Fortune,* September 1, 1968.

Martorella, Rosanne. "A Study of Organizational Authority–A Case of the Routinization of Charisma at the Metropolitan Opera." New School For Social Reasearch, 1968, unpublished.

Merton, Robert K. "Bureaucratic Structure and Personality." *Social Forces* I (May 1940): 560–568.

Mills, C. Wright. "Situated Actions and Vocabulary of Motives." pp 355–366, Printed in *Symbolic Interaction.* Jerome G. Manis and Bernard N. Meltzer. Boston: Allyn and Bacon, 1967.

Mueller, John. "Baroque Datum Hypothesis or Tautology: A Critique of Musical Aesthetics." *Journal of Aesthetics and Art Criticism,* No. 4 (June 1954):421–29.

Nash, Dennison. "The Socialization of the Artist: The American Composer." *Social Forces* 35 (1957): 307–313.

_____. "The Alienated Composer." In *The Arts In Society,* Wilson, Robert N., New Jersey: Prentice-Hall, 1952.

_____. "New York City Opera Company As A National Culture Institution," *Chord and Dischord,* Vol. 2, No. 6, New York, 1950, pp 130–2.

The New York Times. "Fund Cut Curtails Joffrey's Fall Season" March 19, 1973, p. 46.

The New York Times. "Ford Funding Glum on Arts Outlook" March 2, 1969, P. 47.

The New York Times. "Musicians Ask Right to Fire Conductor" April 27, 1963, p. 1.

Perrow, Charles, "Organizational Prestige: Some Functions and Dysfunctions," *American Journal of Sociology,* v. 66, (1961), pp 335–41.

Peyser, John. "Henzel: Where the 'Action' Music Is." *The New York Times,* July 16, 1972.

Phillips, Harvey E. "A Tenor of Line." *Opera News,* 37, No. 9, p. 25.

_____. "Opera in the Bronx? Yes Thanx" *The New York Times,* October 7, 1973, p. 15.

_____. "Will Carmen Bring Opera Recording Back to America?" *The New York Times* November 26, 1972, p. 16.

Raskin, Theodore. "Labor as Performer and Practitioner in the Arts." *The New York Times,* April 9, 1964.

Rich, Maria F., "Trials and Triumphs: U.S. Opera Survey 1979–80," *Opera News,* November 22, 1980, pp. 32–42.

_____. "Opera on the Map." *Opera News,* December 22, 1973, pp. 14–18.

_____. "In the Balance–United States Opera Survey." *Opera News,* December 16, 1972, pp 26–9.

Rizzo, Francis. "Memoir of an Invisible Man." *Opera News,* February 5, 1972 and February 19, 1972.

Rochberg, G. "Contemporary Music in an Affluent Society." *ASCAP Today* 1, sec. 3, (August 1967).

Rockwell, John. "Met: $35 Tickets and a Lingering Deficit." *The New York Times,* September 24, 1975, p. 50.

――――. "City of No Angels." *Opera News,* March 3, 1973, p. 8.

Rubin, Stephen E. "The Eyes of Texas Are Upon 'Figaro'." *The New York Times,* December 9, 1973, pp 19 and 39.

――――. "Understudy Makes It To The Top." *The New York Times Magazine,* September 23, 1973, p. 36.

――――. "Shostakovich. If My Dreams Cease. . . " *The New York Times,* June 24, 1973, pp 1 and 10.

――――. "Andre Kostelanetz–Middlebrow Toscanini?" *The New York Times,* May 16, 1973, p. 17.

――――. "I'm Not A Showman–I Hate All That," *The New York Times,* February 4, 1973, pp 15 and 32.

――――. "What Opera Would I Like Revived?", *The New York Times,* February 2, 1973, p. 17.

――――. "Cutting Opera Down to Size–For Television," *The New York Times,* December 31, 1972, pp 11 and 14.

――――. "Nicolai Gedda–The Case of the Introverted Tenor," *The New York Times,* December 10, 1972, p. 19.

――――. "If the Metropolitan Won't Sing Her Tune, Goodbye, Scotto." *The New York Times,* November 19, 1972, p. 15.

――――. "Whose 'Siegfried' Will It Be?", *The New York Times,* November 12, 1972.

――――. "Pavarotti? Mama Mia." *The New York Times,* February 13, 1972.

――――. "Last of the Red Hot Showmen," *The New York Times,* May 13, 1973, p. 1.

――――. "Kubelik: New Conscience of the Metropolitan?" *The New York Times,* October 17, 1971, p. 17.

――――. "Out Where the Bravos and Boos Begin." *The New York Times,* September 5, 1971, p. 9.

――――. "Ronald Wilford: Muscle Man Behind the Maestros," *The New York Times,* July 25, 1971, p. 15.

Rudel, Julius. "Modern Operas? You Write 'Em, We'll Produce 'Em." *The New York Times,* August 12, 1973, p. 15.

Schonberg, Harold C. "City Opera Unveils Spring '81: Innovation, Tradition (and Miss Sills)." *The New York Times.* February 15, 1981, p. 1.

――――. "The Boulezian Plans in the Spring (Tra La?)" *The New York Times* April 15, 1973, p. 15.

――――. "Did Rachmaninoff Collaborate With God." *The New York Times,* April 1, 1973.

――――. "The Philharmonic Confronts A 'Desperation Gap' " *The New York Times* November 19, 1972.

――――. "Delius' 'Romeo and Juliet', It Will Tear You Apart," *The New York Times,* September 30, 1973, p. 15.

――――. "Cash for Culture Too," *The New York Times,* June 1973.

224   THE SOCIOLOGY OF OPERA

_____. "Was the Cheering Premature?", *The New York Times*, May 20, 1973, p. 17.

_____"He Ran His House As An Autocrat" *The New York Times* April 16, 1972, p. 13.

_____. "On The Risk of Playing It Safe." *The New York Times* September 19, 1971.

_____. "Recipes to Spice Up The Diet at the Metropolitan." *The New York Times* July 25, 1971, p. 15.

_____. "At The Metropolitan, Creeping Socialism." *The New York Times* April 18, 1971.

Serrin, William. "Class Distinctions Add to Discord Complicating Met Labor Problem." *The New York Times*, October 15, 1980, p. A1

Simmel, George. "Psychologische and Ethnologische Studien uber Musik." (Psychological and Ethnological Studies in Musik.") In Lazarus and Steinthal. *Zeitschrift fur Volkerpsychologie*, Vol. 13, 1882, pp. 261–308

Simon, Herbert A. "Inducements and Incentives in Bureaucracy." In *Administrative Behavior*. New York: Macmillan and Company, 1954, pp 327–333.

Stebbins, Robert. "The Conflict Between Musical and Commercial Values In The Minneapolis Jazz Community." Proceedings, 30, sec. 1, 1962.

Stinchcombe, A. L. "Bureaucracy and Craft Administration of Producttion: A Comparative Study." *American Sociological Quarterly* 4, (1959): 168–87.

Stone, H. H., "Mid Nineteenth Century Beliefs in the Social Values of Music." *Musical Quarterly*, 43 (Jan 1957): 38–49.

Strauss, Anselm L. "Professions in Process." *American Journal of Sociology* 66 (1961): 321–34.

Wadsworth, Stephen. "All About Evelyn." *Opera News*. December 20, 1980, p. 11.

Walker, G. " 'You're Singing Too Much' . . . The More I Sing, The Better I Sound." *The New York Times Magazine*, February 27, 1972, sec.6, p. 18.

Williamson, Alix. "Mass Music Minded Men: A Problem in Promotion on the Private Relations of A Business In Publics." 1970 (Mimeographed.)

Zachary, Ralph. "Corsaro." *Opera News*, August 1972, pp 16–18.

Index